Wealth and Well-being

Wealth and Well-being

A National Strategy for the Nineties

John Hart

OXON

First published 1988 by Oxon Publishing
Market House, Market Place,
Deddington, Oxford OX5 4SW

Copyright © John Hart 1988

Cover design: T. Haws

Typesetting: Ransom Typesetting Services, Woburn Sands

Printed and bound in the United Kingdom by Billing & Sons Ltd,
Worcester

British Library Cataloguing in Publication Data

Hart, John
    Wealth and Well being.
    1. Great Britain. Economic conditions
    related to social conditions
    I. Title
    330.941'0858

    ISBN 1–870677–03–X

Contents

Acknowledgements

I thank Juliet Clark for her unstinting support throughout the project. For their valuable and constructive comments on the draft manuscript, and assistance in other ways, I am grateful to Terence Allott, Patrick Ballingall, Sheila Colbeck, Dave Copsey, Geoffrey and Norah Corson, Robert Cummins, Phil Davies, Sue Granger, Joe Hart, Chloë Jameson, Paul Kelly, Ken Kingsbury, Chris Mundy, Geoffrey Pearson, Sue Preston, Rosalind Richard, Derek Sharman, Michelle Warden, David Warrell and Gerry Wisher. I am also grateful for the assistance of my former employer, Amersham International, particulary Jolyon Lea and the staff of the library, Charlotte Priestley, and Barry Hough.

I am grateful to *The Economist* for permission to reproduce a number of figures from its informative pages.

The opinions expressed in this book are, however, my own, as is responsibility for the accuracy of the information presented.

For her unflagging and cheerful efforts at the keyboard, I thank Glynis Sutton, and for the comforts of home during the final writing period, I thank my mother.

Overview

Off the northern coast of mainland Europe lies Britain, a country consisting of a small group of rainswept islands on which dwell about one and a quarter per cent of the world's population. It is the seventh most crowded place on earth.

The British cannot feed themselves and, though they have ample coal and oil, lack many other raw materials. They must trade to survive but their record in past decades has been poor, and even their own people will often not buy domestically produced goods. In consequence their prosperity has declined relative to that of their neighbours, the French and Germans.

Though they have a distinguished past, the present could be improved. There is perennial talk of unemployment, rampant crime, social divisions leading to deprivation and poor health, collapsing cities, despoiled environment, philistinism and unsympathetic rulers. National morale is not buoyant.

The British tailspin down the economic ranking seems to be turning in the late eighties into a level, though bumpy, flight. What is needed is a flight plan to send the nation's prosperity into a steep vertical climb. Fortunately one has become available. Here it is.

Summary

Britain has endured multiple decline. For over four decades we have suffered economic decline relative to other nations, but less well acknowledged has been relative slippage in the areas of personal health and some types of accidental injury, crime, average educational attainment, the environment, social cohesion and libertarian standards. A Wealth and Well-being strategy is proposed to improve our national performance. Prosperity will be raised by boosting manufacturing industry and by a concerted attack on the world market for financial, information-related and leisure/arts services. The quality of life will be improved by reducing threats to well-being in the areas of health, crime and accidents. A scheme is suggested for alleviating unemployment as part of the creation of a convivial society – this latter being summed up as 'fun and profits with care'. Political and other reforms are recommended. With economic and social improvement will come a resurgence in national morale and a cultural revival.

In the 1950s Britain was the second most prosperous industrial nation in terms of gross domestic product per head. Now, after dropping a further couple of places in the decade to 1985, we are barely in the top 20. We have grown economically, particularly in the south-east of the country, but our competitors have grown faster. By some measures, we are now poorer than the Italians.

The main failing has been industrial: manufacturing has not held on to its share of the world market and has even lost a significant part of the domestic market. It has failed to make and sell goods effectively. Service industry has also lost market share, though it has retained most of the home market.

The objectives of the Wealth and Well-being strategy are to improve prosperity, raise the quality of life and restore national morale. In the economic sphere, a gross domestic product aspiration is suggested of £700bn at current prices by the year 2000, requiring an annual growth rate of nearly 6 per cent. This would imply a doubling of incomes, bringing us up to the level of our more advanced neighbours. Although we are in the early stages of the post-industrial era when the majority of jobs are in services, most wealth will continue to be significantly associated with the making and selling of goods. It is vital, therefore, for Britain to become more successful as a manufacturing nation.

The 'Two Sectors/One Future' economic sub-strategy calls for vision and commitment. It gives priority to boosting the industrial sector (manufacturing) and co-ordinating the 'post-industrial' sector (globally-orientated financial, information-related and leisure/arts services). The aim is to win a 10 per cent share of world trade in both goods and services by the end of the century, up from the present level of below 8 per cent.

The keynotes of the economic sub-strategy, acronymically memorable as PRINCE, are Pioneering, Reinforcement of success, Individual excellence, National roots, Clear goals and Europeanism.

A crucial feature of that part of the sub-strategy bearing on the industrial sector is that individuals and companies in manufacturing will enjoy tax benefits ('M-ratedness'). Mortgage interest relief will be abolished and support given instead to industrial investment, research and training, the tripod on which rests the crucible of the future. Other measures are recommended to assist manufacturing industry.

The post-industrial sector, centred on London, requires strategic co-ordination to exploit overseas markets fully. A new body should be established in the capital dealing with so-called 'invisible exports' called Invisible Enterprise. This would oversee the City of London's financial services, a new London Idearium (a centre for information-related services) and foreign currency earning activities in the leisure/arts area and tourism. The London Idearium would act as a national meeting place and a clearing house for suggestions, symbolising a nation reborn through ideas. London should seek to become 'European Capital of the Future'.

The equivalent body to Invisible Enterprise for strategic co-ordination of overseas trade in 'visibles', i.e. goods, will be called Visible Success.

A lifestyle sub-strategy complements the economic sub-strategy. Its intention is to improve the quality of life by reducing threats to well-being caused by ill-health, lawlessness and accidents. A centrally co-ordinated National Programme for Risk Reduction should be developed based on the mostly preventive tenets of 'risk engineering': eliminate risk at the 'design' stage; target big risks and high-risk groups; encourage personal responsibility by 'reconnecting' people to the consequences of their actions.

The British are an unhealthy lot as judged by international comparisons on the basis of indicators such as heart disease, lung and cervical cancer, infant mortality, and longevity. Profound social inequalities in health exist here which have been tackled better abroad. A parallel organisation to the National Health Service should be set up dedicated to preventive medicine. Called 'Lifestyle 2000' this would foster healthy lifestyles by educating the public and the media. It would take over the NHS's preventive activities, initiate novel screening programmes and develop a quantitative approach to health using a new Health Quotient concept. The aim would be to improve the nation's health by 10 per cent by the end of the century. Efforts should be made to reduce smoking (the premier cause of health damage) and excessive drinking (the premier cause of social damage) by raising prices through taxation and by other measures.

Britain appears to have become one of the most criminal nations in Europe. We should aim to reduce offending by one-third by the year 2000. This can be achieved by targeting young offenders (e.g. with a new penalty based on delayed age of majority) and criminals at the top of society (for 'moral multiplier' effects). Preventive measures are recommended (e.g. expanded Neighbourhood Watch schemes, thief-proof cars). Victim compensation and support should be given a high priority. Sentences should be made more consistent.

Thousands die needlessly in accidents each year, millions are injured. Accidents to children on the roads and in the home are particularly prevalent. Work accidents are on the increase again after years of improvement. To halve the toll by the end of the century we should, for example, improve home accident publicity, bolster the Health and Safety Executive, improve road and car design, introduce stiffer penalties for drunk-driving, and aim to discourage the use of motorcycles.

A snapshot of strategic objectives and economic and lifestyle policy recommendations is given on page 144–5.

The 'One Future' of the economic sub-strategy is suggested to be the 'convivial society'. This is encapsulated as 'fun and profits with care'. Industry and individuals must prosper, but caring values must also be fostered. In line with this, a 'post-industrial programme' (PIP) is recommended for the unemployed offering the dignity of pay and the opportunity to opt out of fruitless job-orientation in order to serve the community. A hand up, rather than a handout.

Our democracy, though old, is immature. This is evidenced by excessive secrecy at the centre and an inequitable voting system. Society has become more stratified into rich and poor and there has been social erosion (e.g. the rise of one-parent families, increased violence at sporting events). Educationally, we are the 'thick man of Europe'. Scientifically, our influence is waning. Our performance has been poor as regards the environment, whether inner city, rural, littoral or atmospheric. Defence spending is disproportionately high.

Britain's past achievements are remarkable. Revival from multiple decline is perfectly feasible with implementation of the Wealth and Well-being strategy and associated reforms. With success will come improved morale. The core of our self-esteem will be economic pre-eminence and continuing radical innovation. A cultural rebirth can be forecast as Britain heads for the third millenium. A new renaissance.

Part I
Wealth

1
Analysis

In this first section we are going to look at a nation in relative economic decline – Britain. This is necessarily a rather depressing subject so to cheer you up I have made a list of some of Britain's past achievements and famous people (Appendix I). When, as you read the following pages, the black bile of despair or the red bile of anger rises in your gorge, remember that no nation on earth has made a bigger contribution to the modern world than Britain. If you don't believe me, read the list. And the good news, as we shall see, is that we can rise again. But first it is important to understand our present plight and how we found ourselves in it, before deciding what we should do in the future. Hold your nose and plunge in – you are about to suffer.

Post-war Decline

Britain has been on the blink for decades. While we have grown richer, other nations have grown richer still, such that we are now the poorest of the major industrial nations. And the truth is that we deserve to be.

At the end of the Second World War, Britain doffed gas mask and tin hat and stumbled victorious from its air raid shelter into what promised to be a new dawn, but what turned out to be a protracted economic twilight. A few short years after the war we were the second richest nation in terms of gross domestic product (GDP) per head – though it may not have felt like it at the time. A few short decades later we are towards the bottom of the top 20 and still on the way down. We also then had a quarter of the world's trade in manufactured goods, but by the mid-1980s our share had clattered down to below 8 per cent by value, a smaller proportion than Italy's. In the race for post-war prosperity through trade, we have seriously lagged behind.

Britain is now in the third division of nations in terms of standard of living. This was the conclusion of one analysis in the notoriously difficult area of comparing national incomes. Up there at the top were the United States, West Germany, Switzerland, Sweden, Canada and some favoured smaller nations such as Kuwait. In the second division were the likes of Japan, France, the Netherlands, Austria and Denmark. We were classed in the third division alongside Hong Kong, Puerto Rico, Yugoslavia and the Soviet Union. We were reported to earn significantly more than these nations but were grouped with them. That is the humiliating scale of our post-war defeat.

In 1960, we were still the richest country in Europe. Twenty or so years later, the economist Sidney Pollard was able to write that the gap between Britain and West Germany in terms of income was as wide as the gap between Britain and Africa. Italy is probably the most recent nation to overtake us. On trend we will eventually be overtaken by Spain and after that Greece and Portugal. From being the rich men of Europe we have become a nation of also-rans.

So striking have our problems been that the post-war world was given a medico-industrial condition, the 'British disease.' This was characterised by economic sloth and a failure to thrive. We were under-performing as a trading nation and the crucial component of this related to manufacturing industry. We were not making and selling things successfully enough for home and foreign consumption. The result was relative decline.

The key word here is 'relative'. This might explain why the British have not been galvanised by failure. In real terms our disposable income has doubled since 1950 and materially most of us are quite obviously better off, particularly if we live in the prosperous south-east. Even in the half decade to 1985 household income increased by 11 per cent after allowing for inflation. Also disguising our true position is the experience most of us have of rising income through life with promotion and so forth. It is only when travelling abroad that prosperity differences are obvious. We do seem rather poorer.

Does it matter that we have lagged behind? Emphatically yes, because it affects our access to material comforts, the quality of public services and our very well-being, as I shall argue later in the book. Moreover, in a society strapped for cash, those at the bottom of the heap can be crushed.

We have prided ourselves in the past on the way we do things, the 'British way of life', but some such idea as 'never mind the width feel the quality' is an offshore island myth that has become increasingly hard to sustain. The lives we lead are *not* better than those of people in other industrial countries. Certainly, our emigrants don't think so – between 1971 and 1983 half a million more people left our shores than arrived at them.

Money is necessary for the good life: materialistic but true. Here is a comment on wealth and decline by Robert Skidelsky, Professor of International Studies at Warwick University:

The conclusion is that we are locked into a system in which growth in wealth has overtaken all other objects of human striving. Individuals may opt out: many do. But societies cannot safely do this without offering something else. There are many candidates, but few takers. In the competition to produce more wealth Britain has been doing increasingly badly. If 'standard of living' is defined in terms of what the contemporary world has to offer, the British are getting a decreasing share of it. This is the only meaning of decline which makes sense in our world: but it does make sense.

Decline matters, too, because it means loss of national self-confidence. Ralph Dahrendorf, sometime director of the London School of Economics put his finger on it when he described the clinical depression of the British people. Robert Skidelsky, writing as recently as 1985, has described living in Britain as akin to being in a social hospital. When self-belief declines nothing becomes possible.

How did we get into this parlous state? Notably we squandered the enormous head start we had over almost all our industrial competitors in the immediate post-war years. Squandered, too, the Marshall Aid of which we were greater recipients than West Germany. We had ample coal reserves and in the decades ahead were to discover oil. We had excellent sea and air communications, access to advanced technology, and a relatively well-educated, law-abiding populace. We also boasted a high level of scientific and technological creativity and, indeed, we rank only behind the Americans in providing radical innovations in the post-war period (for examples, see Appendix I). And we have gained more Nobel Prizes for science per head than any other country. Our extraordinary fertility in ideas is matched only by our failure to exploit them for commercial gain – a wealth of opportunities squandered.

On the evidence, Britain's failure to partake fully in the long post-war boom has been an achievement of sorts itself, albeit a negative one. How did we do it? Here is a masochist's check-list of some of the main reasons which have been given for our failure: bad, ill-trained management; stroppy, strike-prone, over-unionised workforce, resistant to change; persistent under-investment in industry; short-term profit mentality, combined with a failure to understand the long lead-times involved in high technology; poor pay, status and clout of engineers; over-investment in property at home and abroad; poor productivity; lack of coherent industrial strategy; the brain drain overseas and into the universities; anti-business, anti-technology and anti-enterprise cultural attitudes not encountered elsewhere; ineffective partnership between government, finance and industry; resources allocated to the creation of a welfare state when our competitors were building wealth-creating industries; financial sector favoured ahead of industry; high exchange and interest rates; high defence spending particularly on research and development (R&D) to the detriment of civil research; a technically illiterate, amateurish civil service; pendulum, class-based politics and stop–go policies; an unfair electoral system producing unrepresentative governments failing to command wide support; anachronistic institutions; an anti-utilitarian education system dominated by a liberal arts tradition; inadequate technical training as sponsored by both government and industry; poor design, marketing and delivery of goods followed by rotten after-sales service; laziness, sloppiness and lack of attention to detail as national characteristics; too high individual expectations; chronic tendency to over-pay ourselves; loss of captive empire markets; backward orientation, nostalgia; divisive class system; obsession with City froth rather than with building a robust industrial base; too few fleet-footed small companies, too many lumbering industrial mastodons; and so on and on.

Two features stand out from this remarkable and sorry catalogue: a failure of solid commitment at all levels of British society to the growth of industry; and a failure to achieve a common vision of the future, i.e. to agree a target. On the first point, the historian Martin Weiner has described in the nation that gave the world the industrial revolution a decline in the industrial spirit. This conjures up a picture of the industrial spirit rather like a raw material which we exported round the world and which is now exhausted. But we take his point. There is, in this country, a disdain for the making and selling of things which is not found abroad.

As for a common vision of the future, we seem to be perennially a nation at odds with ourselves. There has, however, been at least one area of agreement – what Robert Skidelsky has called the quest for national efficiency. This has provided what consensus there has been in British politics in the twentieth century. But governments and institutions have come and gone with barely a change in the trend of relative decline. For the last 150 years, British economic growth has averaged about 2 per cent per year, regardless of the policies of the day.

Novelist John le Carré, writing in *The Sunday Times* in March 1986, has given us a bleak view of the post-war years:

> For as long as I have been alive the hopes of every British generation have been dashed. The war generation saw the victory taken from it. In the dreary seesaw between failed socialism and failed capitalism that has followed since, there is enough motive for any number of angry or despairing gestures.

In case you thought that we enjoyed remission from the British disease during the Second World War, Corelli Barnett's *The Audit of War* seeks to alter your view. The author, an historian, bludgeons to death the comforting myth of war-time industrial efficiency wrought under the threat from Hitler's Germany. The familiar symptoms were there, even midst shot and shell: managerial incompetence, poor labour relations, innovative science and technology but severe production problems, and over-reliance on foreign manufacturing technology. Notably there was a lack of technically qualified personnel at all levels, a result of the lamentable uselessness of Britain's 'liberal' education system. The prime focus of post-war resource allocation was on achieving not an economic miracle but a social one based on equality, financial security, health for all and good housing – a 'New Jerusalem'. In the concluding sentence of the book, Corelli Barnett turns his sour gaze on the nation at peace:

> As that descent took its course, the illusions and dreams would fail one by one – the imperial and Commonwealth role, the world-power role, British industrial genius, and, at the last, New Jerusalem itself, a dream turned to a dank reality of a segregated, subliterate, unskilled, unhealthy and institutionalised proletariat hanging on the nipple of state maternalism.

Most contributors to the capacious literature of decline agree that the part of our economic life which has suffered most in the post-war era is manufacturing industry. We can gain some idea of our performance by considering briefly steel, cars and shipbuilding.

Iron and steel were at the heart of Britain's industrial supremacy of the nineteenth century – but the heart has beat less strongly since. A decade after the Second World War, Britain's and Germany's steel production were at about the same level, while France was producing half as much. By 1986 our production had dropped by a third, France was producing one-fifth more than us and Germany was producing two-and-a-half times as much.

In the 1950s we were, after the US, the world's largest producer of cars. Subsequently we were overtaken by West Germany, Japan, France, Italy, Canada and, recently, Spain. UK production, after doubling in the 1960s, has now returned to the level of the mid-1950s. The only remaining British-owned mass producer, Rover Group (formerly BL), had less than 16 per cent of the home market in 1986 and lost nearly £900 million. It has become increasingly reliant on a link-up with Honda of Japan.

As for shipbuilding, we were the world's largest builder of merchant ships in 1955. Today, we are struggling to keep in the top 20 with less than 2 per cent of world output.

Overall, in the late 1950s, we were exporting almost three times as many goods by value than we were importing (Figure 1). Now we are exporting slightly less and are net importers of finished manufactures for the first time since 1600.

If the car and steel industries narrowly survive, other bits of industry have, like shipbuilding, been less fortunate. The British industrial graveyard boasts headstones marked Motorcycles, Optics, Electronics, Typewriters and Consumer Durables. Places have been reserved for fork-lift trucks, machine tools, medical equipment, and bicycles. Over there are two graves that were nearly filled by Rolls-Royce and the textile industry. Under that long mound is British Rail's advanced passenger train. This part of the cemetery here I have reserved for Britain's civil nuclear power programme and Concorde, two particularly notable failures. Alongside Concorde are laid to rest other would-be aviation coups: Comet, Brabazon, Britannia, Princess flying-boat, Vickers Vanguard and the VC10. And here, in this particularly spacious area, are the last resting places of assorted military howlers including TSR2, Blue Streak, Black Arrow and a more recent arrival, under the fresh earth, the Nimrod airborne early warning system. No flowers by request.

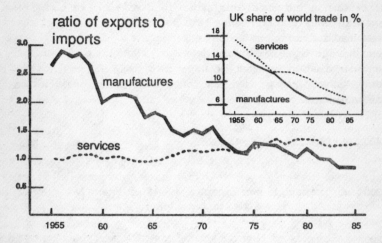

Figure 1. Manufacturing and service industry: ratio of exports to imports and shares of world trade
Source: *The Economist*

Britain has declined industrially but, looking back, we should beware of self-delusion. Our role in the nineteenth century as the 'workshop of the world' can be overstated. Despite our lead in industrialisation, it now seems fairly clear that by mid-century our exports were already concentrated in a small number of products based on the use of unskilled labour in relatively low wage industries. The key examples here are cotton and woollen textiles which accounted for 54 per cent of exports in 1851. Britain was 'overtaken' industrially by the US and Germany in the last quarter of the nineteenth century and was soon to be overtaken by other nations. *This said, it is important to note that our identifiable rapid decline vis-à-vis other nations is a phenomenon of the post-war years.*

Manufacturing's share of GDP has sunk from 37 per cent in 1955 to less than a quarter now, a sharper decline than for any other major industrial nation. The same is true of manufacturing employment which now accounts directly for just one in four jobs. There has been a trend towards service industries in all advanced industrial nations but the shrinking role of manufacturing has been especially striking in Britain. We are now probably better described as an industrialised service economy than an industrial nation.

In recent times relative industrial decline has turned into absolute decline. Note this well: *we were producing less in the mid-1980s than we did in the early 1970s.* No other nation has suffered this shrinkage; when times were hard, as they were in the early 1980s, other countries merely grew more slowly.

The decline in industrial production in Britain in the eighties is unprecedented this century. Figures 2 and 3 show the extent of it. Absolute and sustained declines in production are very unusual and it is not possible to argue that our recent performance is part of a continuous trend towards post-industrialisation in what is the world's most mature industrial economy. Rather, we have seen here halted industrialisation or, indeed, deindustrialisation.

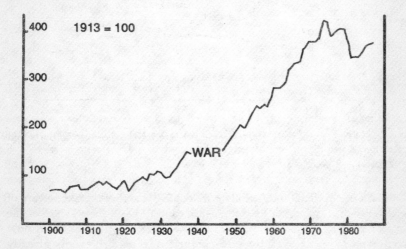

Figure 2. UK manufacturing production, 1900-1986
Source: *Economic Trends*, HMSO

Britain is now a relatively minor industrial power. We produce about one-third as much as the Japanese and just less than an eighth of the US. Our output is below two-thirds that of France and less than half that of West Germany. Can we afford to let manufacturing dwindle? The simple answer is 'no'. Over half of our exports still come from manufactured goods. These cannot realistically be replaced by selling services abroad. For example, City financial services brought in just one-sixth of the foreign exchange earnings of our manufacturers in 1985. They would need to expand 7 per cent just to compensate for a 1 per cent fall in foreign sales of industrial goods. And that ignores the employment issue. Over five million jobs still depend on manufacturing directly and twice as many again indirectly.

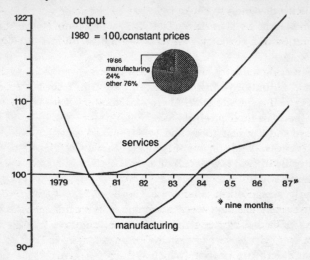

Figure 3. Manufacturing and service industry output, 1979–85
Source: *Economic Trends*, HMSO

What if we threw up protectionist barriers to shield our surviving industries? We would probably be hurt more than most other nations if there was retaliation as about 30 per cent of our income derives from exports. We would probably have to act in concert with our European partners. An economist working for the investment bank Goldman Sachs concluded that a full-scale trade war between the European Community and America could reduce output in both places by up to 20 per cent. This would have a disastrous effect on both employment and living standards.

We are a trading nation *par excellence.* We are not self-sufficient in food or raw materials; we need to trade in goods. To do this we need a successful industry. As the Henley Centre for Forecasting has said:

> On all conventional definitions, a continual contraction of the manufacturing base of the UK is not consistent with sustaining existing average living standards let alone with a real growth in prosperity.

The First Eight Thatcher Years

Recent times have not been kind to manufacturing industry and there have been fundamental structural changes to the British economy. In macroeconomic terms the two most striking phenomena were the slump in world trade in 1980–1 and the subsequent recovery. The slump was triggered by oil price rises in 1979 and was exacerbated for Britain by a loss of competitiveness due to high exchange and interest rates. These had two causes: the pound's petro-status and the new Thatcher government's tight fiscal policies designed to choke inflation by reducing demand – dubbed sado-monetarism by its critics. The rise in the pound was the largest over-valuation of a currency ever recorded by the International Monetary Fund.

Manufacturing industry, the most exposed sector, was clobbered by these factors, and output, investment and employment had not returned to 1979 levels over half a decade later. The manufacturers were partly to blame, however, because their products too often did not have the quality image of Japanese and German goods and were thus too sensitive to loss of price competitiveness. Trade in manufactured goods deteriorated from a £5 billion surplus in 1980 to a deficit of more than £3 billion five years later.

The business cycles of the major non-communist industrial nations became increasingly synchronised after the oil crises of 1973–4 and 1979. Britain seemed to become the 'bow wave' economy: we were first into the recession in the late 1970s and first to emerge from the downturn in mid-1981. The recession was, alas, also heaviest in Britain whether judged by a fall in GDP, manufacturing output (which fell 15 per cent in the first three Thatcher years) or unemployment. With our new status as oil producer we might have expected to do reasonably well out of the oil price rise but instead, as industry suffered, unemployment rose at twice the world level to well over 3 million. This involved an increase between 1979 and 1985 of 8 percentage points here against 4 in France, 5.25 in West Germany, 1.5 in the US and 3 in Italy. Britain in this period suffered over 16 million man-years of unemployment which was some 5–6 million more than France, for example.

Levels of unemployment have been higher in the 1980s than during the Great Depression and leaving aside the social cost, the financial cost has been horrendous. Between 1979 and 1985, the money spent on unemployment benefits was £33 billion. This compares in magnitude with the government's tax revenues from North Sea oil of £51 billion.

By mid-decade, recovery had gathered pace. Growth was a healthy 3.5 per cent in 1985, which was more than twice the annual average for the previous decade. Particularly encouraging was an 8 per cent increase in exports of manufactured goods as against a 6 per cent rise in imports and a 6 per cent growth in world trade. Oil trade also improved to produce a surplus on the current account of £3.6 billion.

We were still behind our main competitors, however, in terms of inflation, unemployment, rise in unit labour costs and interest rates. And the presence of a surplus on the current account masked a disturbing trend in the pattern of trade. Britain ran a deficit in visible trade (i.e. in goods) in 1985 of £2.1 billion, which would have been £10 billion but for £8 billion surplus on the oil account. The deficit on finished manufactured goods was particularly serious at over £3 billion. Fortunately, the overall deficit on visible trade was more than offset by net 'invisible' earnings of over £5 billion from such sources as banking, tourism and foreign investments. Britain has enjoyed a surplus on invisibles in every year since 1948 but between 1982 and 1985 earnings trebled. Several factors were at work.

The trade in financial services via the City of London has been a British success story with earnings doubling in real terms between 1979 and 1985 to about £7.6 billion. At the same time, Britain's travel account (business and tourism) moved into surplus in 1985 following four consecutive years of deficit as Britain played host to 14 million foreign visitors. (Tourism, incidentally, turned over £14 billion in 1985 compared, for example, to the motor industry's £9 billion.)

Another factor in the invisibles boom has been foreign investments. This represents the biggest change in Britain's post-war financial history. Our overseas assets grew much larger than the assets held by foreigners in Britain and as a result we were enjoying a surplus on investment income – from interest, profits and dividends – of over £4 billion by mid-decade. The £80-90 billion we had stashed away abroad was up from £12 billion in 1979. Since the abolition of exchange controls in that year, in fact, money had flooded abroad attracted by higher returns. Incongruously, given our dismal manufacturing performance, we had acquired more overseas assets than any other industrial nation except Japan.

The various contributions to invisible trade made us the world's largest invisible earners in 1985 ahead of Spain (profiting from tourism) and Switzerland (banking). Until recently, America held the title but that nation had converted itself from the world's biggest creditor into its biggest debtor.

A vital factor in our economic equation was the vertiginous drop in the price of oil in early 1986 to its lowest level in twelve years. Britain was going ex-oil with a bang. The surplus on the oil account was halved in that year. At the same time, growth in export earnings weakened and imports boomed. The trade deficit reached £1.5 billion in August alone – an all-time monthly record – and £8.5 billion for the year, another record. Fortunately, the surplus on invisibles increased by a half to well over £7 billion. This included earnings from our foreign assets now valued at £114 billion. Invisibles helped cut the balance of payments deficit, the first since 1979, to just short of £1 billion.

Growth in 1986 was 2.6 per cent. This was the fifth year of economic growth since the recession of the early 1980s. Britain was enjoying its longest, though not steepest, upswing this century. Unemployment remained over 3 million, however, contributing disproportionately to the EC's 'man-mountain' which had reached a record 16.4 million unemployed by the end of 1986.

Inflation fell to 3.7 per cent in 1986. This compared with an average of 2.8 per cent among the member-states of the Organization for Economic Co-operation and Development (OECD), the Paris-based capitalists' club. In spite of reduced inflation, British earnings in 1986 went up by 7.8 per cent.

Margaret Thatcher became prime minister in 1979. She was the first woman to lead a major Western democracy and she was to become better known internationally than most of her male predecessors. A radical populist, Mrs Thatcher was a 'conviction politician' believing in strong government rather than consensus. Her intentions were to make British industry more competitive and market-orientated, and to reverse the nation's historic relative decline. She wanted to reduce the dependence of individuals on the welfare state and foster self-reliance. How did we fare during the first eight Thatcher years?

The short answer is 'not particularly well'. The economy grew at below 1.5 per cent on average each year through two Tory governments to the 1987 election, a slower growth rate than that achieved by most of our industrial competitors. Manufacturing experienced an upturn after the early setbacks, but output in 1986 was still 4.9 per cent below 1979 levels. In the early 1980s we played host to the Western world's worst recession. The government's critics regard it as having exacerbated the slump by following monetarist policies and by over-reliance on market forces. Nearly two million manufacturing jobs were lost during the resulting 'shake-out' and in the years that followed. Some of the companies that survived were undoubtedly leaner and fitter – Jaguar was much cited – but others remained weak and relatively vulnerable to competitive pressures and currency changes. Our share of world manufacturing trade had slipped to an all-time low in 1981 according to Henley Centre calculations, and had hardly recovered thereafter. Britain's share of trade had slipped below that of Italy which on some reckonings had replaced us as the fifth largest industrial economy in the capitalist world.

In terms of relative wealth, the British people continued to lose ground against those of other industrial nations. A GDP analysis was published in 1987 by the EC and the OECD. It comprised a comparison of 19 advanced nations on the basis of per capita GDP at 'purchasing power parities' which allow for different price levels for goods and services in different countries. This is regarded as a fairer basis of comparison than a straight conversion into a common currency of national incomes at market exchange rates. Between 1976 and 1985, Britain became better off but we slipped in the ranking from tenth to twelfth place despite the boon of North Sea oil. Unsurprisingly, Germany and Japan were among the ten nations which improved their position relative to us. We did better against seven countries including France, where growth noticeably faltered in the eighties, and the United States, though both these two remain richer than us.

Figures for the GDP comparison were not available for all the OECD's twenty-four member-states, notably for Switzerland, Australia and Iceland. Assuming, fairly, that these nations were richer per head than us in 1976 and 1985, then our relative position declined from thirteenth to fifteenth. If you take account of rich nations such as Kuwait and Saudi Arabia outside the OECD, then we were barely in the world's top 20 in 1985. Since 1985, however, we have grown quite strongly, meaning that we have probably at least maintained our position in the economic ranking.

The government has claimed success in curbing inflation. This fell to a 17-year low of 2.4 per cent in the summer of 1986 helped by falling oil and international commodity prices. The experience at the start of the Thatcher years was rather different. In 1979, the government doubled VAT and reduced income tax by 3 per cent. This radical package stoked up wage demands, contributing to a rise in the annual inflation rate in May 1980 to 21.9 per cent. During the period 1981-5 Britain's average inflation rate was 6.8 per cent. This was lower than in France and Italy but higher than in West Germany, Japan, the United States and other OECD nations.

We endured historically high levels of unemployment between 1979 and 1987, significantly more than other industrial nations. For much of the time there were over 3 million unemployed with perhaps 40 per cent of these having been on the dole for more than a year. The annual cost of dole payments was running at about £8 billion by the end of the second Thatcher term of office. Precise analyses of unemployment trends became difficult because the government made a score of changes to the statistical basis on which the figures were calculated. Only once did this have the effect of increasing the count and then only slightly.

The government evinced a 'hands off' attitude to job creation in the first half of the decade. Later, when low inflation growth was seen not to be producing jobs, the government developed a considerable enthusiasm for special schemes particularly aimed at the young. This was a popular U-turn.

Social commentators spoke of a huge 'underclass' of the low paid, unemployed and participants in the unofficial ('black') economy. This increased social stratification led to renewed talk of 'two nations'. An increase in the labour force had been accompanied by an absolute decline in the number of jobs in the economy. In late 1986, the employed labour force was 24 million. This was 1 million more than in 1983, the start of the second Thatcher government, but nearly 1 million less than in 1979. We had lost more jobs in the period 1979-86 than the whole of the rest of the EC put together. A sharp decrease in manufacturing jobs, particularly in the north and midlands, had been partially offset later by a rise in part-time and service employment.

During the early Thatcher period when the pound was seriously overvalued and industry suffered such a body-blow in consequence, the government refused to intervene. Later it did so routinely as the pound slithered in 1986 to its lowest-ever level against other European currencies.

The Tories' ambition in 1979 was to cut public spending every year in real terms. This they failed to do. In the late sixties, public expenditure averaged 38 per cent of GDP. By the latter half of the seventies this had risen to 44 per cent. As a result of Mrs Thatcher's 'cuts', public spending accounted for 46 per cent of a larger GDP in the period 1980–5 though it declined slightly as a proportion thereafter. The main increases in public spending outside the welfare system occurred in the areas of defence and law and order where, according to one report, expenditure went up by more than a quarter during the two Thatcher governments. Spending on other services fell by 3 per cent during the same period. The number of civil servants fell from 730,000 to 600,000.

With lower public spending was to have come lower taxes. Instead, taking all forms of tax together, we were paying significantly more by 1987 than we did in 1978–9, Labour's last year, when taxes and national insurance contributions amounted to 33.8 per cent of national income. By 1988, the figure was 38 per cent. Income tax, however, had been reduced from a basic rate of 33 per cent in 1979 to 27 per cent in 1987. Corporation tax went down from 52 to 35 per cent.

The government proclaimed a faith in 'market forces.' This did not spare them from interventionist fiascos such as Lear Fan, DeLorean and Nexos. Economist David Henderson wrote in 1985:

The notion that Mrs Thatcher and those of her ministers who share her views are ardent and consistent devotees of nineteenth century economic liberalism is mistaken. Over wide areas of policy they are convinced interventionists.

Market-orientation, if not invariably practised in areas such as energy, agriculture and housing, was encouraged in others. Several old industries – notably coal, steel and textiles – reduced their capacity, cut their costs and increasingly produced goods their customers wanted at a price they were willing to pay. To quote Correlli Barnett: 'In a word, heavy industry has ceased to be part of the social services'.

During the first eight Thatcher years Britain remained a grudging member of the EC. Mrs Thatcher, concerned by Britain's high contribution to the Community's budget, waged a popular and successful war of words to 'get our money back'. In 1986, for the first time, 50 per cent of our trade (imports and exports) was with the other 11 Community countries. Trade with the EC reached £79.8 billion, exactly half total trade of £159.6 billion.

Industrial productivity increased from an average annual rate of 1.9 per cent a year in the years 1960–80 to 2.6 per cent a year since then. This improvement was partly wrought by job-shedding. According to the International Monetary Fund our productivity improved more slowly than the European average.

Agricultural productivity has continued to increase. Output rose by 2 per cent a year over the decade to the mid-1980s, faster than total GDP. The cereal harvest rose 60 per cent. Farmers' incomes, however, have fallen in recent years. The EC's Common Agricultural Policy was widely vilified for causing massive food surpluses and for its distortive effects (worldwide) on the market for agricultural products. In 1985, 70 per cent of Community spending went on farming. Three-quarters of this amount went to the richest quarter of farmers. Consumers in Europe were beefing up farmers' incomes by $40 billion a year through higher than necessary food prices.

In the mid-1980s, company profits boomed, more than recovering from the 1979–81 recession. Raw materials were cheaper, interest rates, though higher here than elsewhere, were falling, and demand for goods had strengthened. Despite booming profits, investment remained at a stubbornly low level. Industrialists seemed to prefer setting aside money for mergers and acquisitions, and building up financial assets. Investment in plant and equipment in 1987 was 17.5 per cent below a previous peak in 1979, which in turn was lower than the level in 1970.

Between 1979 and 1987, spending by the Department of Trade and Industry had dropped by nearly two-thirds. Some found this a remarkable instance of parsimony for a nation allegedly in the throes of industrial regeneration. Continuity was hardly likely to be helped by frequent changes at the top. The DTI was headed by half a dozen different ministers during Mrs Thatcher's first two administrations.

Company takeovers reached record levels in 1986 at a frothy £13.5 billion and involved some 700 acquisitions. This was up from £7 billion in 1985. Only a minority of acquisitions seemed to have significant industrial justification. Management buy-outs, arguably a healthier activity, also boomed.

The stock market enjoyed a record-breaking boom with share prices more than trebling between 1979 and mid-1987. It was the strongest bull market since the 1920s. The City was deregulated in the 'Big Bang' of 1986.

Sell-offs of a dozen and a half state owned companies raised some £20 billion. As a result of this series of double-your-money privatisations, taxpayers with cash to spare, and the inclination to use it, gained at the expense of other taxpayers. The government was accused of selling off assets cheaply. One justification for the programme was increased competition but this goal was not reached in most cases, notably as regards the megalithic British Telecom and British Gas. Even so, the managements of newly privatised companies seemed to sharpen up at least in the immediate aftermath of the sale – and the scope was increased for international endeavour (e.g. British Telecom's purchase of the Canadian company Mitel).

Privatisation was pioneered in Britain and may yet be regarded as the major achievement of the Thatcher years. It has been widely copied abroad. Turkey has sold the Bosphorus bridge and the Keban dam; Japan, NTT; and France, a large proportion of Elf-Aquitaine and St Gobain. Other examples abound.

Privatisation helped widen the number of private shareholders from an estimated 2.5 million in 1979 to 8–9 million in 1987. The increase in share ownership, the rise in vacuous takeover activity and the boom in share prices led some observers to describe us increasingly as a nation of mini-capitalists in a candy-floss economy.

The number of self-employed individuals rose to almost 10 per cent of the total labour force, a rise of a quarter since 1981. To a government committed to promoting a culture of enterprise this was doubtless a welcome trend. Another related to business start-ups which, expressed as new companies per 1000 people, almost doubled between 1979 and 1987. Bankruptcies, however, were also running at high levels.

Venture capital came of age. Funding rose steeply and reached £400 million a year. We were investing as much proportionately as the Americans and we were well ahead of our European counterparts. The British Venture Capital Association reckoned that the typical new entrepreneur was a former senior manager, professionally qualified and over 35 years of age. Half of the business ventures were in the high-tech field. An encouraging sign this, but among the advanced countries, Britain continued to have one of the smallest small-business manufacturing sectors.

High-tech industry blossomed in some parts of the country, notably along the M4 and M11 corridors in England and in Silicon Glen in Scotland. Service industries expanded rapidly in London and elsewhere, while traditional industrial areas declined. This was true also in mainland Europe, but there, outlying regions saw real growth in manufacturing. Dr David Keeble of Cambridge University's department of geography described this phenomenon as affecting southern and western France, southern Germany and southern Italy. 'The peripheral regions of Europe, with the exception of Scotland and northern England, have been showing signs of industrial buoyancy,' Dr Keeble was reported as saying.

The worst excesses of trade union power were curbed by tough legislation and by governmental resolution in the face of industrial action. Membership of the unions dropped between 1979 and 1987 by about 3 million to just over 9 million. This was in large part due to a decline in manufacturing, but also fewer factory managements were recognising unions and a million fewer workers were in closed shops than in 1980. Working practices had become more efficient. The proportion of Britain's workforce in unions, however, at 43 per cent remained higher than in other comparable economies such as Italy, West Germany, Japan, France and the

United States.

In 1985, there were fewer strikes than in any year since 1938 and the number of days lost was at its lowest level since 1979. The average number of working days lost through strikes per 1,000 employees, however, remained far higher in Britain during the 1980s than in our European neighbours France and Germany. Only Italy's level of industrial disharmony compared with our own.

The miners' strike in 1984–5 was probably the bitterest industrial dispute in the nation's history. The Treasury has since calculated that the adverse effect on the current account was in the order of £2.75 billion. The strike provoked the finest oratory of the day. Speaking before the House of Lords, the late Harold Macmillan, a former Conservative prime minister and the first Earl of Stockton, said: 'it breaks my heart to see what is happening in our country today. A terrible strike is being carried on by the best men in the world.'

Another industrial dispute was that involving the print workers in 1986 and early 1987. The arrival of News International in London's Dockland signalled the long overdue arrival of the national newspaper industry into the latter part of the twentieth century. There were many vicious scenes outside the company's new printing plant in Wapping.

Those in jobs had seldom done better, particularly in the south of the country where GDP per capita in 1986 was 40 per cent higher than in the north. Even in manufacturing, real wages went up 26 per cent between 1980 and 1986. The gap between those on high and low incomes grew. The two Thatcher governments did not experiment with an incomes policy. This was a break with Conservative and Labour precedent.

Men tended to do better out of the rise in incomes than women. In 1970, men in full-time work earned 80 per cent more than women. By 1981 this difference had fallen to just under 50 per cent, but by 1985 it was up to 52 per cent. The preponderance of women in low-paid occupations was as marked as ever.

According to figures from the Department of Health and Social Security, 5.9 million people lived at or below the poverty line in 1979. This had risen to 8.8 million in 1983 and an estimated 10.2 million in 1986. The 'poverty line' in 1986 was the supplementary benefit level of £29.40 a week for a single person and £44.80 for a couple. If people in the next worst-off group were included in the figures – the highest income here being 40 per cent above the poverty line – then over 16 million people were experiencing financial hardship. That was somewhat less than one in three of us – a new record. And poverty was not confined to the inner cities. A quarter of rural households were on or below the poverty line.

Meanwhile, among the better off, consumer spending boomed, particularly on foreign goods. Between 1979 and 1986 the volume of retail sales went up by a quarter but the output of UK consumer goods had declined by nearly 4 per cent. Consumers benefited from increased competition and choice; building societies started vying more with the banks in the area of personal financial services; spectacles became cheaper; so did conveyancing, but the process of house purchase remained as scandalously unpredictable and fraught as ever. There was some progress on air fares and rivalry increased within the bus industry and between bus and rail. An attempt to reform our byzantine Sunday trading laws was flunked. Efforts to liberalise the licensing laws in England and Wales and bring them into line with those in Scotland also largely failed.

Personal debt increased enormously. Accumulated indebtedness – which embraces everything from credit cards to home loans – increased from 44 per cent of household income in 1979 to an estimated 73 per cent in 1986. A call by Mrs Thatcher for a return to the 'Victorian values' – which presumably include thrift and moderation – had evidently fallen on deaf ears.

In 1986, 64 per cent of households were owner-occupied. This was 10 percentage points more than a decade earlier and almost 40 per cent more than in 1945. The trend was welcomed on most sides, but an increasing number of households became overstretched. Mortgage defaults, which numbered 8,000 in 1979, leapt to 60,000 in 1985.

Over one million council houses were sold to their occupants, a popular move. New public housing projects were few. Government expenditure on housing fell vertiginously from £2.1 billion in 1979 to an estimated £650 million in 1986. The number of those 'accepted as homeless' rose 65 per cent by 1985 to 94,000. The cost of putting up the homeless in board and lodging had increased tenfold by 1984 to £503 million. Almost a quarter of Britain's housing stock was reckoned to be substandard. A TUC report, *Britain's Housing Scandal*, was published to coincide with the UN's International Year of Shelter for the Homeless in 1987. The report commented:

> The old social evils of housing shortage, homelessness, squatting, bad and decaying housing, overcrowding, are once more emerging on a large scale. Much of the progress over the last forty years is ebbing away.

In housing and in other fields such as education and rate-setting the power of local government was curtailed and there was a corresponding increase in centralism. This was seen by some as an undesirable trend away from local democracy. 1986 saw the abolition of the Greater London Council (GLC) and the six Metropolitan County Councils. The GLC's assistant director-general in its last three years, Peter Brayshaw, became director of the London Strategic Policy Unit. A year after the demise of the GLC, he wrote: 'Far from "streamlining" local government abolition has been costly, confusing, and for some services not far short of chaotic.'

Education was a continuing cause for concern. The British remained on average the worst trained and most poorly educated people in Europe. This situation was unlikely to have been helped by the public secondary education system which was in a disarray unique in modern times. The pay of teachers had declined in relative terms and their right to bargain with their employers had been curtailed. The resulting industrial action disrupted classrooms in many of Britain's 30,000 state schools. Pupils turfed out of lessons may ruefully have considered that the word 'school' comes from an ancient Greek word meaning 'leisure'. Some educational commentators were saying that it might take a generation to undo the damage. Meanwhile, the private schools were unaffected by the ructions in the state sector and, indeed, steadily increased their share of the (declining) school population during the 1980s.

Higher education was also enduring a bleak period. In the early 1980s, student places were cut and resources were withdrawn and in some cases university departments had to close. The number of teaching and research staff in universities declined by one-tenth in the period 1979-87. We were educating fewer of our young people to graduate standard than most other industrial nations, and the proportion was lower than in 1970. Overseas students, charged full-cost fees since 1979, had declined 40 per cent by 1985.

The universities were forced to seek money from industry and from commercialising the fruits of academic research. By 1987 there were 26 campus science parks housing 380 companies. The brain drain from industry into the universities had stopped as academic rates of pay fell in relative terms. There were shortages of lecturers in some subjects such as electronic engineering and shortages, too, of appropriately qualified graduates. In the mid-1980s, Britain was producing 270 engineering graduates per million of the population, compared with 350 in the US and 630 in Japan. Most of these engineers were men; just 3 per cent of British women graduates emerged with engineering degrees in 1983.

Cut-backs, poor pay and scarce promotion prospects were driving 1000 trained scientists and engineers abroad each year in the eighties, according to the Royal Society. Observers of the education scene claimed to have detected a new twist to the long-running and oft-exaggerated brain drain saga – a haemorrhage of arts and humanities professors from Britain to America. According to Steven Lukes, fellow of Balliol: 'Americans believe they are seeing the most sustained academic immigration since Jewish scholars fled Hitler.'

The research councils had to draw in their horns. One-third of top-rated research proposals were being turned down. The Advisory Board for the Research Councils, the body that co-ordinates science funding in Britain, was quoted in early 1987 as saying: 'The country's investment in its science base is falling further behind the investment made by other OECD countries.' It was said that civil research spending was being run down as a proportion of national income as a deliberate act of government policy. Sir

George Porter, President of the Royal Society, claimed that there was clear evidence 'that the country's scientific output and prestige are declining in relation to our competitors'. British scientists were publishing less than formerly and their publications were being cited less by other scientists.

Industrial science, like academic science, was also in relatively poor shape. There was a dramatic slump in R&D spending in the early 1980s coinciding with the recession, and the rate of spending had not fully recovered by 1985. In 1981, there were 195,000 people in industrial R&D establishments according to Department of Trade and Industry statistics, and this number had fallen 20 per cent by 1985 to 157,000. British firms seemed as myopic as ever when it came to investment in research.

Work started on Britain's first US-style pressurised water reactor at Sizewell in Suffolk following the longest inquiry in the nation's history. The power station would cost an estimated £1.5 billion and was expected to be in operation by 1995. The PWR design was favoured over a power station based on the British-designed advanced gas-cooled reactor or on the use of coal.

Attempts were made to bring the Channel Tunnel closer to realisation. Private funding was sought.

Defence spending was buoyant at well over 5 per cent of GNP in 1986, the International Year of Peace. This was higher than that of France or West Germany and lower only than that of the United States among the major Western nations. A decision to adopt the Trident missile system was taken; critics argued that this eightfold expansion of Britain's nuclear deterrent promoted the arms race and had as much to do with national self-delusion as national self-defence. On present evidence, they said, the judgement of history on this *folie de grandeur* would be scathing. During the 1980s, Britain signed an agreement to participate in research on America's remarkable and controversial Strategic Defence Initiative and contracts were won by a number of British university research teams.

The Falklands war was fought over 74 days in 1982 and won. The subsequent military consolidation seemed empty of hope for a sensible long-term solution.

The Nimrod early warning airborne radar system was cancelled after costs had been incurred over a decade of about £1 billion.

A major achievement of foreign policy was the 1984 agreement between Peking and London on the restoration of Chinese rule in Hong Kong in 1997. Another achievement was the transfer of Rhodesia (now Zimbabwe) to majority (black) rule, and a third was the signing of the Anglo–Irish Agreement on Northern Ireland.

Overseas development aid was quietly curtailed. Aid consumed half a percentage point of GNP in 1979, but this had dropped to one-third of a percentage point by 1984. Britain had earlier accepted an OECD

Development Assistance Committee target for aid of 0.7 per cent of GNP without setting a date for achieving it. By 1986, aid had fallen over 15 per cent in real terms. Most other industrial countries were managing to be less parsimonious than us.

Britain's reputation internationally for tolerance and as a haven for refugees declined with new nationality laws and other moves to restrict immigration.

At home, race relations remained as poor as ever. In 1985, Britain's worst-ever race riot occurred on the Broadwater Farm housing estate in north London when a policeman was killed. According to the Policy Studies Institute, a third of employers were turning down job applicants on the basis of skin colour. In some inner city areas Asians slept soundly in their beds only after flame-proof letterboxes were fitted. The social and political ethos of the eighties seemed to offer unimpressive resistance to intolerant racial attitudes.

Crime grew to record levels (see Part II), and the inner cities erupted, notably in 1981 and 1985. More of us were in jail than ever before and the Tories embarked on the first major prison building programme of modern times. Police powers were increased, while civil liberties were eroded, particularly as regards the right to protest. The government was hauled before the European Court of Human Rights on a wide range of issues. We were found to have undermined the right of privacy, the right to freedom of conscience, the right to freedom of expression, and the right to freedom of association.

There were a stream of spy scandals and the Official Secrets banana skin was brought out from time to time for the government to slip on. Other brouhahas (e.g. over Westland Helicopters, the City, and so on) abounded. Public confidence in the probity of politicians was as low as ever.

The Black Report of 1980 on social inequalities and health was shelved. The poor continued to suffer a disproportionate amount of sickness and premature death. Meanwhile, private health care expanded rapidly after 1979 and private health insurance covered 10 per cent of the population by 1987.

So in summary we can see that after two terms of what the government's critics were regarding as school-marm Thatcherism, the report card (on the headmistress and her staff) made rather indifferent reading. A poor verdict seemed particularly apposite on the grim early years when industry suffered so much – 600 firms of reasonable size went to the wall – and before scorched-earth monetarism was finally abandoned, to be replaced by fiscal expansion and exchange rate depreciation.

Arguably, a significant positive impact was made by the Tories in the following major areas: income and corporation tax, City financial activities, privatisations, company profits, share ownership, trade union reform, inflation, sale of council houses, foreign policy, foreign investment, promotion of an enterprise culture, defence (including the Falklands war), police and prisons, and looking after the better-off two-thirds of the population.

The Tories were vulnerable to criticism in the following areas: wealth and industry (relative economic and industrial decline unhalted), unemployment, public spending, tax (other than income and corporation tax), sterling (overvaluation in the early 1980s), education, science, agriculture, regional disparities ('north–south divide'), race relations, inner-city decay, local government, infrastructural investment (roads, railway, sewers, etc.), civil liberties, crime (including that in the City), inequalities in health, and failure to look after the worse-off one-third of the population.

The first eight Thatcher years provided multiple ironies: the party of business presided over an absolute decline in manufacturing output; the position of women in society (e.g. as regards relative earnings and employment rights relating to maternity) worsened under the tenure of Britain's first woman prime minister; and leadership by a sometime scientist and ex-minister of education had not prevented decline in science and education – two areas on which many felt Britain's future depended.

The fortuitous bonus of North Sea oil buttressed the wealth of the British people in the 1980s. As the oil years pass, the economic picture shows financial strength (e.g. those overseas assets) offset by industrial weakness. Britain increasingly seems a nation of bankers, waiters, foreign investors and creatures of (enforced) leisure. The government's critics saw it as having squandered oil revenues on unemployment benefits and as having promoted foreign investments rather than in reversing the decline in our industrial base which we alone have suffered among the industrial nations. In this analysis, the Tories have lacked vision. The crucial deficiency of post-war Britain, the weakness of manufacturing industry, has not been adequately corrected. By this criterion, if by no other, the first two governments of Mrs Thatcher, like all post-war governments before them, have to be judged as failures.

Another Term for Mrs T.

In the June 1987 election, Mrs Thatcher's Conservatives were returned to power with a 101-seat majority gained on a better than 43 per cent share of the vote. The election campaign had been dominated, as ever in Britain, by discussions on the distribution of wealth rather than its creation. At election time economic growth was running at over 3 per cent but the visible trade deficit, Europe's worst, was at an annual rate of about £8 billion. Manufacturing output at last surpassed the 1979 level in mid-1987. In October of that year, the stock market plunged sharply as part of a worldwide trend. In the event, this did not stop the government's sale of its remaining 31.5% stake in Britain's largest company, British Petroleum, as part of its third-term privatisation programme.

In 1987 inflation was 3.7 per cent while average earnings rose by over 8 per cent. Unemployment at 2.7 million by year's end represented 9.4 per cent of the workforce. Industrial production grew 3.7 per cent in the year to November. The current account was in deficit for the year by over £2.5 billion. Sterling had appreciated against the dollar to reach a five-year high.

The 1987 visible trade deficit was £9.1 billion, which was the world's second largest after America's, and a new national record.

2
Objectives

Having endured the heavy seas of national self-analysis, we can now move into calmer, more reflective waters. The current position has been described, and now we have to decide where we want to be as a nation in the future, as we approach the third millenium indeed.

One great failing of post-war Britain has been the absence of a shared vision of the future. Another, related failing has been the lack of an agreed, long-term industrial strategy. With these deficiencies in mind, we must be sure to frame clear objectives and then describe explicit strategies to achieve them. Before describing the objectives, however, let us agree on the basics and the context.

Planning for the future, of course, assumes we have one. For the purposes of this exercise I am assuming that Europe, at least, remains at peace. I also assume that most of us would agree on what can be called the 'motherhood and apple pie' basic requirements of life which include: adequate food, water, clean air, shelter, fuel and material goods for everyone; blooming health; good environment; high level of civil liberties and freedom; maximum opportunity for happiness, freedom and significant endeavour (including work); adequate leisure; reasonable density of people; political, economic and social stability; minimal (preferably non-existent) crime; low risk of accidental death; and so on.

These are the basics, now the context. We live, of course, in an increasingly interrelated world. Our scope for independent national action is limited. As Barbara Ward has put it 'no nation, no race, no culture can escape a truly global destiny'. This was said in the context of the environment and resources debate but is as true in other spheres such as economics and politics. We are to some extent at the mercy of factors outside our control – but fortunately the news in the near future should be fairly good.

Most commentators agree that there will be sufficient food, energy and raw materials in the world over the next 25 years on any likely projection of world population growth. There will be the usual distribution problems, however, and these will be particularly crucial where food is concerned and cruel in their consequences for the poorest nations. That is, of course, unless appropriate action is taken.

The world economic picture looks relatively promising. The early 1980s were a period of low growth and high inflation. Growth then picked up and inflation fell. The prospects in the future could be even better. Here is how the Henley Centre for Forecasting sees it:

> Even the briefest examination of the economic prospects for the 'big' economies leads to the conclusion that future growth rates that are at least as high as the experience of the 1960s are not merely feasible but plausible – even though the undoubted difficulties of the period from early 1970s have inspired many people to believe that zero or low growth should constitute the vision of the long-term future.

Another factor needs to be mentioned – technology. The signs are that we are about to be engulfed by a wave of technology-led economic expansion focussing on the increasing use of microelectronics which could, among other things, lead to the establishment of the much-heralded information society of the future. Also of significance are developments in biotechnology, manufacturing, transport, energy and so on. Some pundits have correlated long, cyclical economic surges in the past with clusters of technological developments. Henley again: 'if the reader is impressed by the long-cycle theories, it should be noted that many interpretations of the apparent cycles *do* date the next long upswing from the late 1980s'. If we catch this wave, we will truly be surfing.

This then is the favourable background against which we can state our objectives. But note: with sufficient determination, the objectives should be attainable even if the world economic situation stays very much as it has been in recent years. The key words here, of course, are 'sufficient determination'. The truth is that since the Second World War we have failed, at least in terms of relative prosperity, because we have deserved to do so. We must deserve to do better before we will do better. Banal but true.

What, then, are the objectives? They are quite straightforward and uncontroversial:

1. increased prosperity
2. improved quality of life
3. restored national morale

I have put them in this order because that is the order in which I am going to deal with them. It is clear, though, that prosperity, at the head of the list, is the most obvious thing wrong with contemporary Britain and that, to an extent, the achievement of the other objectives depends on improving this. There is more to life, though, than vulgar materialism and more to put right than relative poverty.

Some feel that the quality of life has declined in Britain in recent times. There is mention of inner city decay and civil disturbances, crime, social slippage, a 'hardness' in politics, increased vulgarity in popular entertainments, football hooliganism, environmental damage, social divisions, a too-ready resort to violence, job losses and so on. This kind of analysis can be pushed too far – and political utterances can lead us to lose a sense of proportion. On one side are the reflex criticisms of opposition politicians; on the other, the emollient reassurances of the government of the day. We do not have to agree, however, on whether the quality of life has actually declined, only that there is substantial room for improvement.

Aspects of the quality of life will be dealt with in both Part II and Part III. The latter will also consider the important subject of national morale.

One striking feature of modern Britain is a lack of self-confidence and an air of defeat. Forty-odd years of failure have taken their toll. This deterioration must be reversed.

We can all share the objectives I have described which can be summed up as follows: 'I want myself, my family and friends, and my fellow countrymen to be better off through honest endeavour, to enjoy a better quality of life, and I want us to feel good about ourselves.' This is very commendable, I am sure you will agree. But how does our present approach differ from that of a long series of post-war governments, all of which have had as their goal the revitalisation of Britain? Two things: clearly stated targets, our progress towards which can be monitored, and explicit strategies free of woolly-mindedness.

The target for prosperity – the subject of this section – should be described fully and given a value in pounds sterling. Let us set our sights on reaching the (ever-rising) level of prosperity of our more advanced European neighbours by the end of the century, and in the process resume our place in the front rank of nations. As GDP in 1987 was about £350bn, let us aim for £700bn, at current prices, by the year 2000. Given our relatively stable population, this is a doubling in income for each of us and represents an annual growth rate of nearly 6 per cent. This is very hefty growth indeed by British standards, but we have a lot of catching up to do. In stating this GDP aspiration we may be a pioneer: perhaps the first western nation to announce such a target over a span of more than a decade. How are we to achieve it? This is where the explicit strategies come in.

3
Economic Sub-strategy

I am proposing a Wealth and Well-being strategy which comprises sub-strategies for economics and lifestyle, together with a package of political and other reforms. The economic sub-strategy, which will be described here, has as its themes *vision* and *commitment*: vision in anticipating what the future will be like, deciding how we can succeed and believing we *can* succeed; commitment to those parts of the economy in particular which will give us the greatest chance of success.

The economic sub-strategy derives from an analysis against a world background of Britain's strengths and weaknesses. Some of the more important of these, relating to economic and other spheres, are shown in Table 1.

The 'Two Sectors/One Future' sub-strategy, as I call it, focuses on two crucial parts of the British economy. The first, the 'industrial sector', consists of manufacturing industry. The second, that I will call the 'post-industrial sector', consists of those parts of service industry selling financial, information-related and leisure/arts services abroad. Important aspects of the 'One Future' emerge in the course of the detailed description of the economic sub-strategy and in the complementary 'lifestyle' sub-strategy outlined in Part II. I will draw these threads together and give one vision of a desirable future for Britain in Part III.

The first priority of the economic strategy is to boost the industrial sector by putting the full weight of the nation behind it for the first time in British history. I recommend a package of financial and other measures to reverse the trend towards deindustrialisation that has characterised recent times. We have quite simply got to make and sell things better.

The post-industrial sector is presently in much better shape than manufacturing, but requires co-ordination to exploit fully the possibilities offered by the emerging global financial and information society. The role of London will be crucial in any efforts in this area and, accordingly, I recommend the founding of a new London-based co-ordinating body for invisible exports.

We will achieve our GDP aspiration of £700 billion by raising our present share of world trade in both *goods* and *services* of below 8 per cent to 10 per cent for each category by the year 2000. This is the '10/10 aim.' To set it in context, look at the inset graph in Figure 1 (p. 8).

Table 1. British strengths and weaknesses

Strengths	Weaknesses
Language	Import penetration of market for manufactured goods
Inventiveness	
'Invisibles' (financial services, overseas assets)	Loss of export markets for goods
	Union negativism
Financial institutions	Managerial amateurism
Ability to win wars	Unemployment
History/heritage	Poor investment (equipment, R&D and training)
Political stability	
Democratic tradition	Low morale
North Sea oil	Lack of common vision of future
Theatre	Education (lack of funding, arts bias)
Literature	Defence (over-funding)
Cinema	Class consciousness (fortunately waning)
Television	
Sport	Appalling popular press
Science	Northern Ireland
Air and sea communications	Electoral system
Individualism	Adversarial politics
Bulldog spirit	Institutional resistance to change
Sense of humour	Declining standards of social behaviour (e.g. violence, crime)
Looted treasures	
Freedom from natural disasters	Infrastructure/inner cities
Island stronghold	Nostalgia
Mild climate	Cultural antipathy to business and technology
	Social and regional inequalities
	Commercial failure of grandiose projects (e.g. Concorde)
	European unpopularity (arising from e.g. political obstructionism, acid rain, football hooliganism)
	The British Sunday
	High divorce rate
	Brain drain
	Public catering
	Inequalities in health
	Poor housing stock
	Rape of the countryside

The sub-strategy, besides having the two themes of commitment and vision, has six keynotes, royally personified as PRINCE. These are:

- Pioneering

  Britain as the birthplace of the future

- Reinforcement of success

  Exploit our strengths – except for manufacturing which remains vulnerable and should be assisted

- Individual excellence

  An emphasis at the personal level on quality and style

- National roots

  Found the future on British talent, culture and geography – go with the native grain

- Clear goals

  No reliance on muddling through

- Europeanism

  The island race, yes, but a European destiny

We will encounter our handsome prince frequently in our travels through his soon-to-be-revitalised kingdom. Let us first visit what, for our present purposes, are the two most important of his provinces, the industrial and post-industrial sectors.

Industrial Sector

So here we are in the industrial part of the kingdom and there is something not quite right. There is a lack of robust self-confidence which is more reminiscent of those who have averted failure rather than those who have gained success. This is not surprising, for while the rest of the economy has grown, manufacturing output is not much different in the late eighties from what it was in the late seventies – even in spite of a growth in world trade. Industry has been fighting a rearguard action. If it went into full-scale retreat again as it did in the early eighties, then the impact on the economy would be disastrous at a time when North Sea oil production is past its peak and the oil price in inflation-adjusted terms has fallen to 1960s levels. Ex-oil and ex-manufacturing, Britain could quickly become ex-tinct.

Our dependence on manufactured goods is still high; they account for somewhat over half of foreign earnings. If we ceased to export goods, services could not fill the gap. The world market for services is much smaller than that for goods, and at any realistic level of penetration would not deliver enough prosperity, let alone replace the millions of jobs directly and indirectly related to manufacturing. The conclusion that we need manufacturing industry, and a successful one at that, is irresistible. Here is Lord Gregson of the excellent House of Lords Committee on Science and Technology:

> The manufacturing industry is absolutely vital to the economic well-being of the United Kingdom and the stupidity of saying otherwise must stop.

It is important to note, as we said previously, that the decline of manufacturing in Britain is not part of a trend towards a post-industrial society. It is industrial failure – deindustrialisation. And it has occurred only in Britain. As Robert Skidelsky has put it, 'we have given the world a new spectre, the failure to stay modern'. This is a piece of pioneering we can do without.

We saw in the analysis that the main reason for Britain's failure in the post-war period has been industrial. We earn less than our European neighbours because our manufacturing industry has done less well. Even our home market has been lost to foreign goods. In fact, however, we remain one of the top half dozen exporting nations in the world. Unfortunately, we are also one of the world's largest importers. That will not surprise you as you probably drive a foreign car and watch a foreign television.

In 1985, we exported less per head than the West Germans but more than the Japanese. In terms of dollars – this being the international currency of comparison in these matters – the figures were: Britain, $1,800 worth of exports per person; West Germany, $3,000; and Japan, $1,450. As for imports, these were: Britain, $1,930 per head (i.e. a larger figure than that for exports meaning a trade deficit); West Germany, $2,600 (a healthy surplus); and Japan, $1,070 (another healthy surplus). Note that the Germans export more than twice as much per head than the Japanese and import more than the British. The route to success taken by the Germans and Japanese thus differs: the Germans have high exports and moderate imports; the Japanese, moderate exports and low imports. The Japanese trade surplus in the twelve months to November 1987 amounted to $96 billion. The West German surplus was $64 billion which, given the difference in population, means they did about as well.

We suffer from import penetration, which is another way of saying that we have lost our home market. This is one factor in our poor trading performance. We now import 35 per cent of the manufactured goods used in industry and the home, which is twice the level of 1970. We could throw up protectionist barriers to reduce imports to achieve a 'Japanese-style' trade balance. If we did this, though, it would almost certainly induce retaliatory action which would hurt us as much as anyone else.

The other approach is to become more competitive to win back markets at home and overseas. This would be a 'high exports, moderate imports' style of trade balance which would suit our national penchant for consuming foreign goods while delivering an excellent standard of living.

The key to raising exports and reducing imports, of course, is *competitive manufacturing*. To this extent our future lies in the hands of businessmen who, in time-honoured fashion, will aim to achieve efficient production of products well-tailored to customer requirements, reasonably priced, delivered reliably, and for which suitable technical and after-sales support is provided. They will increasingly regard Britain as just one part of a lucrative world market, and a small part at that.

Particularly important for manufactured goods are quality and design. There has been an avalanche of books and papers on these subjects in the last decade. Though some progress has been made there has not yet been a sufficient improvement in our products to restore pride in the 'Made in Britain' tag.

A major problem is that manufacturing has not taken centre stage in our national life as it is in the life of other, more successful, nations, and the fact that we had to set aside 1986 as Industry Year proclaimed as much. We have not given manufacturing the support and encouragement it needed. What I propose therefore is that the industrial sector be made to feel what it is – special. It is the first priority of the economic sub-strategy to restore the health of manufacturing. It must be helped because on its success all our livelihoods ultimately depend. *Everything else in the economic sphere must take second place to manufacturing*.

To quote Alistair Graham of the Industrial Society:

> We will turn the economy round by first of all placing the expansion and the improvement of manufacturing industry as the central concern of everybody in the country. Until the achievement of such an objective is the prime concern of government, management, trade unions and individual workers, I doubt we will make any progress.

Giving priority to manufacturing is the basis of the concept which can be dubbed 'total peace'. It is not a comment about nuclear disarmament or defence spending, but it *is* analogous to the concept of total war. The entire economy must be mobilised to ensure the success of the manufacturing sector. A climate must be created in which manufacturing industry has the first claim on talent and resources. Cultural attitudes which view with disdain the making and selling of products must be rendered impotent by a package of measures designed to make manufacturing the centre of excellence in the British economy.

The most important element in the package relates to financial incentives. From the moment we declare total peace, a favourable tax status would be given to the five million people working in manufacturing companies, regardless of who owns the company. Workers in manufacturing would pay a moderately lower rate of taxes than workers in other parts of the economy. They are the front-line combatants and should receive special rations (tax advantages). This is particularly important because manufacturing jobs at shopfloor level can be unpleasant.

Corporate taxes and rates would also be lower for firms manufacturing in Britain. This would be to improve the financial robustness of manufacturing companies so that they can compete better. There would also be an improvement in the 'tone' of industry if it was seen to be conspicuously in the limelight. The name of the game here is 'M-ratedness', i.e. manufacturer-rated tax and rate reductions which could perhaps remain in force till the end of the century. The aim is to reapportion the tax burden, not increase it overall. The message would be clear to everybody in the land: manufacturing is the important sector. And to people in industry: you are the important people. This approach is in line with the fifth of the 'princely' virtues, clear goals.

Although all forms of manufacturing should be favoured, particularly important is the supply of high 'value-added' products. The concept of adding value is crucially important. If I sell you sheets or bars of metal you will pay a certain price. If, however, I first fabricate the metal (and other crucial materials) into a computer, you will expect to pay much more. I can be said to have 'added value' to the raw materials by the exercise of (in this case) electronic engineering skills.

You will recall that reference was made in the analysis to Britain's exports in the nineteenth century. Even then, when we were hailed as the 'workshop of the world', a large proportion of our foreign earnings arose from a few, relatively low value-added products. Now, when we are supposed to be an advanced industrial power, the position shows only moderate improvement. Too many of our products are still too easy to make. This exposes us to competition from countries where labour is less expensive. It is as simple as that.

Our industry spends too much time minimising the cost of existing production techniques instead of developing new and better products and in applying new manufacturing technology. This was the predictable conclusion of a report prepared for the British Institute of Management in 1986 by the respected Cranfield School of Management. It was the follow-up to a study a decade earlier, and showed little progress. Management perspectives tend to be short and there is pressure from the City for a rapid pay-back on any money spent. If your balance sheet weakens, you become ripe for takeover. These factors hamper long-term strategic thinking, particularly in relation to market share dominance and new technology.

The key words here are *research* and *investment,* and they affect everyone. For example, to keep your wardrobe up to date you find out in the research phase (or passively notice) what is fashionable (or at least will not expose you to ridicule). In the investment phase, you buy the appropriate clothes. If you do not research and invest, the 'production' which suffers is your image. Metaphorically, much of British industry is still wearing flared trousers and kipper ties.

If research and investment are low, so too is the commitment to training. British companies spend on average less than one-sixth as much on improving the skills of their employees as their American counterparts and the differential is even greater between British and West German companies. One British company in five employing over 1,000 people was found by one study to make no provision at all for management training. Three-quarters of smaller companies were similarly negligent. Training, research and investment form the tripod on which rests the crucible of our industrial future.

We must halt what the Henley Centre for Forecasting has described as the downward path to specialisation in low value-added, non-skilled-intensive products and services. The sure way to economic success is through highly skilled people doing high value-added things.

I recommend that research, investment and training by companies in the industrial sector become eligible for M-rated tax relief. The drop in tax revenue from companies would be made up from individuals by abolishing mortgage interest relief. This subsidy of the nation's 8 million or more mortgage holders costs the country about £4.5 billion a year and has increased by more than 400 per cent since 1978-9. It disproportionately benefits the better-off and stokes up house price inflation. The money should be made available through tax relief to industry in order to boost long-term prosperity. We should redirect national resources *from* buildings, *to* building the future.

The abolition of mortgage interest relief commands the support of much expert opinion. It was one recommendation of a committee set up by the government and chaired by the Duke of Edinburgh to look into the housing problem. The committee presented its far-sighted report in 1986 but its recommendations have not been taken up.

An end to a subsidy on home-ownership will presumably be less popular with mortgage holders than economists. For this reason, espousal of the idea by any one political party may be difficult. An alternative approach might be a manifesto commitment to put the issue to a referendum. This would be a test of narrow self-interest versus foresight. A 'yes' to abolition of mortgage interest relief in favour of manufacturing, would be the biggest psychological boost ever received by industry.

British companies are not at present compelled to declare in their annual report how much they spend on research and development. This is in contrast to the situation in other countries and should be changed. A shareholder or other interested party must be able to appraise a company's attitude to the future by reference to clear information on research – and also on investment and training.

The need for concentrated thought on the future has seldom been greater: a new wave of techno-economic expansion is in the offing. British companies must be in a position to contribute to the vast range of new products forecast for the 1990s stretching over leading-edge technologies in information handling, energy, biotechnology, new materials, earth sciences, robotics, transport and communications. We must seize the opportunities offered by new technology, not least by *applying* microelectronics, automation and biotechnology to productive processes.

The signs are not good. We have fewer robots in our factories than our industrial rivals and invest less in new production technology. We are also running a deficit on information technology (IT) products which reached £1.2 billion in 1985. This was a record among the leading industrial nations and should have set the alarm bells ringing. Our only major computer company, ICL, is not even ranked in the top 12 in the industry worldwide, and we do not have a semiconductor company among the top 30. Our market share in telecommunications has declined over the last two decades from roughly 20 to just 5 per cent. Overall, our high-tech trade balance, expressed as a percentage of GDP, swung from plus 0.49 per cent in 1979 to minus 0.41 in 1984.

One hope for the future is co-operation with our EC partners. This is where Europeanism, the sixth of the princely virtues, comes in. Pan-European research projects, particularly in the costly high-tech area in the pre-competitive phase, may be vital if we are to counter the threat from Japan and the United States. Initiatives already under way include Esprit (information technology), Race (telecommunications) and Brite (other industrial technologies).

Europe is currently the greatest trading bloc in the world with combined exports of £275 billion. This is 40 per cent more than the US, almost twice as much as Japan and six times the Soviet bloc. But Europe's share of the world market for electronic products is reckoned to have declined in the last decade from 25 to 19 per cent and on trend will be just 10 per cent by the end of the century. According to one expert this could lead to a European deficit on IT products of £30 billion and a loss of 200,000 jobs.

Approval of pan-European initiatives should not cause us to fall into the trap of *centralism*, identified by David Henderson in the 1985 Reith Lectures. It is not trading blocs or even countries which compete, but for the most part individual enterprises. It is also not true that the larger states necessarily do best. Within Europe the most economically advanced nations are Sweden and Switzerland. In the Far East, Hong Kong and Singapore are notable successes. The key feature in most of these cases is a large number of individually successful companies performing on the world stage.

Britain has some world-class industrial enterprises, BP, ICI and Glaxo being three. We seem to do well in chemicals and pharmaceuticals where the gulf between science and application is narrowest. Where it is wider, as in engineering, we do less well. We need more world-beaters if we are to close the trade deficit of £9.1 billion which opened up in 1987.

Big companies tend to be better at exporting than small ones which, however, can play a key role in import substitution. The increase in company start-ups in the 1980s has been a welcome trend towards the much-vaunted enterprise culture – but we have some way to go. In America in 1986 an estimated 1.4 million new businesses were started. This is more than the number of all *existing* small businesses in Britain. And in America, failure apparently carries little stigma; it is a springboard for future success. That is an attitude we would do well to foster here.

A raft of tactical actions can be suggested to improve industrial performance: continue efforts to link pay – or part of it – to performance ('profit sharing') to improve commitment and results and to break down 'them and us' attitudes; cut defence spending – there is a well-documented inverse relationship between industrial success and defence expenditure – and rechannel funds from defence research (which represents almost half of government spending on research) into civil research; continue privatisation, but make the criterion of selection of candidate companies their improved ability to win in domestic or export markets, rather than just the need to fund tax cuts; designate a cabinet minister as the voice of science and technology; increase the proportion of graduates in engineering subjects above the present level of 12 per cent and give them (and their lecturers) M-rated grants; create a Royal Society of Industrial Excellence to boost the status of world-beating manufacturers, and invite the increasingly impressive Prince Charles to lead it; publicise an Industrial Index on the lines of the stock market's FT Index, so that everybody knows how we are doing industrially; and so on.

Given commitment and investment, the prospects are really quite reasonable. Take modernisation, for example. Many parts of British industry are below the level of foreign competition in terms of equipment. This, surprisingly, is a great opportunity, particularly in the low-wage economy that Britain has unfortunately become. As economist Sidney Pollard has put it:

> One important advantage of installing the latest plant in a backward economy is the opportunity of setting up the unbeatable combination of low wages with high technology until such time as the general level of wages creeps up to the level of other advanced countries with the general transformation of the economy.

On these terms we can even compete successfully with the newly industrialising countries of the Pacific Basin such as South Korea and Taiwan. But we have a long way to go. The average British worker in manufacturing produces less than half the average American, German or Japanese worker and we will not succeed until this improves. (Incidentally, and ominously, the Koreans are said to describe the Japanese as the 'lazy Asians'.)

Factories of the future must rise from British soil. These will be highly automated affairs using computer-aided design and capable of producing short runs of customised goods using machine tools linked into so-called flexible manufacturing systems. This type of manufacturing of high-quality personalised products, made possible by new technology, is perfectly in key with the third of the princely virtues, individual excellence. Industrialisation bred uniformity; automation breeds diversity.

The function of industry is to make things and create wealth, not create jobs. Industry should not be used as an instrument of social policy, notably regional planning. The choice for international companies seeking access to the European market is often not between south-east England and the north, but south-east England and another country altogether.

Manufacturing jobs are attractive because they have large 'multiplier effects', that is, knock-on jobs are created in other private and public organisations. This should not lead us to mislocate industry in areas of high unemployment by using special subsidies and grants. Manufacturing should go where its competitiveness will be most enhanced. Job creation in less favourable areas should be confined to service jobs which in any case are cheaper to create. This means that industrial firms will flourish where it is most fitting for them to do so – with due deference to environmental considerations. That will often mean near southern motorways and ports, in London and so forth.

The approach advocated here is designed to facilitate industrial success while maintaining free trade. Public spending will be largely unchanged and there will be only minimal government intervention. I am mindful of David Henderson's verdict on this latter subject:

> The same imperviousness to evidence can be seen in the industrial policies pursued over the past four decades by successive British governments. I believe that the long and continuing sequence of assisted programmes, subsidized ventures, officially arranged mergers, support for lame ducks and selective aid for special cases has had, and will continue to have, adverse effects on British economic performance.

M-ratedness and the other measures will encourage success, but a resurgence of British industry will finally depend on the cumulative effect of individual improvements at the company and personal level.

As the lesson of the early 1980s showed, governments have a greater capacity to do harm (for example, by supporting overvaluation of the currency and high interest rates) than good. Robert Skidelsky:

> Repeated failure has been disillusioning. Many people are wondering today whether governments should be in the revival business at all... it may be that the first duty of government is not to make matters worse than they would otherwise have been by inflicting costs in a vain effort to secure revivalist gains.

So scalpel cures are out. Steady political will is, however, required: 'a firm commitment to keep to reconstruction as the first priority must ultimately derive from the government', as Sidney Pollard has pointed out.

A particular area of poor performance by successive governments has been large-scale projects. David Henderson regards Concorde and Britain's second nuclear power programme as 'two of the three worst civil investment decisions in the history of mankind, the third being the Soviet counterpart to Concorde'. These kinds of disasters impoverish us all. If we must embark on large projects let us observe the fourth princely virtue of going with the native grain. For example, to generate power why did we not put a barrage across the River Severn to harness the world's largest tidal drop, rather than opt for a PWR nuclear reactor at Sizewell based on a foreign technology which finds no other purchaser?

With the right conditions manufacturing can succeed. What we should aim to create is a world-beating industrial sector led by a well paid super-elite of technologists, managers and financial experts deploying first-class skills of hand and mind. With this, and the favourable world economic conditions, we can surf in on the next wave of techno-economic development and in the process secure the 10 per cent of world trade in goods which should be one of our aims.

To set the right tone I suggest the creation of a body to co-ordinate the marketing abroad of 'visibles', that is, goods. This would be called Visible Success and would be the dynamic and better funded successor to the British Overseas Trade Board. The case for such a body was made by Edward Heath in an Employment Institute pamphlet published in 1986:

> our export promotion effort is ill-co-ordinated ... our competitors devote far greater resources and effort to ensure that their firms are properly supported in overseas markets, that as far as possible they do not cut each other's throats and that they co-operate as closely as possible to present a cohesive package.

At home, there is a persuasive case for a new organisation to represent the interests of manufacturers and act as their public voice. The Confederation

Confederation of British Industry is industry's current lacklustre champion. Within this organisation there is a strong contingent of importers and service sector companies such as banks whose interests can be divergent to those of home-based manufacturers. The CBI has also seemed in the eighties to be too closely identified with Tory governments practising political neutralism towards manufacturing, a sector of the economy ostensibly regarded by government as small and unrepresentative. There is a pressing need for an effective and independent voice for manufacturing industry. Fortunately, the recently formed Campaign For Industry may fulfil this role.

Can we do it? Can we rebuild our industrial base? Sidney Pollard certainly thinks so:

> British industry has sufficient going for it such that it could without difficulty launch Britain on a course of rehabilitation to catch up with the advanced world by the end of the century.

'Without difficulty' the man said, and he went on to say:

> As far as the material pre-conditions are concerned, therefore, nothing stands in the way (as nothing has stood in the way during the past decade) of rejoining the advanced countries of Europe by an upward spiral of modernisation, output rise, cost reductions and the recapture of market shares at a rate comparable with that of other catching-up economies.

So the message is quite unequivocal: WE CAN WIN, IF WE WANT TO.

Montgomery's famous words to the demoralised 8th Army in 1942 should be remembered: 'Plans for withdrawal will be burnt.' He and his army went on to victory – and so can we.

Post-industrial Sector

We have toured the industrial sector of the kingdom, now let us visit the second province, the post-industrial sector. Here, the first and second princely virtues are to the fore: Britain as pioneer and reinforcement of success. The post-industrial province has London at its centre and involves that part of service industry dedicated to the provision of financial, information-related and leisure/arts services for overseas consumption. Before outlining our strategy in this area, it is worth glancing at the historical background before considering the role of services today.

In historical terms we are in the third phase of human economic development. In the first phase, wealth was primarily associated with agriculture, in the second, manufacturing and trade. Now, in the third phase, the jobs and prosperity of most of us are linked to the provision of services and a key economic resource is information. In the emerging global information society, so the pundits tell us, it will not be what you make that matters so much as what you know. But more of this later.

First, what is a service? A definition is difficult, but in crude terms, if it does not graze or grow in a field and is not made in a factory, it is a service. Included here, then, are transport, communications, retailing, education, health, entertainment, and the rest.

During the past 35 years, service employment has jumped in Britain from 43 to 65 per cent of the total workforce, while the proportion in manufacturing has fallen from 40 to below 25 per cent. Only in the United States is there a greater proportion of the workforce in the service sector, nearly 70 per cent in fact. In the past decade or so services have generated about 1.25 million jobs at a time when manufacturing has been shedding them at an unprecedented rate. Half a million of these were in the City during a period of massive investment in new technology, proving, incidentally, that unemployment and new technology are not necessarily synonymous.

Services now account for nearly half of our GDP and they have boomed as people have spent a smaller proportion of rising incomes on food and durable goods. The trend has been helped along in any case by the relative reduction in the price of manufactured goods with improvements in productivity. In national economic terms the service sector is good news because we make a profit on our trade in services with the rest of the world, an edifying £7.2 billion in fact in 1986. This compared with a deficit on manufacturing trade of £8.5 billion. Manufacturing provides over half our foreign earnings but in this sector, as we have seen, import penetration is high. In services, by contrast, we have retained much of our home market and make substantial sales abroad.

The home market for services is in truth less easy to lose than that for goods because much of it is locally-based and involves low wages. Hairdressing is a good example. The opportunities for exporting are also consequently less and, in fact, only just over one-tenth of service 'output' is exported, compared to one-third for manufactured goods. But sell services abroad we do and the main focus for this is London.

As we saw in the analysis, the surplus we earned from services in 1985 arose mainly from three sources: City-based financial services; earnings from our mountain of overseas assets; and a modest positive balance on the travel account. All this sounds healthy enough until you realise that our share of the world service market has declined even more for services than manufacturing, from 18 per cent in 1955 in fact, to around 7 per cent now (Figure 1, p. 8).

What should we try to achieve for services? This can be quite simply stated: first, hold on to our domestic market; second, exploit to the full our opportunities overseas and, in line with the 10/10 aim, obtain 10 per cent of the world market by the end of the century. We can do this by exploiting the post-industrial sector, as we shall see later, but first let us briefly inspect our foreign assets and meet those camera-festooned tourists.

Britain's investments overseas of well over £100 billion far outweigh the investments of foreigners here and money continues to flee abroad. In 1985, £21 billion left our shores in search of profitable investment opportunities overseas. There are some signs that this exodus has slackened since, which is just as well if we are to rebuild our industrial base. The way to stop the flow is not by regulation, though, so much as creating exciting investment opportunities at home. This is our challenge for the future and depends largely on the regeneration of industry.

As for tourism, or at least the 'travel account' comprising business and personal travel, the success of 1985 was short-lived. 1986, like the four years prior to 1985, saw a deficit. American visitors were fewer due to terrorist scares. This will probably prove to be a 'blip' on the upward trend in tourist numbers. By 1992 it is estimated that we will receive 20 million overseas visitors a year and that tourism will be turning over some 16 billion. It is already Britain's fifth most important industry and also the fifth largest tourist industry in the world providing 1.5 million jobs.

We can reinforce this success by better marketing abroad and by making Britain more attractive. Here are some suggestions for improvements: fully reform Britain's nanny-state licensing laws (e.g. all-day opening on Sundays); reform the regulations covering shop opening hours to permit Sunday trading; clean up our litter-strewn landscape and continue efforts to persuade the British not to use their countryside as a wastepaper basket; further improve the eating out experience (90 per cent of catering employees have no qualifications or training; around 100 people suffer food poisoning each day); improve hotels (e.g. more en suite bathrooms required) and make travelling around easier (e.g. increase the number of road signs giving place-names); reverse the decline of the pub by rescuing our hostelries for conversation; clean up our hideously dog-dirty streets and recreation areas (and meet the cost of clearing away the million kilos of canine faeces deposited every day in Britain by fining dog-owners and by levying a sizeable licence fee); raise spending on the arts, so beloved by tourists (just one-third of one per cent of public expenditure goes on the arts); improve the inferior wines on sale in pubs (kept inferior by the big brewers anxious to maintain beer sales); radically improve service by encouraging attendance of 'customer care' training courses like those designed for sales and marketing personnel in industry; clean up our filthy beaches; rename the boring-sounding 'Bank holidays'; and mount a campaign to discourage tipping for anything other than *exceptional* service. These changes would be good for foreign visitors, but, more importantly, good for us too.

We are lucky with one thing: the quality of our customers. Our cultural and other attractions appeal to upmarket visitors. Some other nations with more basic amenities attract the less distinguished type of travellers – including the ghastlier of our own revellers.

With determination we can achieve a steady surplus on the travel account but there is unlikely to be a bonanza. Against the attractions of our rich heritage and marvellous, life-enhancing rain, foreign sun and ski slopes attract hordes of Brits abroad each year. Tourism is a useful earner but it is not the answer to our economic prayers. Or as Sir John Harvey-Jones, the former head of ICI, put it in a BBC Dimbleby lecture:

> If we imagine the UK can get by with a bunch of people in smocks showing tourists around medieval castles, we are quite frankly out of our tiny minds.

One part of the travel account is particularly successful and that is civil aviation. In 1984 our net earnings were about half a billion pounds. Apart from running some profitable airlines such as British Airways, we have in Heathrow and Gatwick the first and fourth largest airports in the world handling between them over 40 million passengers a year. London is a major 'hub' in the international travel network and we should do all we can to keep it that way. This chimes neatly with the role the capital can play in the world financial, information and communication networks to which we can now turn our attention to.

Taking the financial area first, London is up there with New York and Tokyo as a financial centre and has, of course, been doing it for far longer – 500 years, in fact. The City has retained its pre-eminence in the increasingly integrated world market for several reasons, not least because it is the centre for the enormous Eurodollar market which dwarfs the stock exchange and which is Europe's largest capital market. It is also the biggest international banking centre, with all the world's top 100 banks represented.

The City's overseas earnings, which account for somewhat over 4 per cent of Britain's total exports of goods and services, arise from banking, insurance (with Lloyd's at its centre), brokerage and commodity trading. The real star here is banking whose overseas earnings have almost quadrupled since 1979. But even here the old story of lost market share recurs.

A survey published in early 1987 by the Bank for International Settlements, the central bankers' bank in Basle, showed that in the rapidly expanding market for international banking, Japanese banks had replaced those in the US as the most important national group. West German banks, like the Japanese banks, had improved their share of the market while the shares of the British and the Americans had declined. Ominously, Japan held nearly a third of the market according to the survey. The world's top five banks as judged by assets are now all Japanese and no British bank is in the top 15. The Nomura Bank of Japan is larger than all the British banks put together.

What is true of banking – lost market share – is true of services as a whole. This decline is disturbing given that the City in particular has consistently, we are told, been a magnet for Britain's brightest and best, never more so than since the financial revolution in 1986, 'Big Bang', blew salaries through the roof. Two suggestions can be made to help stop the rot. The first is to replace the British Invisible Exports Council and the second is to improve company reporting.

The British Invisible Exports Council functions for the export of invisibles as the British Overseas Trade Board does for goods. It is limp, underfunded and restricted in scope. It should be replaced by a more go-getting outfit which could appropriately be called Invisible Excellence. This would co-ordinate the marketing of all foreign currency earnings services, including the non-financial ones to be discussed, and tourism. The new organisation would have as its stated aim recovering for Britain a 10 per cent share of the market for services by the year 2000.

The second suggestion is more modest and is designed to puncture corporate self-delusion relating to success. At present one notable absence from the annual reports of many companies is information on world market share, past and present. Corporate growth is usually given but the growth characteristics of the market itself are often crucially omitted. If a company is growing at 20 per cent a year, that sounds impressive. If, however, the market is expanding at 100 per cent a year then the company growing at 20 per cent a year is in fact a relative failure. That, after all, is what has happened to British exports as a whole since the war. Market share has been lost. We should consider making it a legal requirement that world market share information be prominently displayed in company reports – a rule that would apply to manufacturers as well as service sector companies.

Underpinning international financial services such as banking, credit-cards and insurance is the flow of information around the globe whether by telephone, telex, fax, satellite, cable or forked stick. The nations of the earth are interconnected as never before, and the amount of information pelting around is colossal. This is partly due to the spread of multinational businesses and, indeed, 70 per cent of international information is estimated to be the internal communications of multinational corporations. Britain can gain from this information flow both by acting as a 'switching station' (that is, a communication centre) and as a source of new information.

The point about information being a key economic resource deserves further examination. As Tom Stonier, Professor of Science and Society at Bradford University has declared: 'Wealth is created when a non-resource is converted into a resource as a result of information.' For example, wind becomes a resource only when you invent a sail or a windmill. And what is information? Simply knowledge in all its forms. Stonier again:

> If during the nineteenth and twentieth centuries Britain's global economic role was that of industrial machine shop, it must now become its post-industrial technical-managerial consultancy and information provider.

From workshop of the world, in fact, to talking-shop.

In the post-industrial world, so the theory goes, the brain and service industries will increasingly dominate the economy. These activities will be the net providers of jobs. This is just as well given that our manufacturing industry must be lean to be competitive. As Stonier says, in manufacturing (as in agriculture before it) the material needs of the many can be met by the efforts of a few – perhaps by as little as 10 per cent of the population by the end of the century, he reckons, compared to rather less than a quarter now.

Looked at from the point of view of jobs we are arguably already in the information society. If you define information workers as all those employed in the production, storage, retrieval and distribution of information, whether it comes in the form of a good or a service, then one in every two jobs already falls into this category. As information workers are set to increase in number, information exchange seems likely to become the latter-day equivalent of taking in one another's washing.

One particular aspect of the information society has been described by Peter Large in the *Guardian*:

> products of the mind – from computer software to videos – do not show any sign of reaping their logical inherent reward. Their profit still hangs on the hardware and the economic structures that distribute them.

This feature of the contemporary brain industry will certainly change.

Information society analyses can be overdone and more plausibly relate to jobs rather than wealth creation. In Britain for the next couple of decades manufacturing will have to make the bulk of the money or our straits will be dire indeed. Earnings from selling services abroad on any likely sales forecast will just not be enough to sustain us at a decent level of income. To adapt the old exhortation on exports: 'manufacture or die'.

With this in mind we must emphatically not become *only* the world's talking-shop. Rather, we must be providers, firstly, of high technology and other goods and, secondly, of internationally orientated services. To support the latter part of this let me introduce the magic formula: 'London, European Capital of the Future, pioneer of the post-industrial era'. In this scheme, the metropolis must become Europe's principal information-broker and communications centre to match its role as centre of financial services, air transport, tourism, etc. London was the financial capital from the eighteenth century to the Great Depression and briefly achieved fresh prominence in the swinging sixties. It can become the place to be again, the forerunner of a new age.

If knowledge is going to be the key economic resource of the future then we must be prepared to generate and trade in it if we are to prosper. What is required, above all, is co-ordinated effort. With this in mind, I propose a single focus for Britain's assault on the world information market involving the establishment of a co-ordinating and creative body called the London Idearium. This organisation, as the name suggests, would be based in London and dedicated to the generation and dissemination of ideas, information and knowledge. It would be the centre of a concentrated marketing effort to exploit the opportunities of the information society. And it would be symbolic of a nation reborn through ideas.

One function among many of the London Idearium would be to co-ordinate what Stonier called the 'technical-managerial consultancy' role. Britain still has a fine network of research and science establishments, consultancies and experts even in spite of the neglect, or actual depradations, of recent times. Though the primary role of this network should be to regenerate industry at home, money can be made selling our specialist knowledge abroad.

The Idearium would assemble databases and so-called 'expert systems' for use internationally. At home, we would gain access to this information via a broad-based computer communications network linking homes and business throughout the land and having the Idearium as its centre.

Another function would be operation as a clearing house for ideas, a national suggestions box. Over the portico in fact would be the words 'New, True or Important'. Ideas from any source, including the general public, offering new ways of doing things or new products or services, would then be channelled to the appropriate recipients.

The Idearium would represent a national meeting place, something which is currently lacking. Here, industrialists, trade unionists, academics and any one else could meet if they wished to hammer out ideas, devise marketing strategies, resolve disputes, discuss important issues, speculate on the future, and so on. It is clear from this that the Idearium is not meant to be characterised by a uniform sepulchral hush. Parts of the Idearium will be filled with the din of creative discussion, other parts will be devoted to reflection and research. Either way, Britain will be fulfilling its traditional role as innovator (see Appendix I). As Harold Macmillan put it in 1951, 'The genius of the British has always been originality'.

Many disparate organisations would wish to be housed in the Idearium permitting a multitude of fruitful connections within what would become a national 'think-tank'. And the Idearium would have strong links with other 'ideas' centres such as the patents and trade-mark people, museums and libraries.

Education and training would be other Idearium functions particularly in the realm of thinking skills. A Fellowship of the London Idearium could be created on the lines of the Royal Society to enhance the status of creative thinkers in whatever sphere.

The pioneering novelty of the London Idearium would need to be embodied in the building in which it was housed. Modelled on the human brain, the design would be in the shape of a split hemisphere with 'step pyramid' sides. 'The Brain' – as the building would doubtless become known – would be an architectural parable of the lobes and fissures.

Although large, the Idearium would contain myriad meeting places on an intimate scale as well as conference rooms and lecture theatres. Needless to say, it would feature any number of electronic aids to information retrieval, processing and dispersal. It would be a centre of technological excellence, albeit unobtrusively so. The key feature would be people having and discussing ideas, that is, exhibiting individual excellence, the third of the princely virtues.

Co-ordination of the foreign earnings activities of the London Idearium would be necessary to enable full exploitation of commercial opportunities. This would be one function of Invisible Excellence. Another function of this body would be to co-ordinate export marketing activities in the leisure/arts area, to which we can now turn.

The role of London is paramount in the leisure/arts field. The capital is the largest art market in the world ahead, narrowly, of New York. It is a centre for the publishing industry which puts out 50,000 titles a year and in the process generates £2 billion worth of sales, half from exports. Theatre thrives here with successful companies taking their shows abroad, notably to Broadway. London is the world's leading conference location. It is also a centre for television programme production and the various television companies, including the BBC, the world's biggest producer of television programmes, seem reasonably well placed to exploit the emerging opportunities offered by satellite-based transnational television channels. International radio is already with us in the form of the BBC's long-established World Service. Meanwhile, London's advertising and public relations agencies are well represented in the race for 'global accounts'.

If London is to become 'European Capital of the Future', it will need revitalising. People and businesses have fled the metropolis. London is the only great city in the world whose population has shrunk during the past 35 years. The redevelopment of Docklands is encouraging but many other areas are run-down, unappealing and crime-ridden. The number of homeless people on the capital's streets is greater than at any time since the war, and unemployment is rife. Since the late 1970s, 135,000 jobs have been lost and there were estimated to be well over half a million people looking for work in 1986. London has some of the worst deprivation and poverty in Britain. This needs to be corrected.

An advantage we have over other nations is the English language. This is the foremost language for trade, science, aviation, diplomacy, information technology, shipping, sport. As the number one speakers of English we are uniquely privileged. It gives our film-makers, writers, database organisers, consultants, businessmen and others, a superb advantage over their international competitors. For this reason, English is arguably the nation's greatest asset.

> The amazing demand ... for our language, culture and education must be seized and not lost through lack of vision and imagination.

So said Sir John Burgh, the retiring director-general of the British Council, in 1987. The council is one arm of our cultural diplomacy, the other being the BBC's external services. It maintains cultural bureaux abroad and sends artists, writers, actors and exhibitions on tour. According to Sir John, the British Council's independence had been threatened by government interference, while its effectiveness had been impaired by a 21 per cent budget cut in the eighties. This is an appalling waste of a fine asset. The Council is the softest of soft-sells for British talent and products and as such is part of the invisible export drive. It should report to the newly created Invisible Enterprise rather than the Foreign Office as now. There, its true worth will be recognised as an invaluable shop window for Britain's potentially vast range of attractive cultural products. It will be appreciated, too, as a bait for tourists, four out of 10 of whom give the arts as their main reason for coming to Britain. Links with museums, the National Trust, academe, the private sector (e.g. television and publishing) will be strengthened so that the British Council, like the nation itself, can reach its full potential in the nineties.

With commitment and vision, Britain and its capital can reach a new level of prosperity. Together, a resurgence in manufacturing industry and prowess in the post-industrial sector – Visible Success and Invisible Enterprise – will see us begin an exhilarating climb from near the bottom of the top 20 in the league of prosperity to near the top.

Part II
Well-being

4

Analysis

Money and access to material comforts are very desirable, but still more important is a sense of well-being. By this I mean mental and physical health, happiness and freedom from fear, and a feeling of caring and being cared for. All of this bears on the quality of life which, with increased prosperity and restored morale, was one of the national objectives described in the previous section.

The lyrics of one of Bing Crosby's songs are handy for indicating the approach adopted here: *You gotta accent-uate the positive/Elim-inate the negative/Latch on to the affirmative/Don't mess with Mister In-Between*. In Part II, as regards quality of life, we are going to eliminate the negative by seeking ways to *reduce unhappiness*. In Part III we will accentuate the positive – and latch on to the affirmative. Nowhere will we mess with Mister In-Between.

Leaving aside economic and employment matters, and personal relationships, the commonest kinds of misery-inducing events can be grouped under three headings: ill-health, crime and accidents. I am going to concentrate on these in this section because the opportunities for improvements are particularly strong – which is another way of saying that as regards health, crime and accidents the news for Britain is not good.

If we have been earning less than the citizens of other advanced nations then we are also increasingly shorter-lived and less healthy. We are currently world leaders in coronary heart disease and lung cancer, and infant mortality continues to exact a grimmer toll here than in many advanced nations. We are also increasingly lawless and more likely to be the victims of crime. Furthermore, if ill-health and crime aren't bad enough, accidents at home, on the roads and at work continue at unacceptable levels.

Before going further, it is important that we establish the historical background and understand the concept of risk, so this is where we will begin.

Risk: the dangers of modern life

In the modern world we face unprecedented risks. True or false? False. Most risks have fallen to historically low levels and we are living longer than ever before.

Since the Second World War the number of centenarians in the population has increased ten-fold and some 15 per cent of the population are now over 65. This has been brought about by growing prosperity, better nutrition and living conditions, and medical advances – probably in that order. Like other industrial countries, Britain is moving into the age of the four-generation family. Even now lots of grandparents are still around for their grandchildren's weddings. Increasingly, they will be there to see their great-grandchildren's early years as well.

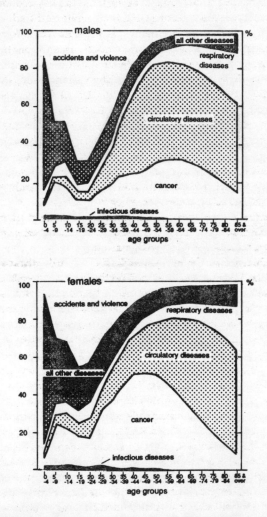

Figure 4. Causes of death: by sex and age, 1983, United Kingdom
Source: *Social Trends*, HMSO

The main threat to our lives used to be infectious diseases. Now – and AIDS notwithstanding – the risk picture is dominated by chronic, non-communicable diseases such as cancer and heart disease (see Figure 4). As John Urquhart and Klaus Heilmann say in their book *Risk Watch*, risk has fallen to an all-time low:

> ... a fact that is frequently obscured by a vocal minority who loudly proclaim the horrors and risks of modern technology and industrialisation. But the facts are that we have traded in big risks for small ones over the past three generations, drastically reducing the risk of premature death but not altering the fact that everyone ultimately dies.

In earlier times, if you lived to an advanced age, there was a good chance you would outlive your children. Queen Anne certainly did, she outlasted all seventeen of hers! Death used to occur at any stage in life. Now it has been confined mainly to the aged. The three traditional scourges of mankind – war, pestilence and famine – have receded, at least in the West. We have made the transition from short, disease-ridden lives to the long, healthy lives that most of us enjoy today. Yet many still feel beset by danger. Urquhart and Heilmann again:

> For unclear reasons, many people's risk-consciousness has grown concomitantly during this period when the risk of premature death has fallen rapidly, with the paradoxical result that risk has declined greatly but fear has remained, or perhaps even increased from the times when a tenth of all babies died and most people died before age 50.

Urquhart and Heilmann pin part of the blame on the media and what they call its victim-orientated reporting. Horrific incidents are reported in a way which creates anxiety out of proportion to the dangers.

Each year, in fact, somewhat over one per cent of the British population dies. We do not die of nuclear accidents, food additives and drug side effects – but we do worry about these things, excessively. There is a tendency to overestimate risks and underestimate benefits. How do we gain a sense of proportion? Certainly, no sense of the priority hazards is gained from listening to what people are talking about. Urquhart and Heilmann cite an American example: in 25 years no one has died as a direct result of the US civil nuclear power programme. In the same period one million have died in traffic accidents. Which is discussed more?

The best way to find out what diseases and misfortunes befall people, and to determine what they are dying of, is to examine hard evidence. What that comes down to is a study of causative factors and statistics. In the field of health, this means aetiology (the study of the causes of disease) and epidemiology (the study of diseases across populations).

The statistical approach can seem cold-hearted, even callous. But as epidemiologist Richard Peto has put it, we must make a deliberate effort to stand back from the welter of human suffering to gain a broad view, otherwise every disease that kills hundreds of people will seem incomprehensibly bad and a proper ordering of priorities will be impossible. We should maintain our sense of humanity, though, even while attempting to establish the facts.

When you look at mortality and morbidity data, consistent patterns emerge year after year. For example, about 5,000 or so people die annually in road accidents. Why is it not 100 one year and 100,000 the next? It is the case that something which may be rather unpredictable at the individual level (e.g. will he die of a heart attack?) becomes much more predictable the larger the group. This is so providing the ground rules are known – typical incidence rates, but also the relative importance of various influences that make an undesirable outcome more likely, that is, the 'risk factors'. At the level of a whole population, the incidence of a particular disease and the number of deaths from specific causes become very predictable. If this were not so, life insurance would be unobtainable and planning for health needs impossible.

The encouraging corollary to this is that small changes in individual risks can yield significant dividends at the societal level. Thus, for example, seat belts make only a small contribution to the safety of individual drivers but for the nation as a whole save hundreds of lives a year. More encouragingly still, if *big* risks can be diluted for individuals then society yields commensurately larger rewards.

Some of the great triumphs of public health have come from the population-scale approach of epidemiology. For example, it was studies of this kind that revealed the relationship between smoking and lung cancer (though some people – smokers mainly – still weirdly refer to this correlation as 'only statistical').

Reliable data can be a fine corrective to anxiety pollution, and to disproportionate perception of risk. For example, in the area of violent crime, surveys usually show that those most fearing attack are old ladies, but statistically this group is least at risk. Reliable data can also be a good antidote to the many myths that seem to abound in the area of risk perception.

One such myth is that technology represents a unique source of danger. This has led to the phenomenon of 'technophobia'. Of course, technology has its blacker side – none blacker than nuclear weapons. But overall it has conferred and still confers enormous benefits upon us to which tragic disasters such as the Chernobyl nuclear accident in 1986 should not blind us. Technology has given us safe drinking water, sanitary sewage disposal and centrally heated homes. It has made rodent and insect control possible, transformed agricultural productivity and been the basis of countless medical advances. And benefits have sometimes come from unexpected quarters. Consider the humble refrigerator: it is reckoned that this unassuming piece of domestic technology may have played a part in the steady reduction in the number of stomach cancers in our society over the decades because it reduced the need for smoked, pickled and salt-preserved foods.

Another example of a risk myth is the belief that 'natural' or 'organic' equals 'safe'. Perhaps the classical example of an unsafe natural product is unpasteurised milk. During the 1970s and early 1980s there were 50 epidemics of salmonella poisoning in Scotland due to unpasteurised milk. These affected 3,500 people and caused 12 deaths. Since legislation was introduced in 1983 banning its sale, there have been 15 outbreaks affecting 100 people in the farming community, which still has access to the untreated product, and none in the general population. There have been no deaths.

If unpasteurised milk is dangerous, consider – in a lighter vein – the following natural products. Carrots contain carototoxin, a rather strong neurotoxin, and myristicin, which can cause hallucinations. Radishes, onions and broccoli contain substances which cause goitre, enlargement of the thyroid gland. Apples contain phlorizin which can disturb kidney function. And so on.

A related myth is that the past was better and safer. This, as we have seen, is completely untrue as regards health and disease. A sub-myth of this relating to crime and civil disturbance is that Britain was once a peaceful and law-abiding society and that since then it has gone to pot. This is nostalgic distortion; we never were the idyllic, crime-free society some of us seem to think we were.

We can keep risk in perspective, then, by considering the historical background and also by remembering that in the West we lead privileged lives compared to many in the developing world. If things have generally improved, however, we in Britain could certainly do far better. The old story of our industrial decline is repeated here. We had an early world lead in identifying and doing something about risks to well-being and we have made some notable strides. But more recently other nations have done better, such that we are now bearing a greater burden of injury, disease and premature death than they.

In the following analysis we are going to look at the subjects of health, crime and accidents through the eyes of a personage who might be called a 'risk engineer.' This individual, a latter-day social engineer, seeks to identify and eliminate threats to well-being. The emphasis is on prevention and thus on identifying causative factors and those individuals most at risk.

Ill-health

Of the 600,000 or so deaths in Britain each year, half are due to coronary heart disease and cancer. Britain, alas, leads the world in the former and in the most prevalent kind of the latter, lung cancer.

Our life expectancies are similarly unimpressive. Between 1970 and the early 1980s, life expectancy in the US for men and women taken together rose from 71 to 74 according to the World Health Organization. In Japan, the figures were 72 rising to 76. In England and Wales, average lifespan in 1970 was 72 years. A decade later it had risen just one year to 73.

The Japanese are now reckoned to be the longest lived nation ahead of the previous leaders, the Scandinavians. In 1984, life expectancy at birth in Japan reached 75 years for men and 80 years for women. In contrast, the British male could look forward to 72 years and the British female 78. They're not only making more cars than we are – they're living longer!

Life expectancy at age 45 in Britain is among the worst in the developed world. A Scottish man of this age can expect to live 26.5 years, compared with 28 in England, 29 in France, 30 in Norway and 33 in Iceland. For women aged 45, life expectancy in Scotland is 32 years, England 34 years, France 35, Norway 36 and Iceland 37.

A report on the nation's health entitled *Charter for Action* was published in 1986 by the Faculty of Community Medicine which is part of the Royal College of Physicians. It pointed out that the number of deaths in Britain from heart disease is not only the world's highest but is not falling as it is in other countries. The annual death rate has fallen in America by 40 per cent since 1950 and in Finland, which used to occupy Britain's place at the top of the table, it has come down one-third in just over a decade.

Coronary heart disease, our biggest killer, claims 25,000 men and 7,000 women a year under the age of 65 in England and Wales. Taking all age groups together, heart disease kills one in three men and one in four women. That is one death every three minutes.

Infant mortality in Britain over the last 35 years has declined less than elsewhere. In 1983 it was 10.1 per 1,000 live births which was higher than in other comparable countries such as France (8.9), Denmark (8.0) and Japan (6.2). In Britain infant mortality is still markedly dependent on where you live and to which ethnic group you belong. It is also affected by social class. The perinatal mortality rate in 1984 for social class 5 (the poorest) was 14.1 per thousand births, compared with 7.1 for social class 1. And while the other classes have shown continuous improvements, social class 5 infant mortality rates have recently started to get worse again.

The number of deaths from cervical cancer has hardly changed in the past 15 years in Britain, although the numbers have been halved in other European countries. This is in spite of the availability of a cheap and effective screening method – the 'Pap' smear – which offers the possibility of early diagnosis and almost certain clear-up. Two thousand or more women die needlessly of cervical cancer in Britain each year.

Preventable infections such as measles, whooping cough and rubella (German measles) in pregnancy have been largely wiped out abroad but still cause death and disability here, according to the Faculty of Community Medicine. Deaths from alcohol abuse and drugs continue to increase and smoking still takes its toll in lung cancer victims. An increasing proportion of these latter are women, among whom lung cancer now rivals breast cancer in incidence.

Overall, the Faculty of Community Medicine sees great scope for improvement:

> That much of the excess burden of premature death and disability could be reduced is shown by the much better control of these health problems in other countries...

Lest we take a too-sombre view of Britain's recent performance in the health field, it is important to bear in mind what we have said about the historical background. There has been an enormous improvement in the health and longevity of the British people. A baby born today can expect to live a quarter of a century more than one born in 1900. Water-borne diseases such as typhoid have been eradicated, as have childhood infections such as diphtheria and scarlet fever. Immunisation has virtually wiped out poliomyelitis and contributed to the decline of whooping cough and measles. Tuberculosis has been reduced to the ranks from being 'the captain of the men of death'.

Maternal mortality associated with childbirth has been drastically reduced and the same is true of infant mortality. The causes of deficiency diseases such as scurvy and rickets have been identified and these diseases largely eliminated. Effective drug therapies have been developed for a range of conditions including pneumonia, gonorrhoea and syphilis. New methods of contraception have been introduced. More people are surviving trauma with improvements in surgical techniques and in methods of intravenous feeding and blood transfusion. (The second case described in Appendix III illustrates the remarkable achievements made possible by modern surgical techniques.)

Perhaps the crowning achievement in the conquest of infectious disease has been the relatively recent eradication of smallpox. The World Health Organization campaign was initiated in 1966 and used immunisation to break the thread of transmission of this disease which spreads only from person to person. Eradication of the smallpox virus cost around $300 million and involved thousands of people in 22 countries. The inspiring defeat of the most devastating pestilence in human history is a major triumph of public health and preventive medicine. It shows what we can do if we try.

We are now well into the era of what has been called the therapeutic revolution in which drug treatments exist for a multitude of clinical conditions previously without effective treatment. Drugs such as antibiotics, anti-hypertensives, anti-cancer drugs, anti-arthritics and centrally acting (brain) drugs of one kind or another have brought real benefits to people's lives. But it is important to appreciate that the major gains in health and lifespan occurred before the therapeutic revolution of the last 50 years, during the so-called sanitation revolution which preceded it.

The decline in mortality and morbidity since the mid-nineteenth century can be attributed more to the prevention of disease than to the development of specific therapies. Of particular importance were improvements in sanitation (e.g. treatment of water and sewage), nutrition, housing, work conditions and standards of hygiene. Family size decreased and the prosperity of the population increased.

Much of the credit for the improvement in the health of the British people must go to engineers, scientists, civil servants, social reformers, farmers and, only to a small extent, the medical establishment. For example, the combined death rate from scarlet fever, diphtheria, whooping cough and measles among children up to 15 shows that 90 per cent of the total decline in mortality between 1860 and 1965 had occurred before the introduction of antibiotics and widespread immunisation. The improvement was largely due to better host resistance, as it is called, a result of better diet. Also important were housing conditions and a possible decrease in the virulence of the causative bacteria.

The combined effect of the sanitation and therapeutic revolutions has been to reduce drastically the number of premature deaths and cause a transition from acute, communicable diseases to the chronic, non-communicable diseases associated with ageing.

To paraphrase medical writer Peter Wingate, medicine came into the twentieth century only in about 1935. It did so courtesy of the nascent pharmaceutical industry and with an uneasy conscience based on a history of crimes against humanity: bleeding, purging, starvation – and the rest of the treatments from the chamber of horrors. From leech-cures to lasers in 100 years. Professor Henderson of Harvard has estimated that 1912 was the first year in human history when the random patient with the random disease consulting the random doctor had a more than 50-50 chance of benefiting from the encounter.

Hospitals used to be regarded as pestholes, and rightly so. Going into one was viewed only slightly more favourably than being shipped direct to the mortuary. In the eighteenth century, the Dublin Foundlings Hospital took in more than ten thousand abandoned babies over a 21-year period. Just 40 of them survived, and these were initially healthy children! That is a mortality rate of over 99 per cent. In historical terms, it is only in relatively recent times that the medical profession has made a net positive contribution to our well-being. Formerly, scepticism towards doctors and their treatments was justified and life-enhancing. It probably still is to a degree. At least 1 in 10 patients is reckoned to suffer some adverse effect from hospital treatment in Britain, while 1 in 18 actually contracts an infection.

Table 2. Deaths analysed by cause (England and Wales), 1984

Cause	Per cent of total deaths
Natural	
Infectious diseases	0.4
Neoplasms (cancers)	25
Circulatory diseases	49
(coronary heart disease)	(28)
Respiratory diseases	10
Digestive diseases	3
Others	9.3
Violence	
Accidents	2.5
(road accidents)	(0.9)
Suicide	0.8

Source: *Office of Population Censuses and Surveys/Annual Abstract of Statistics*, 1986

The contemporary pattern of mortality is shown in Table 2. Nearly 97 per cent of us die of 'natural' causes, the rest being accounted for by accidents of one kind or another and criminal violence. Coronary heart disease is responsible for about 28 per cent of all deaths with other diseases of the circulatory system including strokes accounting for nearly 22 per cent more. This means that about half of all deaths are due to diseases of the heart and the 60,000 miles of tubing comprising the circulatory system.

Cancer accounts for a quarter of all deaths, about 140,000 a year in fact. The commonest cancers are those of the lung, breast and stomach, in that order. A further 10 per cent of all deaths are due to respiratory diseases such as pneumonia, bronchitis and emphysema. The next biggest group is deaths due to diseases of the digestive system (3 per cent of the total). Another 1 per cent of mortalities is caused by diabetes; and mental disorders, diseases of the nervous system and diseases of the genito-urinary system each account for 1–2 per cent more.

Infectious diseases now cause 2,000 deaths a year, just 0.4 per cent of the total. This can be expected to change in the future, however, with the increasing prevalence of the viral disease AIDS (acquired immune deficiency syndrome). Hundreds of male homosexuals and drug addicts have so far died. One government forecast in 1987 estimated that the toll would reach 4,000 by 1990 and that it would include a proportion of heterosexuals. Added to the 2,000 other deaths from infections, the 6,000 total fatalities will represent rather less than 1 per cent of all deaths in that year.

The principal cause of death varies with age (Figure 4, p. 52). Among the young accidents and violence account for a large proportion of deaths. More common among older age-groups are circulatory and respiratory disorders, and cancer – causes which account for four-fifths of all deaths in any one year. These afflictions also contribute to the 17 days of sickness which the average person experiences annually. Other major causes of ill-health are rheumatic diseases, skin conditions, colds and influenza, and mental and emotional disorders. This last-mentioned category has increased strongly in recent times such that as much as a third of the population are now affected in some degree by anxiety and depression. Women tend to be more frequent sufferers than men, this being just one of many intriguing sex differences in the matter of health.

Women live on average 6 years longer than men and, indeed, the 'weaker sex' has a better survival rate at all ages. Of centenarians, 75 per cent are women. But compared with men, women report more health problems when surveyed, consult their doctors more often, spend longer in hospital, and are twice as likely to have an operation.

If there are differences between the sexes, there are also striking differences between the social classes. Semi skilled and unskilled workers die earlier than professionals and managers, and suffer more ill-health. Men in the lowest social class, class 5, live on average six years less than men of social class 1. A report, *Inequalities in Health*, was commissioned by the government and produced in 1980 by a committee under the chairmanship of Sir Douglas Black. It painted an appalling picture of social deprivation leading to disease and premature death.

Labourers and others in social class 5 suffer more respiratory and infectious diseases than professionals and more circulatory and digestive disorders – including ulcers, the classical 'executive' ailment. Cancer was more prevalent, as was mental illness. Sir Douglas Black and his colleagues showed that material deprivation and ill-health are highly correlated.

In follow-up studies prompted by the report, Professor Peter Townsend of the University of Bristol compared death rates in two areas of London. In the poorer area, Spitalfields, the crude mortality rate for the under 45s was three times the rate in an affluent area, Cranham West. In the 45–62 age it was twice as high. Similar results were obtained in the Professor's home town of Bristol.

Poverty has always been a common preventable cause of death, and affluence brought much of the contemporary improvement in health. But the Black Report concluded that there had been no improvement in terms of eradication of inequalities since the foundation of the National Health Service and that, indeed, in some respects the health of the lower social classes had actually deteriorated. For example, in the decade to 1981 a modest overall decline in the death rate from heart disease for all social classes accompanied a one per cent increase for less privileged classes.

The number of people below the poverty line went up 70 per cent between 1979 and 1986. This has undoubtedly increased the burden of ill-health borne by the lower social classes and among those at risk are the unemployed. Figures from the *General Household Survey* for 1984 show that those out of work visit their doctors more often than those in jobs and are more likely to suffer from long-standing illnesses. The enormous increase in unemployment in the 1980s has undoubtedly contributed to ill-health in Britain.

The chief cause of death in Britain – coronary heart disease – involves narrowing and blockage of the coronary arteries which supply the heart muscle. When demands are placed on the heart during exercise, for example, cardiac insufficiency can develop if there is an inadequate supply of oxygen. This may be registered as angina – Latin for 'pain' – or, if areas of tissue actually become damaged through lack of oxygen, the heart may start to pack up all together, a heart attack (myocardial infarction).

According to the Coronary Prevention Group (CPG), 25 expert committees from many countries have met in the last two decades to consider the causes of coronary heart disease. They have identified the following risk factors relating to lifestyle and heredity:

- Cigarette smoking
- Hypertension
- Unhealthy diet
- Obesity and diabetes
- Lack of exercise
- Family history

The effects of psychological factors such as stress are less certain but 'there is growing evidence that they can be important'.

Many people believe heart disease is a manifestation of the prosperity enjoyed by the developed countries, that it is a disease of affluence. Yet in Britain and other countries, the disease is most prevalent in the poorest areas and among the poorest sections of the community.

The number one cause of heart disease is cigarette smoking. This probably accounts for 40,000 or more of the 160,000 deaths each year. The adverse effects of smoking are not so marked as for lung cancer, a disease which is 15 times more prevalent among smokers than non-smokers. But it is still marked; deaths from coronary heart disease are twice as frequent among smokers as non-smokers. As Urquhart and Heilmann have put it:

> Doubling the already leading cause of death means a very big increase in the risk of premature death. This unexpected finding arose in the 1950s. It identified cigarette smoking as the greatest single hazard in contemporary life.

Deaths from all causes due to smoking probably amount to 100,000 a year in Britain according to the Faculty of Community Medicine. That is over 270 a day. The BBC's science correspondent James Wilkinson has pointed out in his book *Tobacco*, that of 1000 young adults who smoke regularly, one will be murdered, six will be killed on the roads, and 250 will be killed by tobacco. The risks of smoking are known rather precisely. For example, a non-smoker aged 35 has a one in 75 chance of dying within 10 years. For a heavy smoker, the odds shorten to one in 22. It is figures like these which have persuaded life insurance companies to offer lower premiums to non-smokers.

A quarter of smokers die 'before their time' because of the habit, and a smoker of twenty cigarettes a day loses an average of five or six years of life. The main causes of premature death are heart disease and lung cancer. Smokers who believe that the relationship between the raised incidence of these diseases and cigarette smoking remains to be fully established are deluding themselves. The links are proven beyond reasonable doubt and there is also evidence that smoking increases the risk of other cancers beside lung cancer (e.g. of the mouth) and other cardiovascular diseases besides heart disease (e.g. strokes).

About 3,000 chemicals have been identified in tobacco. Quite a number of these are regarded by experts as capable of causing cancer or of assisting in the process of cancer formation, while other chemicals are toxic. What causes lung cancer is not known, though tar and other chemicals come under suspicion. As for heart disease, this is thought to be due to the carbon monoxide and nicotine in cigarette smoke.

Although the overall rate of coronary heart disease is doubled by smoking, among heavy smokers the risks are very much magnified. One large study cited by the CPG has shown that men under the age of 45 who smoke twenty-five or more cigarettes a day have a fifteen-fold greater risk of a fatal heart attack than non-smokers. Smoking is, in fact, thought to be responsible for about eight out of ten deaths from coronary heart disease in young men.

People with elevated blood cholesterol levels are at greater risk of developing heart disease and the risk increases with the amount of cholesterol present in the blood. A host of epidemiological and clinical studies buttress this conclusion. High blood cholesterol is believed to be important in the formation of fatty deposits on the walls of the coronary arteries and elsewhere. Less clear is the role of a high fat diet. This is relevant because the saturated fats most associated with animal foods trigger the liver to make and release cholesterol into the blood stream. Polyunsaturated fats do not seem to have this effect. This is why polyunsaturated fats are preferred to saturated fats and why a diet low in saturated fats is recommended by health experts.

Genetic predisposition to high cholesterol levels seem at least as important as a fatty diet. This probably explains why efforts to link fat intake with incidence of heart disease have tended to be unsatisfactory in spite of the apparent conviction of health propagandists that 'fat is bad'. Resort is usually made to cross-cultural comparisons, that is, attempts to compare diseases and dietary habits across different populations. The evidence from such studies is fairly suggestive rather than absolutely conclusive.

Another risk factor in heart disease is hypertension. This is caused by increased 'resistance' from the small arteries ('arterioles'). Even moderately high blood pressure increases the danger of a heart disorder. High blood pressure may cause the heart to function badly – resulting in shortness of breath and other complications – or the problem may show itself more dramatically as a heart attack. The risks are multiplied if other risk factors are present. When combined with high blood cholesterol, the risk is increased fourfold. Add smoking to this and, according to the CPG, the risk is multiplied eightfold.

Besides heart disease, hypertension is a risk factor in other disorders, notably strokes. These are caused by the rupture or blockage of one of the arteries of the brain which can be fatal. Strokes kill 70,000 people each year. Alternatively, a stroke may lead to paralysis, failing speech or loss of memory. The risk of mild or severe strokes is far higher in those with raised blood pressure.

People with very high or rapidly increasing blood pressure are also prone to severe kidney or eye damage if treatment is not given.

The development of hypertension has been claimed to be associated with a high-salt diet. Demonstrating a relationship between any dietary component and a disease state is always difficult; establishing a link between salt and blood pressure has proved no exception. Experiments on animals give conflicting results, while studies on humans have not yet proved fully conclusive. In the treatment of existing hypertension, however, low-salt diets have been reported to be effective in a proportion of cases.

Hypertension is more common in obese people than those of normal weight – and the risk of heart disease in these people is elevated even without hypertension. Nearly 40 per cent of men and one-third of women are overweight and a proportion of these are technically obese, that is, 20 per cent over their ideal weight. A strong influence on this situation is the high-calorie, sugar-loaded British diet. Obesity increases the risk of a variety of disorders including diabetes (itself a risk factor for heart disease), degenerative kidney disorders, arthritis and varicose veins. Researchers at Rockefeller University in New York have shown that obese people with fat abdomens are more prone to obesity-associated illnesses than are those with fat hips and buttocks. This may be a consolation to some fatties!

Scientists commissioned to check out the toxicity of new chemicals sometimes report an odd phenomenon when the chemicals are put in the food of experimental animals. The rats or mice in the treated group receiving a supposedly toxic dose of the chemical live longer than untreated 'controls'. The reason is that the treated group eats less of the food because of the contamination and so maintain a lower body weight. There is, in fact, a well-established relationship in the rat between dietary restriction and longevity. As Hippocrates said of another species: 'Persons who are naturally very fat are apt to die earlier than those who are slender.'

Jerry Morris of the London School of Hygiene and Tropical Medicine reported a higher incidence of cardiac problems in bus drivers than in stair-climbing conductors. This illustrates the role of exercise and sedentary lifestyle in heart disease – and possibly also that of stress, as driving is presumably more of a strain than being a conductor.

After coronary heart disease, cancer is the most common killer. The two principal causes are believed to be smoking and diet. One estimate is that these account for about 60 per cent of the 140,000 cancer deaths each year, the remainder being due to a variety of other factors ranging from environmental pollution to sun and sex (see Figure 5). Radiation, natural and man-made, may contribute to the total. Radon 'outgasses' from the rocks and soil under our houses, particularly in the West Country. This may add to the burden of lung cancers. Meanwhile, 'superclusters' of childhood leukaemia cases have (possibly) been identified around nuclear establishments.

The most prevalent form of cancer among men, and the second most prevalent among women after breast cancer, is lung cancer. Nine out of ten cases are probably due to smoking and lung cancer alone accounts for about 36,000 deaths annually, a quarter of all cancer deaths in Britain. Smoking is the most reliably identified cause of cancer with not only lung cancer to its discredit but also, for example, cancer of the mouth, pharynx, larynx and oesophagus. Other causes of cancer are less well established though there is said to be a very strong correlation between dietary fat intake in various countries and the incidence of cancer of the large intestine, lung and breast.

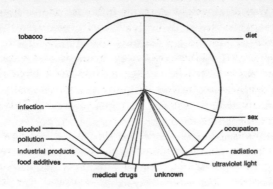

Figure 5. Estimated cancer deaths by cause
Source: *The Economist*

While it is certainly true that a quarter of deaths each year are due to cancer, it is not true to say that we are being engulfed by a wave of cancer deaths. As Urquhart and Heilmann say of the US, cancer has risen from the eighth commonest cause of death to the second commonest today. But as these authors point out:

> Overall cancer mortality has remained about constant (when the ageing of the population is taken into account), and the only group of cancers increasing are those clearly linked to cigarette smoking.

The death rate from cancer – and, indeed, heart disease – has only increased as other causes of death have receded and lifespan increased. Cancer is mainly a disease of old age. Some forms of cancer have actually declined. One such, as we have seen, is cancer of the stomach which may have fallen back due to improved eating habits. This is in spite of the consumption by the average Briton of over 2.7kg of food additives a year in the course of munching his or her way through half a tonne of food. Over 6,000 chemicals are present in food as additives or residues. There are reports of additives causing food allergy problems, irritable bowel syndrome, and Crohn's disease (localised inflammation of the intestine). But whether there is a cancer 'time-bomb' isn't predictable. On balance it seems unlikely. What is clear is that stomach cancer is commoner in non-industrialised countries than in developed countries, as is cancer of the liver and oesophagus.

Another form of cancer for which the death rate has declined is cancer of the uterus (womb). This is due to better diagnosis and treatment. Two other cancers for which effective treatments now exist are those of the cervix (neck of the womb) and skin. These observations point to a more general moral: even if you contract cancer your likelihood of survival is greater now than it was. One study carried out by the National Cancer Institute in the US compared the five-year survival rates for cancer at seven sites – breast, cervix, bladder, prostate, colon, rectum and endometrium (womb lining). Two groups of patients were considered: those diagnosed in 1960–3 and those diagnosed in 1970–3. Of patients in the earlier group, 54 per cent survived for five years. The comparable figure for the later group was 61.5 per cent. A small increase perhaps – but the improvement has been steady over the years and will continue.

For both cancer and heart disease, our top killers, we have identified a particularly common murder weapon: tobacco. However, the indictment of smoking does not end there, as James Wilkinson describes in his book *Tobacco*. Smokers are much more likely to suffer pneumonia, bronchitis and empyhsema – respiratory diseases which account for 10 per cent of British mortalities. Cigarette smokers also run about twice the risk of bladder cancer as non-smokers and there may also be a link between smoking and cancers of the pancreas and cervix.

Over 95 per cent of patients with arterial disease of the legs which causes claudication – pain – when walking, are reported to be smokers. This can lead to gangrene and necessitate radical surgery. A survey in one English health service region in 1981 showed that 225 people had amputations of lower limbs due to impaired circulation. This compared with 32 who had their legs amputated because of injury.

Peptic ulcers are twice as common in male smokers as non-smokers according to an American study and about one-and-a-half times as common in women smokers. Inflammatory disease of the gums is also more likely, which may help explain another finding – that smokers more frequently have had all their teeth extracted than non-smokers.

Tobacco amblyopia is a rare type of blindness which has been attributed to heavy smoking, particularly of pipes and cigars.

One survey cited by Wilkinson showed that people who smoked more than twenty cigarettes a day have to take twice as much time off work through sickness compared with non-smokers. They also visit their GPs more and spend more time in hospital, both as in-patients and out-patients. If they have to have an operation the risk is greater for them than non-smokers.

The risk of heart attack, strokes and other cardiovascular diseases is increased about tenfold in women who both smoke and are on the contraceptive pill compared with non-smokers who are not on the pill. At the other end of reproductive life, women who smoke experience menopause earlier and have twice the risk of osteoporosis, a kind of bone loss that can lead to fractures and spinal deformation.

A woman smoker who wants to become pregnant will take longer to do so on average than a non-smoker. Pregnant women who smoke have a small increased risk of miscarrying (the risk increases with the number of cigarettes smoked), of bleeding and of developing various placental abnormalities. Stillborn babies are commoner as are premature babies. Because these latter are lighter, they tend to have more health problems than normal babies. If the father alone smokes, the baby is still likely to be lighter than average.

It has been suggested that there is an increase in congenital malformation of the heart in children up to the age of seven who were born to mothers who smoke. According to the National Academy of Sciences in the US, children exposed to their parents' cigarettes suffer pulmonary problems such as wheezing and coughing and are more likely to develop pneumonia and bronchitis. There is also evidence that smoky air can stunt the growth of children's lungs. Children of smoking parents are on average 1cm shorter than other children at primary school.

The adverse effects of inhaling second-hand smoke – passive or forced smoking – are not confined to children, of course. Separate studies in several countries have found that non-smoking spouses of smokers experience a risk of developing lung cancer 30 per cent greater than spouses of people who do not smoke. The risk of heart disease is also increased according to a recent study by American researchers. The medical histories of 7000 non-smoking women aged between 30 and 59 were examined. The wives of cigarette smokers were three times more likely to have a heart attack than the wives of non-smokers.

Cannabis is smoked with tobacco but appears to be independently toxic to the respiratory system. Regular smoking of cannabis may damage the bronchial passages and cause acute and chronic bronchitis. A researcher quoted in *New Scientist* said that smoking three to five 'joints' a day caused as much damage to the respiratory system as a packet of twenty cigarettes. Cannabis also has mental effects associated with loss of drive. More seriously, the drug can induce schizophrenic breakdown in people susceptible to the disease. This can involve long-term as well as acute psychotic disorders, according to research at St George's Hospital, London. The research showed that 'one unit' of cannabis and alcohol taken together were four times as intoxicating as either substance taken alone.

Alcohol, like tobacco but not cannabis, is a 'socially approved' drug. It is reckoned to be used by 90 per cent of the adult population, slightly more than consume tea in fact, and far more than smoke. For the demon drink, however, unlike the evil weed, modest consumption is not regarded as harmful. At high doses, it is a different story.

Regular, long-term heavy drinking increases the drinker's chances of suffering liver disease (particularly cirrhosis), ulcers, 'socio-sexual difficulties', traumatic injuries, cancers of the mouth and larynx, heart disease and circulatory disorders, and brain damage. Deleterious effects can occur directly because of alcohol or indirectly because of the lifestyle associated with high intake and dependence. Alcohol supplies calories but does not supply other dietary essentials. Heavy drinking thus encourages obesity with its attendant dangers and an inadequate diet with consequent protein and vitamin deficiencies. In alcoholics, these dietary deficiencies allied with stomach and liver disorders can result in incapacitating brain damage.

Also exposed to brain damage is the unborn child. According to Glasgow's Royal Hospital for Sick Children, alcohol abuse during pregnancy is the most important preventable cause of mental deficiency in the western world. Physical birth defects are also said to be increased among babies born to women who are heavy drinkers.

Caffeine is the third most commonly used social drug after alcohol and tobacco. It is a quite powerful stimulent present in tea, some soft drinks and, of course, coffee. Heavy, long-term coffee drinking has been linked to an increased risk of peptic ulcers and certain cancers, but the evidence is inconclusive. More persuasive is a link with increased risk of coronary heart disease. In a study of male medical students undertaken at the Johns Hopkins Medical Institution in Baltimore, the risk was found to increase with the amount of coffee consumed. Drinkers of more than five cups a day were three times more likely to suffer heart disease than those who drank none. Even one or two cups a day increased the risk by one-third.

Whether caffeine truly poses a risk to normal coffee and tea drinkers remains to be established. One celebrated death attributed to coffee, however, was that of French writer Balzac, who is said to have drunk 50,000 cups of coffee during his lifetime which was shortened as a result.

A section on health would be incomplete without mention of the most prevalent disease on earth, tooth decay. The incidence of this has decreased in Britain, possibly due in part to water fluoridation, an activity which may have influenced other things besides teeth. Recent research suggests that aluminium contamination of food and water may be a cause of Alzheimer's disease, the most common form of senile dementia. Some foods cooked in fluoridated water and in aluminium pans can lead to a very large ingestion of aluminium. It would be a tragic irony if, in trying to save our children's teeth through fluoridation, we had sacrificed our old people's brains.

Law-breaking

Who is the most dangerous person in your life? The answer is simple: yourself. Suicide, self-murder, outnumbers the real thing by a factor of nine to one. In Britain, one in 11,000 of us commits suicide each year; one in

100,000 of us falls victim to murder. After yourself, who should you fear most? Another simple answer: your parents. Five in 100,000 children under one year old are murdered by their parents each year. This is the most dangerous age of all. The next most dangerous age is 16-30 years (1.4 murder victims per 100,000). The safest age is 5-16 (0.6 deaths per 100,000).

The conventional image of the murderer is of a strange man lurking in the shadows of the proverbial dark alley. The sex is emphatically right – 85 per cent of killers are male – but the identity and context are not. In 45 per cent of the 600 or so recorded homicides in 1985, a typical year, the victim was a member of the suspect's family or was the suspect's cohabitant or lover. In fully three-quarters of cases victim and killer were acquainted. The proportion of victims who were not known to the suspect in 1985 was 1 in 6, or just 17 per cent.

A slight preponderance of victims are men; 53 per cent of total murder victims over the period 1976–85 were male. As might be expected from the number of victims and killers who know one another, about half the offences were committed during quarrels or bouts of temper. Less than 10 per cent are associated with robbery or similar incidents.

In half of all murders the killer is drunk. The commonest murder weapon is the knife, classically from the kitchen. Strangling and asphyxiation are the next most common methods, followed by hitting and kicking and then the time-honoured 'blunt instrument'.

The stereotype of the homicidal stranger, the psychopathic killer, applies to the smallest category of murders. Similar misapprehensions apply to rape. Three-quarters of the 1100 reported rapes each year take place indoors. Half of all rape attacks are carried out by somebody the victim knows. As criminologist Jock Young has put it, women look in the wrong direction: 'Murder and rape are committed by your nearest and dearest. Women have realistic ideas of the threat, but transfer it to the wrong people, like strangers.'

For the crime of 'wounding', the pattern is similar to rape; in half of all cases the offender is known to the victim. Furthermore, as for rape and murder, both victim and perpetrator are drawn disproportionately from the lower social classes and the crime is most common in inner city areas. Where the victim of wounding is male, the offence most often occurs outdoors. Where the victim is female, indoors.

About 5 per cent of the several million crimes recorded by the police each year involve personal violence. These crimes include murder and manslaughter, woundings, sexual offences and a variety of assault offences ranging from wife-battering and racial attacks to incidents requiring no recourse to medical treatment or even significant discomfort. The more serious offences – those endangering life plus rape and armed robbery – constitute just one-third of 1 per cent of all offences. The risk of falling victim to serious crime is thus very slight but, although this puts the problem in perspective, it should not prompt us to minimise the impact of violent crime. There are now well over 150,000 offences each year involving violence, 12,000 of the more serious type.

Your chances of being gunned down in contemporary Britain remain thankfully low. This is true even bearing in mind a tragedy such as occurred at Hungerford in August 1987 when a lone gunman killed 16 people. In general, less than one in a million of us are shot dead each year. There were 44 fatal victims of shooting in 1985, representing 8 per cent of all murders. This is a typical figure for the last decade. Compare this with the United States where the annual death toll from hand guns alone is 21,000, including 8,000 murders, 12,000 suicides and 1,000 accidents. Even allowing for the difference in population size, this is a remarkable carnage.

Overall, some 20,000 deaths in the US are due to homicide each year which is about 1 per cent of the annual death toll from all causes. In Britain, as we have seen, the comparable figure is about 600 which represents less than 0.1 per cent of annual mortalities. The comparison flatters us: even with the bullets flying, the average American still lives longer than the average Briton.

It is relatively easy to see that Britain is less crime-ridden than the US, particularly as regards personal violence. Other international comparisons are less straightforward. Over the years, Britain appears to have been moving up the international league table of crime such that now it may be at or near the top of the European league for all crimes taken together, though we occupy a better position as regards personal violence. In a Europe-wide poll conducted not long ago by the Gallup organisation more Britons reported being victims of crime than anyone else.

Crime levels have reached record levels in Britain. In 1985, 3.6 million notifiable offences were recorded, 3 per cent more than in 1984, itself 8 per cent up on the previous year. There is now a crime involving violence every four minutes on our streets and a burglary every 30 seconds. The dismal story of increasing criminality is shown in Figure 6. (This analysis excludes the 1.6 million 'summary offences' triable in magistrates courts which, some far from trivial, include 1.1 million motoring offences and sundry other misdemeanours including cruelty to children, assaulting a policeman and certain drug offences.)

The official figures from the Home Office publication *Criminal Statistics* undoubtedly understate the problem. The British Crime Survey (BCS) reported that in 1983 there were an estimated 12 million incidents involving crime against individuals or their private property. The vast majority were offences against property. Crimes of violence comprised 5 per cent of the total, and a further 12 per cent were common assaults involving negligible or no injury.

The BCS showed that as few as half of all burglaries get into police records, about a quarter of woundings and sexual assaults, and as little as 10 per cent of incidents of vandalism. For shoplifting and some other categories of crime the figure may be as low as 1 per cent. For drunken driving the detection rate may be 0.4 per cent.

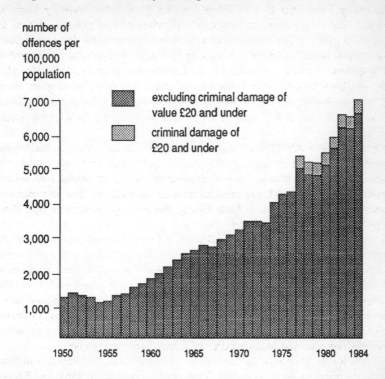

Figure 6. Notifiable offences recorded by the police per 100,000 population (England and Wales)
Source: *Criminal Statistics*, Home Office

While car theft is well recorded, the same is true of only 30 per cent of thefts *from* a car. Perhaps only 10 per cent of 'robbery/theft from the person' is recorded, a category which includes mugging. If the BCS estimate for 1983 of 12 million offences was right, then this means there was almost one crime for every four people in England and Wales in that year. This is a staggering burden of villainy for a supposedly law-abiding society.

The bare statistics showing the growth in crime over the decades are these: the number of recorded crimes has risen from 500,000 in the 1950s to one million in the mid-1960s, two million in the mid-1970s and over 3.5 million in the mid-1980s. This is a seven-fold increase over a period when population grew by just 13 per cent. As we shall see, the official statistics undoubtedly overstate the rise in crime but nonetheless the trend is unmistakably upwards.

Over half of all crime involves theft; this accounted for 1.9 million offences in 1985. A further quarter (0.9 million) involves burglary. The balance is made up of 'violence against the person' (which includes homicide and wounding), sexual offences (which includes rape and indecent assault), robbery (which is theft with violence or threat of violence), fraud and forgery, criminal damage (vandalism), and 'other offences' (which includes drug trafficking). The contribution of these various categories to the overall crime picture is shown in Table 3 and Figure 7.

Table 3. Notifiable offences recorded by the police per 100,000 population (England and Wales), 1985

Offence group	Number
Homicide	1
Violence against the person (excluding homicide)	243
Sexual offences	43
Burglary	1,751
Robbery	55
Theft and handling stolen goods	3,786
Fraud and forgery	271
Criminal damage[a]	710
Other offences	24

Source: Home Office
Note: [a] Excluding 'other criminal damage' valued at £20 and under

For almost all types of crime the main offenders are male. They commit 85 per cent of murders, 90 per cent of burglaries, offences involving drunkenness and motoring offences, and 95 per cent of woundings and assaults. They are also responsible for over 70 per cent of social security offences. Men figure less prominently in the categories of shoplifting and offences involving cruelty to children. The fact that men commit a preponderance of serious crime is reflected in sentencing patterns. Less than one-tenth of the 100,000 women offenders in 1985 received custodial sentences compared with over one-fifth of the nearly 500,000 male offenders.

Males are not only far more likely to commit violence than females, they are also more likely to fall victim to it. In the case of serious wounding which endangers life they are five times more commonly victims than women, and for less serious wounding, three times. The dangerous age for men is 16–24, when the incidence of all types of wounding rises to nearly 1 per cent each year.

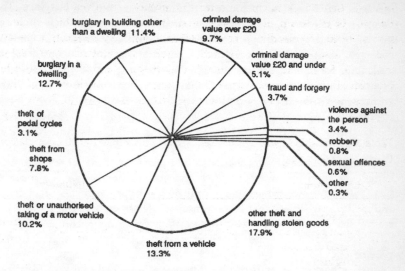

Figure 7. Notifiable offences recorded by the police, by type of offence (England and Wales), 1985.
Source: *Criminal Statistics*, Home Office

While the official statistics show that men are more likely to fall victim to violent crime than women, inner city surveys tell a different story. There is a huge problem of domestic violence, with perhaps three-quarters of a million wife-beatings in London alone each year. There is also a higher incidence of sexual assaults, an almost exclusive female 'prerogative', and women are more likely to be the victims of street robbery than men in inner city areas. All these violent crimes are heavily under-reported to the police. The same is true of the (usually) non-violent crime of burglary. A survey in a North London housing estate showed that single mothers were the most likely victims.

Crime is emphatically a male pastime: 22 in a thousand men offend each year compared with five in a thousand women. Moreover, crime is a *young* male pastime. Some 30 per cent of offences are committed by boys under 17, a further quarter by those under 21. The peak age for crime among males is 15, and by 20 almost a quarter have a criminal record. This rises to over 30 per cent by the late twenties, according to a survey reported in *Social Trends*. One-tenth of these offenders had over 10 crimes to their discredit.

The offences committed by teenage boys are not trivial. More than 40 per cent of burglaries and robberies are committed by those under 17, and overall this group accounts for a quarter of all serious crime. Half of those convicted of rape, wounding and assault are males aged between 17 and 24; three-quarters are males aged between 14 and 29.

These and the other criminal statistics make pretty depressing reading. It is clear that we live in a crime-ridden world. But viewed from the perspective of history, things may not be quite as bad as they seem. Let me set the scene by rehearsing some clichés. Criminals seem to be getting younger. Youth has shrugged aside parental authority. Family life is declining. More women are working to the neglect of their children. Popular amusements are debasing behaviour. Streets are unsafe. Courts are going soft. Does all this sound familiar? Geoffrey Pearson in his book *Hooligan, a History of Respectable Fears* has brilliantly characterised the recurring fears of successive generations and the cyclical nature of nostalgia.

The Golden Age always seems to be twenty or thirty years ago. This beneficent time is contrasted with the unique horrors of the present. Unparalleled crime waves and moral depravity; new levels of violence and civil disturbance – that is the present. Safe streets and docile or easily correctable youth; a law-abiding populace peacably going about its business – that is the past. In short, that is the now imperilled British Way of Life.

In debunking the enduringly stable law and order myth, Geoffrey Pearson takes us back through the generations to pre-industrial Merrie England and shows us in all ages an abundance of crime and violence. There were law and order panics in 1760, 1800, 1829, 1842, 1856, and so on. Just as recurrent were fears of social breakdown and national decline. Friedrich Engels, newly arrived in a Victorian England loud with the clamour of industrialisation found time to shout above the din that 'the British nation has become the most criminal in the world'.

Crime – particularly the street crime of turbulent youth – did not spring from nowhere in the past twenty years or arise since the war, or happen because of the arrival of black people or because the law has gone soft. Neither did it result from the moral laxity of modern education or as a result of television violence. We have not just recently been plunged into an unnatural state of disorder. Crime and violence have always been with us and, indeed, they are a deep-rooted feature of British life. We are a criminal and violent people. And we delude ourselves if we think otherwise.

Teds, mods and rockers, punks, football hooligans, muggers – all have their forerunners of yesteryear. Even that supposedly modern phenomenon the inner city riot has venerable antecedents,though they tended to be bloodier affairs in times gone by. For example, riots in Bristol in 1831 provoked savage reprisals by the dragoons which, on some people's reckoning, left 500 people dead. Compare that with latter-day disorders, disturbing though these may be.

Geoffrey Pearson writes of 'respectable fears – repeatedly accusing the here-and-now present of succumbing to an unprecedented deluge of crime and immorality, while gazing back fondly to the recently and dearly departed past'. Being aware of these historical continuities is a useful corrective to domesday pessimism but it should not be an invitation to complacency. 'It is one thing to wriggle free of the ageless mythologies of historical decline. It is quite another to leap into the arms of the equally pernicious social doctrine that nothing ever changes.' It would, indeed, be a remarkable thing if crime rates had stayed the same over the last 200 years, given the huge social upheavals which have occurred in that period. How to get a reliable assessment? The figures, where available, have to be handled with care.

Probably the most reliable figures when comparing the crime rate in one age with another are those for murder. Most are probably reported and recorded. Adjusting for population, the risk of being a murder victim is now less than it was 100 years ago. In the early 1980s, your chance of being murdered was about 25 per cent lower than it was in the 1860s. However, the danger was lower still in the 1950s, perhaps half the present level.

For crimes less serious than murder, the figures are far less reliable even over recent decades. We have seen that the figures include only reported crime. They are also reclassified from time to time rendering comparisons difficult, and the rules on recording are changed. Different police forces and individual police officers interpret the rules differently, and with the rise in police manpower and the use of computers, more of the reported crimes may be recorded. There is evidence that more crime is reported now than hitherto, perhaps partly due to a rise in telephone ownership.

All this should induce scepticism about the seven-fold increase in crime between the mid-1950s and the mid-1980s described earlier. Attempting to circumvent the problems of interpreting the official crime statistics, a team of four sociologists from Leicester University used local newspapers and interviews with long-lived policemen to establish the trends in violent disturbances between 1900 and 1975.

Industrial violence, the Leicester team found, has declined dramatically since the first 20 years of this century, though it has been rising again since the 1960s. The bitterly contested miners strike of 1984–5 and the print workers dispute at Wapping in 1986 are two examples of recent industrial disputes degenerating into horrific scenes of violence.

Community violence – which in the study covered brawls and street-fighting – has declined this century though not so dramatically as incidents in another category, that of political violence. In the two general elections in 1910 several large riots occurred, some involving thousands of people, rival supporters becoming embroiled in vicious fights. There has been little of this in recent times, but large-scale violence has not been banished from Britain's streets, as witness the urban riots of 1981 and later which set inner city areas in London, Birmingham and Bristol ablaze.

The only category of violence that the Leicester researchers found had increased overall this century fell into the category 'sport and leisure' and particularly related to football. Hooliganism at football matches has been a feature of modern times. British football fans have a justifiably appalling reputation wherever the game is played. The nadir was reached after the period covered by the Leicester study, when to their eternal shame, Liverpool football fans rioted and caused the deaths of 39 rival supporters at the Heysel stadium in Brussels in 1985.

Taking the results of the Leicester study together with other research findings and the criminal statistics, it would seem that crime in Britain described a downward trend from the early part of the century to the Second World War. Since that time crime has risen, giving a picture of recent deterioration against a long-term improvement. Particularly disturbing has been the recent increase in violent crime and the use of firearms.

The more serious offences of personal violence, those entailing the loss or endangering of life plus rape and armed robbery, increased between the mid-1970s and mid-1980s by about 60 per cent. Homicide was up by about 10 per cent a year but wounding was up by 42 per cent. Rape was up by nearly 70 per cent over the decade to 1985 while the biggest increase was in armed robberies which increased 150 per cent to 2,500, with 65 per cent of offences occurring in London.

The increase in rape is almost certainly exaggerated by the official figures. The police are now perceived (fairly) as being more sympathetic to the victims of rape and this may have increased the rate of reporting – which in any case is reckoned to be as low as 10 per cent. According to *Criminal Statistics* this does not explain the full increase, though, which suggests a true rise in incidence. Other sexual offences such as indecent assault have fallen slightly in the last decade to below 20,000, a more encouraging trend.

Sexual assault is one cause for concern, another is mugging. National statistics on mugging are unavailable, but figures from the Metropolitan Police showed an increase from 1,454 offences in 1974 to 7,888 in 1984. About one in ten of these crimes was solved. Given that not all muggings are reported, that means relatively few muggers are caught. The Home Office report *Personal Violence*, published in 1986, commented:

Mugging is an unsophisticated crime. It offers low rewards at the risk, albeit slight, of severe penalties. As such, it is typically resorted to by youths from lower socio-economic groups in areas such as those where large parts of Britain's minority communities are settled.

Old ladies are not the principal victims of muggers. Most victims are young or middle-aged and for those muggings which reach the attention of the police at least, less than half the victims are female.

The number of crimes involving firearms doubled to nearly 10,000 between 1975 and 1985. Apart from the increase in armed robberies, much of the increase was due to a rise in criminal damage offences involving air weapons. Overall, the use of firearms in crime is mercifully rare. In 1985, 0.3 per cent of notifiable offences involved a firearm. The incidence of fatal or serious injury caused by a firearm was still lower at 0.1 per cent. For burglary – a crime many people fear will happen to them – the recorded usage of firearms in 1985 was 2 in 10,000. Your chances of meeting an armed burglar are therefore very low indeed.

Burglary, on the other hand, is very common. The trend suggests there will soon be a million of these a year; they have been increasing at 5 per cent annually. However, the results of the General Household Survey and the British Crime Survey suggest that much of the recorded increase in burglaries was attributable to an increase in the proportion of offences committed which were recorded. Less than a third of convicted burglars are 21 or over, indicating that burglary is a young man's trade – and a common one. A third of the prison population is 'doing time' for burglary.

According to the Home Office an average person aged 16 or over can expect a burglary in the home once every 35 years. He or she can expect to be the victim of a robbery such as mugging once every 450 years; an assault resulting in injury once every century; and the family car to be stolen once every 60 years. In some inner city areas the risk of becoming a victim in each of these categories is very much higher.

The British Crime Survey showed that cars, vans and motorbikes were the most common targets of crime. One in five owners surveyed in 1983 reported having had something stolen from their vehicle or the vehicle itself stolen or vandalised. Theft *from* a vehicle, in fact, doubled between 1975 and 1985. Thefts of cars have increased more slowly at about 3.3 per cent per year. The two car-related categories taken together account for about 45 per cent of all thefts and thus a quarter of all crime.

If you are a victim of crime, what are the chances of 'your' criminal being nailed? In 1980, 40 per cent of crimes were 'cleared up', that is, the police had apprehended somebody. By 1985 this had fallen to 35 per cent, and by 1986 to below 32 per cent. Even these figures overstate the success rate, however, because not everyone who is apprehended is found guilty. Furthermore, many crimes go unreported.

Clear-up rates tend to be high for crimes where victim and offender know one another. Thus in 1985 someone was arrested in 96 per cent of murders, 73 per cent of woundings and other acts endangering life, and 84 per cent of assaults. For all crimes involving violence against the person the figure was 73 per cent in 1985, down from over 80 per cent in 1975.

Someone was taken into custody in 64 per cent of rapes in 1985. This too was somewhat lower than 1975.

The clear-up rate in London, at 16 per cent, is well below the national average. Differences in recording practice are claimed by *Criminal Statistics* to contribute to the low figures, but the lesson from these offence-related statistics seems clear: if you are a criminal, choose a crime with a low clear-up rate (e.g. burglary) and commit it in the capital.

For a supremely bad taste crime on these lines, consider the following cutting taken from the *Guardian* of 28th December 1979:

Thieves stole £1,000 from the London headquarters of the Save the Children Fund at Christmas by breaking into the building while the caretaker was at church.

London is undoubtedly a criminal hot-spot. In 1985, there was a total of 10,257 offences per 100,000 people. Of these offences, 211 were robberies, a crime at which Londoners seem to excel. The next highest robbery rate was in Merseyside at 128 – but here the true speciality was burglary at 3677 offences per 100,000, the nation's top score. The average for England and Wales was 1751. The true 'Shock-Horror Capital of Crime', however, was Greater Manchester which had a total of 11,202 crimes per 100,000 residents in 1985. Compare this with the law-abiding, rural area of Dyfed Powys which had a mere 3734 offences for every 100,000 people, half the national average.

London aside, the north of England tends to have higher crime rates than the south – and the difference has become more accentuated over the years. Divergencies between the two parts of the kingdom in material standard of living may have a bearing here. A recent Home Office report concluded that key factors in the rise of crime were poverty and the decline of the inner cities. This was a less than staggering contribution to the immemorial debate about the causes of crime which, like nostalgia for a peaceful bygone era, has its timeless elements. The political Left traditionally seek explanations in social injustice and deprivation; the political Right in 'permissiveness' and the breakdown of family ties and codes of behaviour. Either way, however, most victims of social injustice and the majority of 'permissive' people (whoever they are) do not commit crimes. Many of us, though, worry about becoming victims.

According to the British Crime Survey, which started in the early 1980s, anxiety about crime is widespread. Rape emerged as a considerable source of worry for women, followed by mugging. Fear for personal safety is an urban problem, particularly an inner city one. It can restrict people's behaviour and social lives. Over one-tenth of all inner-city residents said in the BCS survey that they never go out at night because of crime. Half of women do not go out unaccompanied after dark. In the poorest council estates and multi-racial areas there were especially high levels of fear, which were, however, matched by high levels of risk. This indicates that fear and perceived risk are not necessarily out of alignment.

An example of a group experiencing too little fear is provided by young men. This group paradoxically are the least anxious in the population but are most often victimised by assault. Old people have the opposite problem, coupled with a misinterpretation of the awfulness of the times in which we live. Geoffrey Pearson:

> It is a matter for little surprise (although it is of enormous social consequence) that it is elderly people who are most prone to nostalgia, and who also most fear crime and violence. Research on the victims of crime tends not to confirm their fears – showing, by contrast, that old people are among those least victimised by crime, particularly by violent crime.

Mishaps

Each year, over 14,000 of us die in accidents. In the 1970s this figure was several thousand more, so the position has improved recently as regards this cause of death. Currently, the home claims 5,500–6,000 lives a year, the roads more than 5,000 and the workplace 400 or so. The balance of fatalities occur in sundry mishaps involving trains, planes, drownings, natural disasters, sporting and recreational activities, and so on.

Accidents kill only 0.025 per cent of us each year – which is 2.5 per cent of total deaths – but create a large burden of anxiety particularly where youngsters and road accidents are concerned. More young men die in accidents than from all other causes put together, and most of these die on the roads (see Figure 4, p. 52). Even among young women, accidents are the leading cause of death, though here traffic accidents account for a smaller proportion of the total.

Accidents are particularly significant because of the age of victims. For strokes and coronary thrombosis the average age of death is in the mid-70s. For accidents it is in the mid-40s. Accidents thus account for more *lost years* than either of the other two causes, though strokes and heart disease are more prevalent causes of death.

An average of 15 people die in the home each day – and a further 8,500 sustain injuries requiring medical attention according to the government's Home Accident Surveillance System. The deaths occur mainly among the very old and the very young. The old die in falls – and this accounts for 60 per cent of domestic fatalities – and the young die of choking or suffocation. Accidental poisoning and asphyxiation account for some 500 deaths annually. Domestic fires also claim hundreds of lives a year, the two main causes being electrical malfunctions and unextinguished cigarettes.

Smoking is believed to be the cause of about half the fires that the fire brigade has to deal with, according to James Wilkinson. Between 1970 and 1980 there were 7,400 non-fatal casualties in Britain and almost 2,000 deaths in fires started by smoking materials. This is about a quarter of fire deaths each year. Such fires are not confined to the home, of course, but also occur in factories, hotels, places of entertainment and even at sporting venues. When a cigarette butt or a match was carelessly discarded in a stand at the Bradford City Football Club in 1985, 56 people died in the ensuing blaze.

Britons seem to be four or five times more likely to die in fires than the Swiss, though we are less likely to perish this way than North Americans. Expressed as fire fatalities per 100,000 population, the figures for a range of countries in 1980–1 were: Switzerland 0.51, Sweden and Japan 1.70, Britain 2.24, Hungary 2.68, United States 2.84 and Canada 3.45. We have got a long way to go to equal the best.

More than one person is killed at work every day. The most dangerous places of employment are mines, quarries and construction sites, followed by farms and factories. Deaths from accidents at work declined by nearly 30 per cent in the period 1961–84 according to *Social Trends*, but this encouraging figure masks a deterioration in recent years. According to the Health and Safety Executive, the incidence of fatal and major injuries in manufacturing industries rose from 71 per 100,000 workers in 1981 to over 87 in 1984. In the construction industry, the rate went up by almost half from 164 per 100,000 employees to 233. Those who have jobs in industry are facing increasing risks. There has to be the suspicion that employers are caring less about the safety of their workers.

The most common non-fatal industrial injuries are broken bones from falls on building sites and fingers lost in machinery.

Vastly more deaths and injuries occur on the roads than at work. About 1.5 million accidents occur on Britain's roads each year which result in over 5,000 deaths, 70,000 serious injuries and more than 240,000 slight injuries. These are the official figures. Hospital checks show that the police records on which the accident statistics are based under-report slight casualties by about 35 per cent and serious casualties by about 20 per cent, although it is probably the less severe of the serious casualties that evade the figures.

The real total for deaths and injuries on our roads is probably over 400,000 a year. This is an enormous human cost – and the economic cost is also pretty frightful. Taking into account police and medical costs, damage to property, lost output and so on, the bill is running at £3 billion a year. That is over £50 for each one of us, annually.

Your chances of being killed each year on Britain's road are somewhat over one in 10,000. There is twice the risk on America's roads where fatal traffic accidents account for 3 per cent of all deaths each year. Our figure is nearer 1 per cent. Not only is driving safer in Britain than America, it is safer than in many European countries. The most dangerous place to drive is Portugal, where there were 300 deaths per million people in 1983, followed by Austria (over 260), France and Luxembourg (each about 235), and Belgium (about 215). The safest place to drive is Scandinavia followed very closely by Britain with 100 deaths per million people.

At all ages males have a far higher risk of being killed in traffic accidents than females. In Britain in 1982 the ratio of males to females killed was 2.4 to 1. The difference in rates is greatest for the 15–24 age group where the ratio in 1982 was 4.1 to 1. In terms of road accident risks, as in so much else, women are a different species.

The risk also increases down the social classes. An unskilled manual worker, for example, is four-and-a-half times more likely to die in a motor vehicle accident than a self-employed professional. Remarkably, the manual worker is 16 times more likely to be killed while walking.

The number of deaths on our roads is at a 30-year low. This is a considerable achievement when you bear in mind the growth in motorised traffic over the decades. To go back over half a century, consider 1931 when 2.2 million cars caused 6,700 deaths. Now, nine times as many cars cause three-quarters as many deaths. Those who look back fondly to a time when it was safer to play in the streets are deluding themselves. As we have come to terms with the car the human cost has fallen.

We can be encouraged by the improvement in road safety, but we should beware of topsey-turveydom. A US Secretary of Transportation, quoted in *New Scientist*, announced that deaths had declined by 1 per cent in 1985 by saying: 'More lives than ever before are being saved on the nation's highways.'

The most striking improvement in the safety of car-drivers and front-seat passengers in recent years has been wrought by seat belts. These are reckoned to be saving perhaps 400–500 lives a year since their use was made compulsory at the beginning of 1983. Since then, deaths among drivers have gone down by a fifth and among front-seat passengers by a quarter. This demonstrates the advantages of preventive medicine enshrined in law. Or does it? Being in a car may be safer but other road users may be picking up the tab. John Adams, a controversial road safety expert, has claimed in his book *Risk and Freedom, the Record of Road Safety Regulation* that belted drivers may be induced to drive faster and more recklessly at the expense of other road users. As the author puts it, the response of motorists 'leads to potential safety benefits being consumed as performance benefits'. Whatever the explanation, it seems true that the benefits of safer travel are not being enjoyed by pedestrians and cyclists (Table 4).

The particular tragedy of pedestrian and cyclist accidents is that they disproportionately involve children; a third of deaths and serious injuries among those on bikes or on foot involve the under-15s. It is also true to say that of all children who die, a high proportion do so on the roads. In London, traffic accidents account for 50 per cent of all child deaths.

Child pedestrians are at greatest risk between five and nine years old. More cyclists are killed and seriously injured between the ages of 10 and 14 than at any other time. The trend of inexperience and risk, in fact, runs throughout the road accident statistics. More people are killed and seriously injured on mopeds at 16 and on motorcycles at 17 than at any other age. Similarly, the greatest toll among car drivers is at the age of 18 and 19. Whether on wheels or on foot, you are at most risk when you have least experience. Just as it takes a society time to come to terms with the car, so, too, the individual.

Table 4. Road accident victims killed or seriously injured

	1975	1980	1985
Pedestrians	20,815	19,035	19,470
Cyclists	4,564	5,536	5,652
Two-wheel motor vehicles[a]			
riders	15,059	20,359	16,532
passengers	1,554	2,338	1,640
Cars			
drivers	19,213	18,932	16,722
passengers	15,969	14,309	12,385
All road users[b]	83,488	85,400	76,145
(killed)	(6,366)	(6,010)	(5,165)

Source: *Road Accidents Great Britain 1985*, Table 5, HMSO
Notes: [a]Includes mopeds, motor scooters and motorcycles
[b]Includes bus or coach drivers and passengers; LGV drivers and passengers; HGV drivers and passengers

Road accidents accounted for 76 per cent of accidental deaths and 36 per cent of all deaths in the 15–24 age group in 1980. The great majority of these were young men killed in motorcycle accidents. A typical rider has a 1 in 500 chance of being killed each year. In fact, an extraordinary fifth of all fatal and serious casualties on the roads occur in accidents involving motorcycles, yet motorcycling accounts for only 1 per cent of all journeys made. In 1984, more than 1,100 people were killed in such accidents (excluding mopeds) and more than 50,000 were injured, 18,000 seriously. To a motorcyclist, a serious injury is usually serious indeed; hospital studies show that this class of road user is at greatest risk of severe disablement.

Motorcycles are the single most dangerous form of transport. This makes it particularly unfortunate that it is the favoured mode of transport of the group, young men, least appropriate for bearing additional risk responsibly. The level of anxiety among juvenile riders is predictably low. As John Adams comments:

> Young male motorcyclists, with very high accident rates, appear to be much less concerned about road safety than their mothers, who have very low accident rates.

The causes of motorcycle accidents are not a mystery. Stephen Plowden, an expert writing in *The Times*, has described how high accident rates are associated with reckless, risk-taking and inexperienced youth, and powerful machines.

In general, accidents of all types occur at the busiest times of day. The most notable exceptions to this are the hours between 11pm and 1am on Friday and Saturday nights when the rates peak. Drink is a factor in this effect, and makes the hour between 11pm and midnight the killing hour on British roads when a quarter of all road deaths occur.

Since 1967 the legal limit for alcohol has been 80mg per 100ml of blood. The drink-driving law had a deterrent effect in the early days but since then, according to *Social Trends*, the proportion of fatal accidents involving alcohol has returned to pre-1967 levels. Of drivers involved in fatal accidents, 28 per cent were over the legal limit in 1985. The problem is not confined to those in charge of a vehicle. Up to a quarter of adult pedestrians killed in car accidents are themselves legally drunk.

Over nine-tenths of drunk-drivers are men. Conviction rates for this offence in Northern England are 50 per cent higher than the national average. Northerners have also a greater propensity for speeding and, overall, have a 25 per cent higher conviction rate for all motoring offences taken together. The peak age for offending is 17 to 19, and this group commit three times as many driving offences as any other group.

In spite of 300,000 speeding convictions a year, speed limits in Britain are widely flouted. According to a survey quoted by Stephen Plowden and Mayer Hillman in *Danger on the Road: the Needless Scourge*, half of all vehicles break the speed limit on the majority of roads in residential areas. This is where 75 per cent of accidents occur. Although there are fewer accidents rurally, the ratio of fatalities to all injuries is higher than for urban areas because average speeds are higher. At 30mph your stopping distance is 75 feet. At 50mph it is 175 feet. One study showed that if you hit a pedestrian when driving at about 35mph, your victim has a 1 in 2 chance of surviving. At over 40mph the pedestrian's chances drop sharply to 1 in 10. Children and the elderly are particularly vulnerable.

Speed has a decisive bearing on the outcome of accidents in bad weather. Wet or icy roads are safer in fact than dry roads – though only because of the modified, risk-reducing behaviour of other drivers. More accidents occur in wet and icy conditions but these tend to be less serious because motorists are usually travelling more slowly. Because of drivers' behaviour, 'safe' driving conditions can be more dangerous than 'dangerous' driving conditions.

Motorway coaches are the safest means of road transport. The various forms of transport can be compared on the basis of fatal and serious casualties per hundred million kilometres travelled. The following figures are taken from Plowden and Hillman and relate to 1978–9:

Bus or coach passenger	2
Car passenger	9
Car driver	9
Pedestrian	85
Cyclist	120
Motorcyclist	270

Each kilometre travelled on a motorcycle is 30 times more dangerous than the same distance covered in a car and almost 135 times more dangerous than a bus or coach. Cycling, though safer, is still the second most lethal way of getting about – particularly if you are young.

Broadly, road accidents can be divided into two main types. The large majority are due to miscalculation, inattention or bad luck of one sort or another, including mechanical failure, which on its own accounts for 3 per cent of accidents. The people involved here are a cross-section of drivers though, as we have seen, inexperienced road-users figure prominently in this group. There are also a small number of people who seem to be more accident-prone than others or who seem to go through a period of accident-proneness.

Accidents of the second type involve a breach of the rules, such as disregard of traffic lights or reckless overtaking. A large number of these miscreants are people who defy the law in other ways. Young men are over-represented in this category of driver.

5
Objective

It is clear from the analysis that we Britons are less healthy than our counterparts abroad and that we are dying earlier. More of us are cut down in our prime by heart disease and lung cancer than in any other country. Crime seems to have increased here more than elsewhere, and your chances of becoming a victim have not been as great for decades. Accidents, though in overall decline, are increasing at work – reversing an historic downward trend – and among young pedestrians and cyclists.

We saw in Part I that the wealth of the British people has improved over the decades since the Second World War but that other nations had done better still, leaving us relatively poorer than they. A similar thing has happened to our health and longevity, both of which have improved but relatively more slowly than elsewhere. These two effects – relative economic decline and relative ill-health – seem connected. Affluence is life-enhancing.

Our single objective here is to improve the quality of life. The sub-objectives relate to the prevention of ill-health, crime and accidents, and can be stated quantitatively for the year 2000:

- Ill-health   A 10 per cent improvement in the health of the population (an interesting exercise in quantification this, as we shall see).

- Crime   A reduction to 2.5 million offences a year – a drop of about a third in the crime rate.

- Accidents   A reduction of 50 per cent in fatal accidents, currently running at over 14,000 a year; the number of non-fatal injuries to be reduced commensurately.

The actual targets are less important than the principle that targets should be set.

6

Lifestyle Sub-strategy

The theme of the lifestyle sub-strategy is the reduction of risk to decrease the incidence of ill-health, crime and accidents. This can be achieved by a National Programme for Risk Reduction, the central intention of which would be to reduce *involuntary* risk. The aim is not to eradicate risk in its entirety, even if this were possible or desirable, but to reduce the kinds of risk most of us do not want to face. Examples here would be the risk of murder and crime in general, the risk of coronary thrombosis and other life-threatening diseases, and the risk of accidental death at work or in the home.

Voluntary risk is another thing. Included here are hang gliding, Russian roulette and other dubious pastimes. Of course, between the extremes of involuntary and voluntary risk there is the time-honoured grey area. For example, if you decide to 'do the ton' on a motorbike you are taking a voluntary risk of injury, disablement and death. I, as a fellow road user, would be exposed to an involuntary risk. And the taxes and national insurance contributions of both of us, and many others besides, would be spent in the event of a 'prang'. As ever, it is a moot point where your freedom ends and my rights begin.

In seeking to reduce involuntary risks, the National Programme for Risk Reduction becomes a platform for opportunity. In the matter of health, for example, and the 'doomed genius' kind of analysis notwithstanding, suffering more typically extinguishes the spark of creativity than ignites it. And if there is opportunity there is also freedom: you remain free to choose to expose yourself to as much voluntary risk as you want (within the constraints of the law). If the National Programme for Risk Reduction succeeds in reducing the bad news of life it will also reduce anxiety pollution. So you should be able to take those voluntary risks and frighten yourself in a more carefree mood. This points to a paradox associated with risk reduction. We are risk-averse until risk drops to a low enough level, then we display risky, thrill-seeking behaviour. The same is true of most activities. If it is made safer, people will tend to change their behaviour to bring the level of risk back to where it was. This phenomenon is called 'risk homeostasis'. An example cited by John Adams in the field of road accidents involves car brakes: if you give motorists better brakes they use them later. A safety benefit is turned into a performance benefit. The situation is neatly summed up by a headline from the *The Sunday Times*, quoted by John Adams, describing the improved safety of climbing equipment: 'Risk your life as safely as possible'. Any reform in the area of safety should take into account the human need for risk and the tendency for this to have a 'set-point' in any particular activity.

The National Programme for Risk Reduction would apply the mostly preventive tenets of what I have called 'risk engineering', a discipline whose aim is to reduce threats to well-being. These tenets are as follows:

- 'Designing out' Create the condition for low risk rather than mop up afterwards. Prevention is better than cure.
- Targeting Target big risks (affecting many) ahead of small ones.
  Target the highest at-risk group as a first priority. Determine why certain types of individuals are over-represented in the high-risk population – 'disproportional representation.'
- Reconnection Your fate is in your hands. We should be reconnected to the consequences of our actions.

If politics is the art of the possible and science the art of the soluble, then 'riskology' is the art of the reducible. Measures to reduce threats to well-being will be discussed under the following headings: Lifestyle 2000, Smoking, Alcohol, Crime and Accidents.

Lifestyle 2000

Compare the expenditure of seven countries on health in 1983, as a proportion of national income (GDP):

	(%)
USA	10.8
Sweden	9.6
France	9.3
West Germany	8.2
Italy	7.4
Japan	6.7
UK	6.2

Having journeyed with me this far, you will not be surprised to find Britain at the bottom of the heap, nor surprised to learn that proportionately our health spending has gone up least since the 1960s. Spending in the mid-1980s fell below 6 per cent of our national income, with only the Dutch and Belgians among the major industrial nations spending a smaller proportion. When you recall that we are probably the poorest nation in the list – poorer even than Italy – you will appreciate that even the percentage figure flatters us. Should this relatively low health spending be a cause for concern? The surprising answer is 'no'.

The reason for this cheerful conclusion is that there is a rather poor correlation between what a nation spends on health care and the health of its people. The Japanese live long, healthy lives and yet they spend far less as a proportion (and in real terms) than the shorter-lived Americans. What the American experience demonstrates is another, somewhat stronger correlation – that between national expenditure and the level of medical salaries. Of more interest still, however, is yet another correlation: between the health of the general population on the one hand and *affluence* and *personal attitudes* on the other.

Wealth brings health. The rich Americans live longer than the poor Brits. They have also taken to healthy living with greater vigour. They are eating better, exercising more and drinking and smoking less. These lifestyle improvements are contributing to better health generally and may have contributed to a fall in the rate of heart disease which is very evident across the Atlantic but not so evident here.

The provision of primary health care is seen in its most divergent forms in Britain's version of socialised medicine, the National Health Service, and in the free enterprise system based on private medical insurance in the US. We currently spend about £19 billion a year on the NHS which is over £320 each. In the US, they spend well over ten times as much nationally which amounts to about three times as much individually. For this extra, they live on average a year longer, and, as we have said, have lower rates of heart disease. But other objective indices of health such as infant and maternal mortality tend to be similar. Overall, the Americans throw vast sums of money at the health problem for only a slightly better performance than ours – and a performance, moreover, that has more to do with other factors than primary health care.

This kind of analysis indicates what a value-for-money organisation the NHS is. It is also fairly efficient. One researcher has calculated that 21 per cent of the total expenditure on health in the US goes on administration alone. The comparable figure for the state-run British system is 5 per cent. The difference between these two figures is more than the cost of the entire NHS.

The US health care approach of compulsory medical insurance linked to competitive private provision is a formula for runaway health care expenditure. There is little resistance to cost increases because they are spread over millions of premium payers and because the professionals compete to push every new type of glamour medicine or high-tech gizmo. Political control – which is Britain's alternative to the operation of the market – is revealed to be a better approach to cost containment in medicine. The American experience is instructive as an economic model and because it highlights some of the worst excesses of modern medicine.

The cost structure difference between the US and British systems is illustrated by the commonness of hospital beds designated for intensive care. In the UK, one-hundredth of the beds are so designated. In the US, the figure is one-tenth. This difference is particularly interesting in view of the criticism that has been directed at the intensive care concept. For example, the classical use is for heart attack sufferers, yet the benefit to these patients has proved difficult to establish.

Controversial obstetrician Wendy Savage of the London Hospital College has pointed out that in the US over a fifth of babies are now born by Caesarean section, a reflection of the American medical profession's concern to make money and avoid lawsuits. Yet there is no evidence that Caesareans reduce the number of infant deaths. In the UK, Caesarean sections have risen from 4 per cent in 1970 to 10 per cent in 1983. Research shows, says Wendy Savage, that the presence of a female companion such as a midwife throughout labour reduces the need for Caesarean sections and drugs, and is cheaper as well.

New equipment for 'high technology obstetrics' is often adopted ahead of proof of worth, according to Wendy Savage. Electronic foetal monitors became popular in the 1970s. Proper clinical trials, carried out a decade later, showed, surprisingly, that monitors do not improve the newborn's survival chances. Similarly, randomised controlled trials show no sign that routine screening of pregnant women with ultrasound reduces infant mortality. The Department of Health now advises against routine scans but 75 per cent of women still receive one. At £25 per scan the misallocation of resources is immense.

One of the most recent additions to the doctor's armoury has been the CT scanner for computerised X-ray assessments of lesions to the head and other parts of the body. The US has six times as many of these machines per 100,000 people as we do. But, comments a writer in *New Scientist* (13 November 1986): 'The surprise is that this has not had as much effect on diagnosis and mortality as might be expected.' Other areas of high-tech medicine are cardiac surgery, transplantation and cancer medicine. All of these have been criticised on the grounds of cost, inhumanity and ineffectiveness.

Some 200,000 patients have coronary bypass surgery in America each year. Apparently there remain important questions about the effectiveness of this procedure according to Professor Valerie Mike, a biostatistician at Cornell University. Far fewer of these operations are performed in Britain which presumably means that Americans are going under the knife for mild or minimal symptoms. Eliot Valenstein, a professor of psychology at the University of Michigan, sees a parallel with the history of lobotomy in psychiatry, there being a 'tendency to look for more and more applications once the staff and equipment are in place'.

Hip replacements are comparable in numbers on both sides of the

Atlantic but many other operations are not. Hysterectomies are far commoner in the US where about 700,000 are performed annually. Yet as Valerie Mike says, this operation has never been properly evaluated by researchers. Nor is its use – and that of other operations – uniform across America. There are tenfold differences in the rates of hysterectomies, prostatectomies and tonsillectomies, with, in the words of the good professor, 'no discernible effect on the general health of the population'. This 'provides support for the view that much of today's treatment is ineffective'.

For high-tech excess, the sky's the limit. Medical helicopter services have started up in the US in recent years, such that there are now about 150 of these air ambulances operating mainly in metropolitan areas. Their accident record is poor – 10 lives were lost in 1985 – and the benefits to the patients have not been established. There may even be dysbenefits. The head of the California Department of Health was quoted in *New Scientist* as saying: 'It's not surprising that a heart patient who finds himself loaded aboard a cramped machine with whirling rotors would have problems.'

Free enterprise, American-style, provokes the excessive use of diagnostic tests and treatments alike, a phenomenon also associated with 'defensive' medicine against the threat of medical malpractice suits. The Americans are famously litigious, which is a pity for them because litigation is a ludicrously expensive way of settling responsibility for accidents. A recent report showed that in the US, doctors' medical-malpractice insurance costs had doubled from $1.7 billion in 1983 to $3.4 billion in 1985. Claims against them were also enjoying explosive growth; these had gone up fourfold since 1980.

American doctors are twelve times more likely to be sued for damages by their patients than British doctors. Their liability insurance premiums are consequently greater and can run to tens of thousands of dollars annually. Damages paid to patients in Britain are generally lower. This is true not only for medical mishaps but also product liability claims. In the US, these latter have caused safe contraceptives to be removed from the market and have driven vaccine producers out of business. Liability insurance now accounts for $8 out of the $11.50 charged for a single dose of DPT vaccine (diphtheria, pertussis/whooping-cough and tetanus) – even though the risk to the child receiving it is small and the potential benefit great.

Laws are less in favour of the consumer in Britain, and drug manufacturers have not had damages awarded against them. Even the claims against the suppliers of thalidomide, the drug that caused children to be born with crippling birth defects, were settled out of court.

Demand for medical services seems almost infinite and rises with affluence. Medical costs also seem to rise faster than inflation. Britain has coped better with the pressures than most nations. In America, payments to doctors under the Medicare system have doubled in five years. British doctors have fared much less well, fortunately for the taxpayer.

Britain's NHS is plainly a better approach than the American one to staunching cost haemorrhages and curbing 'iatromegaly' – medical hubris and technological expansionism. One can go further and say that the NHS comes out well in almost any international comparison. It is a genuine British achievement and is arguably the greatest nationalisation triumph of the post-war era. It has brought many benefits other than the obvious ones of providing health care at reasonable cost. For example, a co-operative health culture has yielded excellent statistics on morbidity and mortality and world-leading epidemiological studies. Britain's 'yellow card' notification system used by doctors to report adverse reactions to drugs, though far from perfect, is regarded as the best system yet developed. The supraregional system of clinical biochemistry laboratories is regarded as highly efficient, while the voluntary national blood-transfusion service is exemplary. And finally, the NHS is backed up by another excellent system, the Public Health Laboratories, the 'bug labs'. These are facets of a British success story.

The NHS may be a success, but there is still plenty of scope for improvement. Some parts of the system are undoubtedly overstretched, particularly those having to deal with the demands of the increasing number of old people. Limited resources also show up in other areas. For example, the number of patients on chronic dialysis per million of population is low compared with several Western nations. This probably indicates pent-up demand. Waiting lists also seem unacceptably long in some regions for some operations. In addition, it has been claimed that patients are being sent home too early after operations and other forms of treatment in the cause of greater efficiency in terms of patient 'throughput'.

Allocation of resources to different treatments in the NHS does not seem to be done on fully rational grounds. For example, each year millions of pounds of scarce NHS cash are allocated to heart transplants. This is in spite of better uses for the money. Researchers at York University have developed the concept of 'quality-adjusted life-years' or QALYS. They concluded that heart transplants cost over £5,000 per QALY, compared with £1,000 for coronary-bypasses and £750 for hip replacements. Put another way, mundane hip operations are almost seven times better value for money than glamorous heart transplants.

There is too little accountability in the NHS. Some health commentators think accountability should extend to hospitals publishing performance data to allow the public to evaluate the service it gets. The 3,000 pay beds in the NHS are a perennial bone of contention, many thinking that the sole basis for priority in the public sector should be need.

The health service undercharges for pay beds anyway and is thus providing unfair competition to the private sector – a case of 'dumping' to use trading parlance.

As regards private patients, the activities of consultants continue to attract criticism. These health workers can, and often do, double their NHS salaries by treating people privately. Sam Galbraith, a brain surgeon turned MP, has been quoted as saying:

> Highly paid hospital consultants are allowed in the company's time, and often using the company's equipment, to run what is in effect a rival business.

This in-house moonlighting should be stopped.

To the outside observer, the NHS – like the British economy itself – seems in a perpetual crisis which never quite spills over into terminal disaster. I have indicated some of the usual problems cited relating to under-resourcing, poor accountability and private practice. But a greater problem exists which goes beyond the NHS to embrace modern medicine and the 'cure' mentality.

In his celebratedly excoriating polemic *Limits to Medicine*, Ivan Illich documented the deficiencies of the Western approach to health. His subtitle says it all: 'Medical nemesis: the expropriation of health'. His thesis – no other word can describe this argument which floats on a heaving sea of footnotes – is that the medical establishment has itself become a major threat to health not only because of the so-called 'diseases of medical practice' and drug side effects, but also by fostering, at the expense of self-reliance, a disabling dependency on paternalistic physicians wielding high-tech cures. Health should be given back to the people.

Ivan Illich's brand of wholesale scepticism is immensely invigorating. But there is a danger of throwing out the baby with the bathwater. The case for modern medicine has been made somewhat unexpectedly by Ted Kaptchuk who holds a doctorate in traditional Chinese medicine and who runs the Pain and Stress Clinic in Boston where a variety of 'alternative' medical approaches are tried to help seriously ill patients.

> Western scientific medicine is one of the greatest triumphs of human history. It can intervene dramatically to reverse physiological and pathological processes, maintaining people who would otherwise be dead. It's done tremendous work dealing with the flesh and blood of human beings and deserves only praise ... I've lived in Third World countries where the unattendant consequences of disease are great.

Dr Kaptchuk was quoted thus in the *Guardian*. He also said, with insight:

'Every healing art falls in love with itself'. Western medicine is no exception. What Dr Kaptchuk is particularly keen on, like Ivan Illich, is developing people's self-reliance.

Death rates fell when doctors went on strike in Israel in 1973 and in Bogata in 1976. While this is amusing to relate, it should not obscure the fact that modern medicine can play a vital role in attending to life's casualties. This is as true in Britain as elsewhere – but there is room for considerable change. As many people have pointed out, the NHS is really a national disease treatment service rather than health service. In 1983, less than 6 per cent of the total NHS budget was devoted to prevention. Preventive programmes there are – one thinks of child immunisation – but the fundamental orientation is towards repair. The most emblematic image of the NHS is of a bustling hospital accident department giving on to an intensive care unit with comatose patient abed attended by bleeping monitors, pulsing tubes and the fateful trace of the oscilloscope. Verily, the hospital is the NHS's centre of gravity.

And if medicine is treatment-obsessed, so too is dentistry. It is said that you can identify the nationality of two groups of people by the amount of ironmongery in their mouths: the Russians and the British.

As is clear from an analysis of the nation's health, the major gains are most likely to come from changes in smoking, eating, drinking, exercise, stress and environmental factors – in a word, lifestyle. An improvement in the way we live holds out more promise of reducing unnecessary death, disease and disability than any number of medical advances. We need only apply what we already know if we no longer want to lead the world in heart disease and lung cancer, for example, two of our biggest killers.

Britain's current preventive health effort is patchy, underfunded and undynamic, and, judging by results, not nearly successful enough. Health professionals do not look to preventive medicine to provide glamorous careers. Within the NHS, the preventive services are not regarded as being where the action is. And yet prevention holds the key to the future. By taking sensible measures we can doff the mantle of the industrial world's chief invalid.

What is required is a parallel organisation to the NHS whose main goal is preventive medicine. The new organisation would have four functions:

1. To take over the NHS's preventive medicine activities;
2. To mount screening programmes;
3. To make policy recommendations;
4. To publicise healthy lifestyles and improve media treatment of 'risk'.

An appropriate name for the new outfit would be 'Lifestyle 2000', a conscious echo of the World Health Organization's optimistic campaign 'Health for All by the Year 2000'. The European goals of the WHO campaign are shown in Table 5. Three of these are particularly memorable and important in the context of a preventive medicine programme: add years to life (prevent premature death); add health to life (prevent disease and disability); add life to years (full development and use of physical and mental abilities).

Table 5. WHO Health for All by the Year 2000: European goals

- Ensuring the pre-requisites for health:
  peace – not simply the absence of war but a climate of stability in international relations;
  social justice – the right of every citizen to the protection of the law and to equality of access to the necessities of life;
  adequate and wholesome food and safe water;
  decent housing and sanitation for everyone;
  education for everyone;
  secure employment so that everyone has a valued and rewarding role in society.
- Equity in health so that everyone has the best possible opportunity to develop healthily and to obtain required health care
- The addition of years to life, by the prevention of premature death
- The addition of health to life, so that preventable disease and disability are minimised
- The addition of life to years, so that the highest attainable level of health continues to be enjoyed by both the elderly and those disabled by chronic illness or permanent impairment
- The identification and promotion of healthy behaviour and the discouragement of unhealthy behaviour
- The introduction of policies in all sectors of public life to make it easier to adopt healthy lifestyles and to participate in health policy making; and to enhance the role of the family and other social groupings
- The creation and preservation of a healthy environment
- The development of health services which are appropriate to people's needs and wishes
- Acceptance of these goals by those responsible for research, for service management and for training within the health professions.

Source: *Charter for Action*, Faculty of Community Medicine, 1986

The plan for the European Region of WHO was outlined in the Faculty of Community Medicine's 1986 publication *Charter for Action*. Specific responsibilities were described for central and local government, health

Table 6. Feasible Targets for Health Authorities

- By 2000, ensure greater equity in health
- where differences exist between geographical and/or socio-economic or ethnic groups in the incidence and mortality from specific conditions, these should be reduced by 50 per cent by securing an improvement for the disadvantaged group.
- By 2000, achieve health-related goals which will add life to years, add health to life and add years to life by
- reducing the prevalence of mental illness to the extent that there is a 25 per cent reduction in the prescription of hypnotics, sedatives and tranquillisers;
- reducing by 10 per cent the prevalence of severe mental handicap;
- reducing by 15 per cent the prevalence of severe physical handicap at birth and as a result of accidental trauma;
- reducing by 50 per cent the incidence of stroke by the prevention and control of hypertension;
- reducing by 50 per cent the prevalence of total tooth loss in adults (this may be one of the most accessible targets since there is already a reducing prevalence of caries);
- reversing and then reducing the rising incidence of sexually transmitted diseases;
- reducing by at least 25 per cent the number of unwanted pregnancies, particularly amongst women aged less than 20 years;
- reducing by at least 15 per cent the mortality, and disability, from such specific preventable infections as measles, pertussis and congenital rubella (it may be possible to eradicate these diseases entirely);
- maintaining a low level of maternal mortality;
- reducing by at least 20 per cent the perinatal mortality rate and the infant mortality rate (both these rates are much higher than in many other European countries; a sustained and co-ordinated campaign is required to reduce hazards to the child *in utero* and the premature onset of labour, as well as to ensure that maternity services respond sensitively to the needs of their patients);
- reducing by at least 20 per cent the mortality rate from all causes of accident at all ages;
- reducing by at least 20 per cent the mortality rate from cancer in those aged less than 75 years;
- reducing by at least 30 per cent the mortality rates from both stroke and heart disease in those aged less than 75 years.

Source: *Charter for Action*, Faculty of Community Medicine, 1986

authorities, professional bodies, training institutions, industry, trade unions and individuals.

A crucial feature in any proposed prevention programme would be quantified aims understood right down to local level. The Faculty of Community Medicine gives a series of what it calls 'feasible targets' for Health Authorities (Table 6). These would form the sub-objectives within the National Programme of Risk Reduction which is designed to improve the health of the population by 10 per cent by the year 2000 and reduce fatalities and injuries from accidents (discussed under a separate heading) by a half.

How would Lifestyle 2000 be funded? A simple (and predictable) solution suggests itself: increase the sales taxes on tobacco products and alcohol. There is independent justification for these moves, discussed later.

The gains from a preventive medicine campaign could be immense. As a general rule, a fatal disease deprives its sufferer of 10–15 years of life. In terms of lost years saved, a preventive programme could have a big impact. The economic consequence could also be significant. As epidemiologist J. A. Muir Gray has pointed out, more days are lost through sickness than strikes, and the loss is equal to the entire cost of running the NHS taking into account lost productivity, lost national insurance payments and lost earnings.

The first function of Lifestyle 2000, as we noted, would be to take over the NHS's preventive activities, including the immunisation programmes and the 11,000-strong health visiting service. Also brought under the aegis of Lifestyle 2000 should be the school health service, the present state of which is a unsatisfactory. According to a follow-up study to the 1976 Court Report on child health, increasing poverty and declining preventive medical services have led to a deterioration in children's health. The study was carried out by Professor Philip Graham, Dean of the Institute of Child Health, and the findings were made known in 1987. Professor Graham claimed that improvements called for by the Court Report and intended to ensure that the right care was available for all children had still not been made over a decade later. Some districts spend only a fifth as much as others on child health. The quality of the school health service and school meals had both gone down.

Professor Graham also pointed out that co-ordination of those responsible for the health of children had diminished with the abolition during the 1982 NHS reorganisation of area medical and nursing officers. What was required were community paediatricians to organise preventive medical services.

The Black Report on social inequalities and health gave children particular priority:

On the realisation that the problem cannot be attacked on all its aspects at once, the focus of effort with the greatest future potential must be on the health and welfare of children.

Since 1980, with mass unemployment, more families have fallen into poverty. The number of children living in extreme poverty is probably over 400,000, and the children of the poor are smaller and sicklier than the children of better-off families.

To enhance the health of poor children, the Black Report recommended improved access to antenatal and child health clinics, better day-care facilities, and closer links between school health services and general practice. Also called for were improvements in child benefit, an infant care allowance, an increase in the maternity grant, free school milk and adequate school meals.

The health education of children is very important, particularly that of girls. Women who are well nourished during their reproductive years give birth to bonnier babies. There is a well established relationship between poor maternal diet and an increased risk of congenital malformation among offspring. This has been described by Margaret and Arthur Wynn in their book *Prevention of Handicap and the Health of Women*. They have also pointed out that Britain has an unnecessary burden of infant mortality due to respiratory illnesses. This seems to be because we do not keep our babies warm enough – it is as simple as that. This is most true in the lower social classes. (For a further consideration of this issue see Appendix II, 'A breath of fresh air'.) As the Wynns have written:

> The health education of girls must be the main means of reducing the prevalence of these disorders early in pregnancy that produce so much handicap ... There is, too, a very big bonus from such education for all women including those who do not have children. Healthy habits that reduce the casualties of reproduction also reduce the risk of breast cancer, cervical cancer and other types of cancer and heart disease and stroke in later life. The health of married women is also so closely bound up with what we have called family health status ... the risk of men contracting cancer, heart disease and stroke in later life depends very much on the health education of their wives.

The health education of children should be a clear priority for school authorities assisted by such organisations as Lifestyle 2000. This is just one aspect of the challenge facing any new preventive medicine organisation and, indeed, the NHS – to get close to the customers to meet their needs most appropriately.

There have been encouraging trends recently within the NHS away from 'cure' and 'hospital' towards 'care' and 'community'. The new emphasis on neighbourhood health centres is particularly heartening. Such changes will be needed if the NHS is to be converted from a network of repair shops of last resort to the responsive, treatment-orientated component of a proactive disease prevention system.

The NHS and Lifestyle 2000 would be partners dedicated to fostering well-being principally through self-reliance. Hippocrates asserted a couple of thousand years ago that a doctor must teach his patients to care for their own health. This implies that the central medical ethic should be that doctors – and others in the health field – attempt to eliminate the need for their services. This is ethically demanding because in livelihood terms it is a throat-cutting approach. (It need not be – the Chinese are said to pay their doctors only when the patient is well. This is pay-for-performance with a vengeance and presumably makes prevention a very hot topic indeed within the Chinese medical fraternity.)

The second major function of Lifestyle 2000, to mount screening programmes, overlaps to some extent with the first of taking over the NHS's preventive role, as the health service has existing screening programmes for breast and cervical cancer, for example. The rates of these cancers in Britain have remained static in recent years, while in other countries they have fallen. An expansion in screening for early cancer detection is particularly worthwhile since patients treated early respond much better than those caught late.

The Lifestyle 2000 screening campaign would be a much-expanded version of what is on offer now. This is justified because of usefulness – screening technology is coming of age – and need – health inequalities, for example, have widened in the eighties. The screening programme would have three aims: the early detection of disease; reconnection of people to the consequences of their actions by identifying unhealthy elements in individual lifestyles; and quantification of individual and national health. These three aims can be conveniently intermeshed.

One thing people lack is a memorable, quantitative assessment of their health. The 'HQ' concept meets this need. Mooted in *Social Inventions*, 'HQ' stands for Health Quotient. It is a measure of a person's health and well-being on the lines of the IQ measure of intelligence. By definition, average health is 100. The advantage of the idea is that an individual gains a precise view of his health and could establish a clear objective for improvement. The HQ would need to measure objective indicators of health such as blood pressure, but also behavioural elements such as drinking and smoking, and 'well-being' elements such as stress and even the difficult-to-define 'contentment'. Sir Douglas Black, of inequalities in health fame, said in a Christie Gordon Lecture:

Of their nature, 'health statistics' relate to morbidity and mortality, not to 'positive health', which in a euphoric passage we defined as a 'positive expression of vigour, well-being and engagement into one's environment or community'.

The HQ concept could be an integral part of a preventive screening programme. Screening specific groups for cervical and breast cancer is already justified, by smear and X-ray mammography respectively, as is measuring blood pressure to detect hypertension (a Black Report recommendation) and assessing blood cholesterol for predisposition to coronary heart disease. Furthermore, a battery of tests is becoming available from biotechnology companies that enables identification of those who are most likely to succumb to common conditions such as diabetes, emphysema, heart disease, several cancers and even, it is said, alcoholism, long before they actually do so. New pregnancy tests have been developed enabling the identification of genetic disorders such as cystic fibrosis and Huntington's Chorea. A new generation of 'physician office' diagnostic tests are arriving. Among these is a kit allowing plasma cholesterol to be determined in two minutes using a pinprick blood sample. Screening is an idea whose time has come – particularly combined with an HQ component which leads to the adoption of healthier lifestyles.

The HQ part of the screening process might well comprise three stages: a preliminary questionnaire, the test itself, and a follow-up interview. The pre-test questionnaire would seek to establish dietary pattern, behaviour, social circumstances, typical levels of psychological stress, information on vaccinations previously received, present and previous illnesses and disabilities, and use of health service facilities in the recent past. Also obtained would be information relating to disease and death among the subject's parents, grandparents and blood relatives to establish the genetic background.

The HQ test itself would be a comprehensive 'medical'. Conventional height, weight and other measurements would be made together with hearing and eye tests, and so on. Blood and urine samples would be analysed. The hapless punter would also be subject to 'treadmill' exercise stress tests with computer assisted monitoring to assess cardiovascular and lung function. Other screening assessments would be made in what would clearly be an extensive test schedule.

The follow-up interview would inform the individual of the HQ findings and identify the potential for improvements focusing on key risk factors relevant to that person. The 'sub-100' subjects would be given particular attention in this regard. The intention would be to develop a Personal Programme for Risk Reduction, the individual equivalent of the National Programme for Risk Reduction, covering diet, exercise, etc. (To show you what this means, I have developed a generally applicable Personal Programme for Risk Reduction which is given in Appendix II.) The opportunity could also be taken to give information, where appropriate, on family planning, sexual diseases including AIDS, dental hygiene, availability of NHS and personal social services, sickness support groups (of which there are almost 9,000 including one for people with diseases so rare they thought no one else had it), local sporting activities, counselling services, welfare benefits (e.g. heating grants), accident prevention and so on. The HQ follow-up could also be used to improve immunisation take-up relating to polio, measles, rubella and whooping cough (for which new, safer vaccines are becoming available).

Who to screen? A representative sample of the entire population, and members of high-risk groups. The representative sample would enable a 'national HQ' to be determined. This would provide the basis for determining progress against our target of a 10 per cent improvement in Britain's health by the year 2000. It would also facilitate broad-based international comparisons in the health sphere in the way that GDP figures permit in the economic sphere. It will have a further advantage: it will enable us to determine 'productivity' in the health business in terms of the HQ score added by a certain treatment, preventive measure, health team, or hospital. It would provide the much-needed rational basis on which to allocate resources in the health field. At present, according to Professor Alan Maynard of York University, resources are often allocated 'on the basis of emotion and shroud-waving'.

The high-risk groups appropriate for screening can be selected on the basis of *victim-relatedness* and *deprivation*. The victim-related category bears on the observation that those related by blood to disease sufferers are in some cases more likely to contract the disease themselves. For example, genetic factors are implicated in about half the 160,000 deaths from coronary heart disease in Britain each year. Screening the relations of victims for high blood pressure and high blood cholesterol would be more cost-effective than screening the whole population. A group led by Professor Michael Oliver of Edinburgh University traced the family of a man who had a heart attack at the age of 44. The group found 51 first cousins, of whom 46, all in their thirties, were badly affected by the disease. Although this points the moral that life's greatest gift is a good set of chromosomes, it is also true to say that if these people changed their lifestyle as regards diet, smoking, exercise and stress, their risk of premature death would be reduced.

A less well established example of victim-relatedness comes from the field of cancer. One study in Denver, Colorado suggested that the daughters of women with breast cancer had a higher-than-average risk of developing this form of cancer themselves later in life. Of women drawn from the total population, 9 per cent develop breast cancer. Among the daughters of sufferers, the incidence rises to 18 per cent. The results of the Denver study are tentative and await confirmation but indicate that screening those related to the victims of cancer could be valuable in detecting this type of disease at an early stage. Some quarter of a million new cancer cases are registered annually. A proportion of these are identified too late for effective treatment.

The deprivation category of candidates for screening arises from the correlation between economic deprivation on the one hand, particularly when linked to urbanised living, and ill-health and premature death on the other. There is 'disproportional representation' on a large scale. The poor have the highest rates of infant and maternal mortality, respiratory disorders, heart disease and so on. Cancer is also commonest in this group. For example, in Sheffield, women from poor areas are five times as likely to have cervical cancer than women from well-off areas. This kind of disparity has been called the 'Titanic effect'. On the doomed liner, 3 per cent of women travelling first class were drowned, compared with 16 per cent in second class and 45 per cent travelling third.

The rich and poor eat differently and look different. In 1984, those households whose main wage-earner made less than £83 a week bought 18.8 ounces of fruit and 34.6 ounces of bread a week. Those earning £355, bought two-and-a-half times as much fruit and two-thirds as much bread. Different lifestyles show up in stature. The difference in height between children of the professional and managerial classes and those of unskilled labourers is about 2cm at 3 years, but this increases to nearly 5cm at adolescence.

Attention was focused on the social origins of ill-health by the Black Report. The government, reckoning that implementation of the major recommendations of the report would cost over £2 billion, shelved it. Sir Douglas Black has written since: 'These are substantial recommendations, but so is the problem with which we were asked to deal. I am personally convinced they are both reasonable and imaginative.' The government evidently felt otherwise.

Other countries such as Sweden, West Germany, the Netherlands and Finland have made greater strides than Britain towards eliminating health inequalities by improving the health of the poor. In the 1980s, indeed, health inequalities have actually widened here according to *The Health Divide*, a report which appeared in 1987 and which was an update of the Black Report. The health gap could be shown between manual and non-manual workers, between those in and out of work, and between deprived and affluent areas. The major causes of inequality were differences in living conditions, working conditions, income and lifestyle. Health inequalities were possibly wider than at any time since the NHS was set up in 1948. In a foreword to the report, Dr David Player, the then director-general of the Health Education Council, wrote: 'such inequality is inexcusable in a democratic society which prides itself on being humane'.

The problem is an enormous one and needs to be tackled across a broad front. One contribution would be a screening campaign targeted at the poor and leading to early disease identification and awareness of better lifestyles. This would be a start to efforts to 'raise the Titanic'.

The third function of Lifestyle 2000 would be to make policy recommendations to government to 'design out' risk. This is to give preventive medicine its widest interpretation to embrace, for instance, public catering standards, road traffic management, sporting activities, building regulations and fire safety. Lifestyle 2000 would need to work with the Royal Society for the Prevention of Accidents – the largest such body in Europe – the Health and Safety Executive responsible for safety at work, the British Standards Institute and other relevant organisations.

Of particular importance is diet. The food industry has a too-powerful, and – many would argue – inimical influence on what we eat. The government has consistently ignored advice from its own expert bodies on nutrition, and key reports have been censored or suppressed. This is all the more remarkable given that we are regarded as having the most unhealthy diet in the developed world. Food production should be changed for the better by, for example, encouraging trends towards leaner meat.

Another important area is medical research. The number of scientists working in a particular area at public expense seldom seems to match the importance of the disease under investigation – and indeed, there often seems to be an inverse correlation. A leading epidemiologist has pointed out that sixty times more people work in myeloia leukaemia research, for example, than on strokes, even though the latter disease affects more people and the opportunities for advances in understanding and treatment seem greater. Not enough money is spent on improving the quality of life of the old or on alcohol-related diseases. Interdisciplinary research is increasingly required of a type which the structure of university departments does not always encourage. In addition, a fair amount of biomedical research is more about publication-chasing than about making bids to improve people's well-being.

Publicity would be the fourth function of the Lifestyle 2000 organisation. This would have two aspects: publicity relating to healthy living; and efforts to improve risk-related media reporting in order to make people risk-aware rather than anxious. Lifestyle 2000 would supersede the Health Education Authority (né the Health Education Council) as purveyor of health propaganda. This should have a life-enhancing tone and eschew guilt-induction.

Of course, preaching commonly sets up a negative reaction, and people are free to ignore good advice and often do. This is already happening now if an unkind inspection of ourselves and our fellow countrymen is anything to go by. The fact is that the average Briton is – in that excellent phrase – a poor physical specimen. Particularly common in our culture is the Sumo wrestler physique of middle age. Catch people in their twenties and you could influence their shape for life. Young men are of interest in this regard because they seem to neglect themselves. Young women care about their own bodies; young men care about young women's bodies – nobody cares about men's bodies. Women's bodies are more interesting biologically and more can go wrong. In consequence they seem to try harder. If a woman's shape goes it is not so much through neglect but more commonly through childbearing. Men do not have this excuse.

We tend to eat like navvies but live the indolent life of the Dauphin. The mercy is that we do not all end up looking like wallaby-fronted television darts players. Young men in particular could usefully eschew gargantuan blow-outs and liver-crippling wassail sessions. To put it another way, they and others would do well to heed the good advice typically proffered during an HQ follow-up briefing: eat better and less, drink less, maintain an ideal body weight, attempt a graded increase in exercise, and smoke not at all. (Pious advice on these lines is given in Appendix II.)

Although people resist good advice, the time seems ripe for lifestyle changes. This is particularly true in the area of nutrition. In favour, for example, is dietary fibre, which is said to give your digestive system something to chew on. Out of favour are animal fats, which may help clog your arteries. Sales of wholemeal bread and vegetables are increasing while, according to the Ministry of Agriculture, milk and butter consumption is down. Fruit juice intake has reached its highest ever level. Provided we avoid mad healthist diets the prospects for reducing ill-health are very encouraging. Diet probably influences the development of heart disease and certain cancers, leading causes of death in contemporary Britain.

The other part of the Lifestyle 2000 publicity remit relates to 'the dangers of modern life'. The message needs to be got across that in historical terms risk has fallen to an all-time low and should go on falling. 'It's not the world that's got so much worse but the news coverage that's got so much better.' G. K. Chesterton said that between the wars. Media activity has undoubtedly increased from the time in the thirties when a BBC radio newsreader is supposed to have said: 'There is no news today.'

Now, a news edition on the television that does not feature a disaster, a vicious crime or multiple death in some form is unusual. What is also unusual is if any of these events is reported in full perspective and with appropriate contextual information. Urquhart and Heilmann have identified what they call victim-orientated reporting which can be seriously misleading. This, they say:

tends to leave us with free-floating anxiety and dread about such things as – in no particular order – the bomb, the next earthquake, air pollution, car crashes, jet crashes, lead poisoning, toxic shock syndrome, deformed babies, chemical plant explosions, carcinogens in food, asbestos in drinking water, formaldehyde coming out of the walls of our houses, cancer risk of X-rays, passive smoking, mercury in seafood, dioxin, AIDS, radioactive fallout, and so on.

When we read the latest scare story, the black box fright recorder in each of us registers anxiety and dread frequently unrelated to the scale of the danger. Urquhart and Heilmann point out what is required is not only information on how many people suffer the adversity but 'how many were at risk and escaped unscathed'. For example, if a plane crashes with loss of life that is an appalling tragedy, but it is placed in perspective by knowing that hundreds of millions of airline passengers complete their journeys without mishap. In the US in the second half of the 1970s, for example, your chance of being killed in an air crash was one in a million per trip. Again, if a grannie is beaten up in her own home, this is disturbing, but it only becomes *disproportionately* anxiety-inducing to potential victims if it is not recorded that many millions of old ladies went through the day unmolested.

Urquhart and Heilmann have proposed a scale of risk to enable people to get dangers in proportion. The Safety-Degree Scale would be constructed on the lines of the Richter Scale, the logarithmic scale used by earthquake boffins but understood in outline by the public. Urquhart and Heilmann have written:

> Of course, no scale for risk can make irrational people rational, but having a well-understood scale for risk as part of our common language can minimise the ability of the irrational members of society to manipulate others by fear mongering, use of misleading statistics, or other forms of disinformation.

The problem with the Safety-Degree Scale is that unlike the Richter Scale it runs counter-intuitively, that is, the bigger the risk the smaller the number. For example, a relatively dangerous activity like smoking rates a score of 2.8, while your chance of being hit by a falling aircraft in any year would be about 7.0. What I propose therefore is a 'Risk Factor Scale' which runs the other way.

At Risk Factor 1 or 2 would be rare hazards like being struck by lightning. At Risk Factor 5 would be motorcycling, a fairly risky pastime, and beyond that at 7, towards the scale-end, even more hair-raising pastimes such as extinguising oil rig fires and breaking in mustangs. (For the statistical basis of such risk gradings see *Risk Watch* by Urquhart and Heilmann.)

The Lifestyle 2000 organisation would be charged with developing a database to support the construction of this scale and indeed they would centralise all statistics relating to risk in the country. They could then offer a free service to journalists giving figures on at-risk group sizes, risk trends over recent years, the risk factor figure itself, and a statement of what are the principal causes. This is not a council of perfection, this is responsible reporting. This way we may get an improvement in risk reporting in line with the improvement in 'miracle drug' stories.

As an adjunct to the Risk Factor Scale could be a verbal scale similar to that used by doctors contacted by the media in connection with their patients involving words like 'satisfactory', 'serious' and 'critical'. Thus, a journalist quoting Lifestyle 2000 on the risk of being a fatal victim of a certain drug's side effects might say: 'Fairly rare at risk factor 3' or 'a serious danger at risk factor 6.'

Lifestyle 2000 would seek to reduce anxiety – of which there is a disproportionate amount – and redirect it to priority hazards. It would liaise with other organisations such as the British Medical Association which has distinguished itself with campaigns against smoking and boxing and in favour of seat-belts in cars. (The medical profession has come a fair way since discussing as late as 1878 in the *British Medical Journal* whether the touch of a menstruating woman could make a ham go bad!) Bodies like the BMA and Lifestyle 2000 would assist the public in getting risks in proportion – and also in giving due weight to benefits. Disasters can have drastic negative effects. For example, the thalidomide tragedy led to great delays in introducing new drugs into the US. One such group were the life-saving beta-blocker heart drugs. Because these were not available earlier, lives were lost. It has been estimated by the Food and Drugs Administration that 17,000 Americans died prematurely each year during the five-year delay. This is far more than the toll from all known drug disasters in modern times worldwide.

We worry about some things and not others. We are deeply suspicious of drugs yet are less risk-aware about surgical procedures, some of which, like hysterectomy and coronary bypass surgery, as we have seen, are less well established than they might appear. Food additives are another area of enormous concern, yet rather few adverse effects have been successfully attributed to these to date. Organic foods may be more wholesome, but freedom from preservatives may mean licence for bugs.

Where attitudes must be changed, the message should be highly targeted in a marketing sense for maximum effect at a reasonable price. For example, why send the nation's pensioners an AIDS leaflet intended to discourage promiscuity and popularise the use of rubber contraceptives as happened in early 1987? Surely the concurrent television advertisements were enough for this low-risk group? In Wales, some old people who received the pamphlet during a winter cold spell tried to exchange them for money at the local post office under the impression they were cold weather payment vouchers. The leaflet was printed in Welsh, a language none of them could read.

Smoking

Imagine a fully-laden Concorde crashing onto the Houses of Parliament with no survivors among the plane's passengers or among our esteemed legislators. That is the scale of the carnage wrought every week in Britain by cigarettes.

Each year 100,000 people die from smoking, which thus accounts for 15–20 per cent of all mortalities. Cigarettes also cause an enormous burden of non-fatal disease and minor ailments.

The response of successive governments to the premier cause of preventable death and disease has been pretty puny. The link between cigarettes and lung cancer emerged in the 1950s. In 1920 there were 250 recorded deaths from lung cancer. Between the early 1930s and 1955, the number of deaths had risen from a couple of thousand to over 17,000. In 1956, the Minister of Health had been advised by the standing Medical Advisory Committee that he should urgently 'inform the public of the known connection between smoking and cancer of the lung, and of the risks involved in heavy smoking'. Statistical studies had shown that heavy smokers were 20 times more likely to contract lung cancer than non-smokers. But under pressure from a Treasury aware of the revenue implications of a decline in smoking, a special committee set up to draft a statement on the issue produced a heavily watered-down statement of the risks. It said that although cancer-producing agents had been found in tobacco smoke, 'whether they have a direct role in producing lung cancer, and if so what, has not been proved'.

The record since then has been similarly unimpressive. A secret report on smoking and health prepared by Whitehall officials at the start of the 1970s was subsequently leaked to the *Guardian*. The report claimed that a reduction in smoking would be paralleled by an equal reduction in invalidity and premature deaths, but that the consequences of such an improvement in the health of the nation would be unacceptable. The men from the ministry pointed out that if two out of every five smokers kicked the habit, the state would eventually face the problem of caring for an extra 100,000 old people every year. Moreover, if people stopped spending so much on tobacco they would have much more money left for the purchase of other, less revenue-producing goods such as food, imported stereos and foreign cars. The committee calculated that over a five-year period a 20 per cent reduction in cigarette consumption would reduce the balance of payments by £50 million at 1970 prices. That was obviously not on, was it?

The economic importance of tobacco has long tempered the reaction to the consequences of its use. After it was introduced into England in the second half of the sixteenth century, there was a fierce debate about its properties and benefits. But by 1625 the extent of tobacco revenues had led even King James I to moderate his fanatical opposition and accept its widespread use. His previous condemnation of smoking is justly celebrated: 'A custom loathsome to the eye, harmful to the brain, dangerous to the lungs, and in the black stinking fume thereof, nearest resembling the horrible Stygian smoke of the pit that is bottomless.'

The high-point of governmental addiction to tobacco revenues has passed. According to Joy Townsend of the Medical Research Council's epidemiology and medical care unit, cigarette taxes in the early 1950s provided no less than a sixth of government revenue. Now the figure is a modest 4 per cent, though even that is over £4000 million a year.

If the government has become less dependent so has the general public. Of men, 36 per cent were cigarette smokers in 1984. The figure for women was 32 per cent. In 1972, 52 per cent of men were smokers and 42 per cent of women. Smoking is increasingly concentrated in the lower social classes. Among unskilled male manual workers almost half smoke, as do 35 per cent of women in the same class. This compares with 17 per cent of men and 15 per cent of women in professional jobs.

Young women now favour smoking more than young men. Among 16 to 19 year olds, 32 per cent of girls smoked in 1984 compared with 29 per cent of boys. Cigarette makers see young women as a major growth sector of the market, judging from their promotional activities. Since the turn of the decade, deaths from lung cancer in women have gone up by 20 per cent. Most smokers start young. Nearly 10 per cent of 13-year-olds smoke at least one cigarette a week. A quarter fall into this category by age 15 and the proportion rises thereafter. Most people who become smokers are hooked by the age of 21.

Because of the penalties in ill-health and premature death, smoking is the most important public health issue of our time. Action must be taken to reduce its incidence if we want to lose our reputation as the world capital of heart disease and lung cancer. We should beware of overreaction, however – in the seventeenth century in the German principality of Luneberg the penalty for smoking was death!

The first recommendation which can be made is to double the price of cigarettes with immediate effect by increasing the sales taxes on these products. This is not as draconian as it sounds; according to James Wilkinson, the BBC's science correspondent, the real cost of cigarettes has actually come down in recent decades. By early 1984 cigarettes were 40 per cent cheaper in real terms than they were in the 1950s. Doubling the price would merely have the effect of bringing it back to the immediate post-war level. The MRC's Joy Townsend has claimed that a fall of 20 per cent in smoking could be achieved this way in the next five years without any loss of government revenue. In fact, in the early period it would probably produce extra revenue on a significant scale, particularly with supra-inflationary rises in successive years. The amount should be enough to make a large contribution to the funding of a preventive medicine organisation such as Lifestyle 2000. An explicit statement on cigarette packets and elsewhere that this was the intended use of the extra revenue might in any case make the price rise more acceptable. It would be appropriate from the inflationary point of view if cigarettes were removed from the Retail Price Index.

Price rises would hit one group particularly hard – the poor. As Joy Townsend has said, 'it is likely that the differential in social-class smoking would be considerably reduced'. This is all to the good.

About a third of adults now smoke. We should aim for this to be less than 10 per cent by the year 2000. The Norwegians are aiming for zero smoking by the end of the century but, given the addictive nature of the habit, this is unlikely to be an attainable goal. A crucial element in reducing smoking will be health education from Lifestyle 2000. As Peter Wingate has noted, the crime-sheet of tobacco-related diseases is so long as to invite disbelief, yet all the claims are solidly based. The danger is that publicity in the hell-fire mode can induce a negative reaction. As Henry Strass, later Lord Conesford, put it: 'I have every sympathy with the American who was so horrified by what he had read of the effects of smoking that he gave up reading.' The opportunities for a supremely bad taste anti-smoking campaign are good, particularly if aimed at the young. After all, smokers are more likely than others to be toothless, blind amputees of low intelligence living in poor circumstances – and they are shortening their lives by five-and-a-half minutes every time they light up. They are also more prone to divorce, they have more car accidents and they are more likely to take drugs and be heavy drinkers. The image of glamour and sophistication projected by smoking advertisements is gapingly at variance with actuality. If you need convincing, take a look at the next ten people you see smoking in the streets.

To complement the lifestyle publicity there should be a total ban on the advertising and promotion of *all* tobacco products. Surveys show this would be a popular move. The ban would apply everywhere including the point of sale. Sponsorship of sport on television particularly sticks in the craw. According to the Health Education Council, sponsorship of snooker alone gives cigarette makers publicity which was running at the rate of nearly 550 30-second advertisements a year in 1986. This involves the BBC, the channel that is not supposed to carry any advertising at all, let alone that for tobacco products. The HEC reckons that cigarette firms are getting about £500 million a year of advertising space on the public service network some two decades after cigarette advertising was banned from television altogether.

Well over £100 million is spent each year by the tobacco industry on advertising and promotion according to James Wilkinson. This colossal sum compares with the puny couple of hundred thousand pounds deployed by Action on Smoking on Health and a proportion of the Health Education Council's £9–10 million budget. In 1981 nearly a quarter of all poster advertising was promoting tobacco products as was a substantial proportion of sponsorship of the arts and sport. The latter is youth-orientated. Given this, the linking of sport and cigarettes is especially offensive. If sporting organisations cannot find alternative sponsors then they must simply cease to operate. Better that than more than a million premature deaths by the end of the century.

Banning tobacco advertising and sponsorship might prove controversial. Why not alcohol and fast cars, too, for example? James Wilkinson has the answer to the objectors: 'They fail to point out, of course, that all these other products are safe when used properly and barring accidents. Tobacco is the only advertised product which is hazardous when used as intended.' He might have added: 'At all doses.'

The Black Committee recommended that tobacco companies should be ordered to submit plans to stage themselves out of the smoking business within 10 years. The government, far from urging them to do this, is reported to have given £5 million in selective aid between 1979 and early 1985 to several tobacco companies including Carreras Rothman Limited, Imperial Tobacco Limited and J.R. Freeman and Son Limited, firms with a large share of the £7 billion a year British market for tobacco products.

In Japan, anti-smoking campaigns aimed at the young are deemed insufficient. There, the habit is outlawed among minors. In our less conformist culture this would probably be unenforceable even if desirable. A tightening of the law on availability might, however, be useful. At present, selling any tobacco products to children under 16 is prohibited, yet nearly nine-tenths of young smokers are said to get their cigarettes this way. It is not an offence, of course, for children to buy, possess and smoke tobacco. We should raise the age at which youngsters can be sold cigarettes to 18. Of 4,000 respondents to one survey of smokers and non-smokers, 65 per cent favoured raising the legal age. In addition, the penalties for selling smoking materials to under-age smokers should be increased. Vending machines selling cigarettes should be outlawed. Alcohol, another drug whose use is restricted to those over a certain age, is not sold this way at all, and rightly so.

In Iceland the display of cigarettes at the point of sale is against the law. We might consider this approach, though it would exasperate tobacconists. We could also strengthen health warnings on cigarette packets. One American warning, quoted by James Wilkinson, reads: 'Smoking by pregnant women may result in foetal injury, premature birth and low birth weight.' We might also put warnings on matchboxes, like the Greeks. Every little bit of propaganda helps.

Many nations are clamping down on smoking. Singapore has introduced a National Smoking Control Programme which, it is hoped, will ultimately lead to a nation of non-smokers. The government is considering laws against smoking if persuasion fails. Among the big fry, America has increasingly turned to legislation to curb smoking in public places, on public transport and in the workplace. There is a new emphasis on smoking as the abnormal behaviour requiring specially designated areas, rather than non-smoking. This approach can be thoroughly recommended for Britain to preserve the health and lives of non-addicts and to improve cleanliness while reducing burn-damage and fire risk. Non-smokers might also appreciate emerging from pubs, for example, without being sore of throat, red of eye and smelling like the underside of a garden bonfire. Curbs on smoking in public places will be resisted, of course, by the 'freedom to smoke' lobby.

Many smokers have a peculiar view of freedom. The matter is quite straightforward and relates to the hierarchy of freedoms. My right to fresh air supersedes your right to pollute my air by smoking in my presence. Similarly, your right to drink clean water supersedes my right to empty a bucket of cess into the only water supply available to you. Your right to inhale unhealthy smoke or drink filthy water alone or with other consenting adults is not in dispute.

The relationship between cannabis use and cigarette smoking among the young is of interest. The use of this drug is far less common among non-smokers than smokers. A rejection of tobacco might be expected to have a 'knock-on' effect by reducing the use of cannabis, the most popular of drugs controlled under the Misuse of Drugs Act. This would be useful because as we learned in the analysis, cannabis may have a respiratory toxicity of its own, independent of the tobacco usually smoked with it. For this reason, 'joints' are regarded as more dangerous than cigarettes. Other adverse effects have been claimed for cannabis, including undesirable personality changes associated with loss of drive and motivation.

A reduction in the use of a mild drug like tobacco (in fact, nicotine) and a 'soft' drug like cannabis may help in developing a climate of opinion among young people in which 'hard' drugs like heroin are even less acceptable than they are now. These trends can certainly do no harm.

After National No Smoking Day in 1985, Joy Townsend of the MRC calculated on the basis of surveys that the publicity had saved 1,889 years of life at a cost of £199 per life-year saved. This compares with the cost of coronary bypass surgery as a treatment for severe angina at £800 per life-year saved or a heart transplant at £5,000. Prevention is excellent value for money.

Alcohol

Alcohol is a scourge of society – but it is also a pleasurable social lubricant. It causes cirrhosis of the liver and premature death among heavy drinkers, but occasional or moderate drinkers seem to live slightly longer than teetotallers – a delightful observation which must vex some health propagandists. On the one hand we have the foaming flagons of pleasure; on the other, the undoubted physical and social damage which fills hospital wards and police cells alike.

Since the immediate post-war period, the average Briton's consumption of alcohol has more than doubled (Figure 8). Each individual over 15 now downs an average of about 8 litres of pure alcohol a year. That is the equivalent of about a pint of beer a day or a couple of glasses of wine. Given that we all know abstainers or light drinkers, it is clear that even 'moderate' drinkers are slaking a mighty thirst. We are drinking more than our parents and they in turn drank more than their grandparents. The main reasons are growing prosperity and the falling relative price of booze.

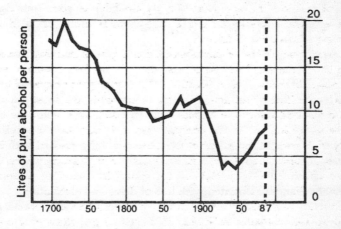

Figure 8. Annual alcohol consumption per person
Source: *The Economist*

As a nation we spend £16 billion a year on alcohol. That is about £400 per adult liver. Most drinking is harmless; some isn't. Alcohol takes its toll. Deaths reportedly associated with alcohol abuse number at least 4,000 a year, and probably many more go unreported. There are 14,500 admissions annually to NHS hospitals in England and Wales for the treatment of alcoholism, and convictions for drunk driving are now running at 100,000 a year.

There are estimated to be one million 'problem drinkers' in Britain. Half of these can be described as 'alcoholics', a group over-represented in Britain's floating population of 100,000 down-and-outs, the inhabitants of 'Skid-Row'. There are 100,000 arrests each year for public drunkenness. Many of these arrests involve alcohol-dependent men.

Alcohol is one of the causes of cirrhosis, 'a condition in which the liver becomes shrunken, hard and knobbly and may not function'. This is a quotation from a landmark report prepared by a special committee of the Royal College of Psychiatrists, *Alcohol: Our Favourite Drug*. In one-tenth of patients, liver cancer may develop as a late complication. Deaths from chronic liver disease and liver cirrhosis, to both of which alcohol contributes, are now of the order of 2,300 a year. The rate of mortality from these causes in Scotland is about twice that in England and Wales. As the RCP puts it: 'The reasons for this surprising and long standing difference are not clear.'

Excessive drinking is associated with an increase in the risk of cancer of the mouth, throat and oesophagus. There is also a risk of brain damage, fatal pancreatitis and hypertension. Strokes are three times more common among heavy drinkers. Sexual dysfunction is also prevalent in this group as is depression, which in extreme cases can lead to suicide.

On the other side of the equation, alcohol taken in light or moderate doses may have a modest protective effect against heart disease. This perhaps contributes to the slightly greater longevity of social drinkers compared with abstainers.

One quarter of men and a sizeable minority of women in general medical and surgical wards have alcohol-related problems. About a third of casualty attendees have excessive levels of alcohol in their blood, and this can provoke violence. In one survey of over a 100 violent incidents experienced by staff in accident and emergency departments, 70 per cent were shown to involve drunkenness.

Intoxication can lead to violence because of a loss of 'impulse control'. Violence can go beyond anything originally intended or be so out of character as to suggest personality impairment. Half of all murderers are intoxicated at the time of the killing, and the victim, too, often will have been drinking. Alcohol is involved in other violent crimes and also sexual assaults. These latter may result from a disastrous loss of restraint and the playing out of fantasies normally under tight control.

Different studies of prisoners in England and Scotland quoted by the RCP have suggested that half to two-thirds of the men and about 15 per cent of the women have a serious drinking problem and most were petty recidivists (repeat-criminals). This does not indicate causation, of course, but implicates alcohol in the 'causative system'. Heavy drinking is a frequent precursor of both violent and non-violent crimes. The perpetrators of 30–50 per cent of burglaries are under the influence of alcohol when they commit their crime. Much football hooliganism is also related to drinking.

Drinking can be criminogenic in a more subtle way because it is an expensive habit. This can lead to 'white-collar' financial crimes like embezzlement.

Alcohol also causes untold misery in the home. A survey of Alcoholics Anonymous, cited by the RCP report, showed that drinking had broken up marriages in about a third of members. Half of battered wives report that their partners engage in excessive drinking. The problem can drive women to desperate measures. One-third of women who have tried to take their own lives by a drug overdose have a complaint about their husband's drinking. Sometimes a drunken husband will be assaulted by his wife, and in rare cases, killed. These are fragments of an appalling picture of lives ruined on a large scale, of broken homes and disturbed children. Alcohol is the largest single factor in the break-up of families and, overall, is the premier cause of social damage.

When men and women become dependent on alcohol they risk accidents at work, sackings and long spells on the dole. At one drink counselling centre, 43 per cent of those interviewed believed that their excessive resort to alcohol had contributed to an accident at work. Over 60 per cent of members of Alcoholics Anonymous have been sacked at some stage for drinking. The result for these people was a loss of standing and a further spiral downwards through social rejection to personal degradation.

Alcohol is implicated in accidents in the home, a fifth of all drownings and over 40 per cent of deaths from falls and fires. A Scottish study showed that 60 per cent of victims of head injuries sustained in assaults and falls were under the influence of alcohol at the time. Among those in their 50s and early 60s, 30 per cent of accidental deaths involved drinking. On the roads, drunk drivers are responsible for some 1,200 fatalities yearly.

What is the economic cost of this catalogue of disasters? In 1983, an estimate was made which took into account the productivity and other cost penalties to industry, NHS expenditure on alcohol-related diseases, and the cost of social services, traffic accidents, criminal activities, alcohol research, and so on. The figure arrived at was over £1.6 billion. Recall that each adult spends £400 directly on drink. Now add to this an additional £40 as the indirect cost of mopping up the damage. And this is a conservative estimate – the cost may be twice as much according to other estimates.

The adverse effects of alcohol at the personal level are dose-dependent. That is to say, the more an individual habitually drinks, the greater the likelihood of developing cirrhosis, of being involved in accidents, of losing a job, of becoming physically dependent, and so on. What is true at the personal level appears to be true at the societal level; the ill-effects of drink rise in step with the per capita average consumption. This was a fundamental insight provided by the Royal College of Psychiatrists' alcohol report. The increase in average drinking has been paralleled by an increase in average risks. And with more people slipping into the at-risk group, more undesirable effects have been observed. It is exactly as if every motorist drove 10mph faster. The fastest drivers would continue to experience the greatest hazards but if everyone accelerates, everyone incurs additional risks and their margin of safety is reduced.

What I am describing here is the analogous situation to the safety argument outlined in the analysis. It was noted that a small increase in safety at the individual level makes an unpredictable contribution to personal safety. But it will make a predictable contribution to *average* personal safety – likewise risk.

The 'risk model' of alcohol hazards is at some variance to the old notion of 'alcoholism'. In this earlier view, which has prevailed for half a century, weak or predisposed individuals are seen as resorting to the bottle and suffering the consequences. Alcoholism could be looked on as a disease and the sufferers as unfortunates to be treated by the caring professions. The rest of us could go on our bibulous way, albeit at a lower level of intake, as 'normal social drinkers'.

The new view does not recognise two discrete populations, the 'at-risk individuals' and the 'at-no-risk' individuals. Rather – given the ubiquity of alcohol consumption – there is just one 'at risk' population and two sub-populations: the 'at-great-risk' individuals and the 'at-less-risk' individuals. Almost anyone's drinking, in this view, could get out of hand, with potential dire consequences for themselves and others. There are no common psychological traits, as we shall note later, that makes someone vulnerable to the claims of alcohol and someone else invulnerable. We are all at risk.

'Alcoholics' do not do most of the damage. As the RCP report says: 'Paradoxically, moderate drinkers, because they are relatively so numerous, make the major contribution to the overall level of alcohol problems in a population.' Much alcohol-related damage is not due to the dependent category of drinker but other drinkers who occasionally become intoxicated. No less than 15 to 20 per cent of men admit to drinking at what the RCP regards as a 'harmful' level.

In historical terms there have been large changes in the pattern of alcohol consumption. Towards the end of the nineteenth century consumption of beer, wines and spirits had risen rapidly, in part due to legislative changes. After 1900 consumption started to fall, slowly at first then steeply during the First World War as more men were called up and in the face of controls on licensing hours imposed by Lloyd George who was determined to curb drunkenness in munitions factories. After the war, and with partial relaxation of controls, consumption began to rise again but the rise was halted and then reversed by the prolonged economic depression of the 1930s. Drinking remained at comparatively low levels until the late 1950s. Over the next twenty-five years, consumption per head rose steadily, virtually doubling between 1959 and 1979. After that there was a slight fall then the trend resumed its upward path.

Parallelling the post-war rise in bibulousness has been a rise in the personal and social harm. Some consequences of excessive drinking are better documented than others. Thus, a clear upward trend is identifiable during the period in convictions for public drunkenness and drunk driving, deaths from cirrhosis of the liver, and mental hospital admissions with a primary diagnosis of alcoholism. Rising also, but less well documented, are alcohol-associated effects such as wife and child battering, other types of violence, crime, and accidents at work and elsewhere.

The rise in drink-related damage during times of economic prosperity, when consumption rises, usually induces efforts to curb the damage. The publicly visible consequences of drinking become obvious and unacceptable. Public attitudes harden until the problem subsides. These cyclical changes in attitudes associated with changes in drinking habits are known to social scientists as the 'long waves' of alcohol consumption. We are probably approaching the top of such a wave when social intervention is appropriate to control the ravages of booze. Alternatively, consumption may fall of its own accord with increasing concern for a healthier lifestyle, the ageing of the population and increasing public revulsion at the horrors perpetrated by drunken football fans and car drivers.

Economic recession may also intervene to reduce drinking. It was noticeable that a slight sobering up coincided with the recession of 1979–81. Predictably, the adverse effects of alcohol also lessened during this period, to rise later with increased drinking.

Alcohol is our favourite recreational drug and make no mistake, drug it certainly is of the psychoactive, mind-altering, kind. It is off prescription, and most of us are drug-takers.

Attitudes to alcohol change over time and different societies have viewed it differently. In Britain it is socially approved; in Saudi Arabia, proscribed. These kind of inconsistencies are not confined to alcohol, of course, and are encountered with other drugs which affect brain function. For example, until 1868, cannabis could be bought perfectly legally in Britain, not only from pharmacists but even grocers' shops. The same was true for opium which was legally grown and harvested in East Anglia. Laudanum, an alcoholic extract of raw opium, was taken for fevers, colic, nervous exhaustion – and even for fun. Now, cannabis and opium are both outlawed.

One society will accept a certain drug as a harmless pleasure, another will outlaw its use as a harmful or even deadly vice. Beer-sellers are called publicans; cannabis-sellers, 'pushers'. Alcoholics are suffering from a disease or are unlucky. Drug addicts are victims of the destructive and degrading effects of an alien drug.

Alcoholic drinks – actually ethyl alcohol and water – have been the chosen intoxicants of Europeans for two or three thousand years. It appears to have stimulant properties because it can make people loquacious, libidinous and loutish. In fact, it is a depressant of the nervous system, rather like chloroform, and the behavioural changes are properly described as 'disinhibition'. Anxiety and self-criticism are deadened. Irresponsible or anti-social behaviour may occur and suppressed feelings of aggression and hostility can be released. Not only do people get involved in more arguments and accidents when 'under the influence', but assaults are also more common.

Tests of reaction times and manual dexterity of those who have had access to alcohol invariably show impairment. This is true not only for occasional tipplers but also habitual drinkers as well. The contrary belief, according to the RCP, 'is to a great extent a dangerous myth'. Judgement is also impaired. Apparently bus drivers given several drinks have been shown to be more likely to try to drive their vehicles through gaps that were too small.

Alcohol is not only a psychoactive drug, it can also provoke dependence. This effect, contrary to widespread belief, is not confined to spirits. Beer, cider and wine can induce dependency just the same. The majority of so-called alcoholics are beer drinkers simply because this remains Britain's favourite hooch.

Alcohol addiction has far greater negative impact on society than heroin addiction, for example. Deaths related to alcohol each year outnumber deaths from heroin by as many as 50 times.

Though women are catching up, alcohol abuse is more a male problem than a female one. Beer-drinking has long been part of the male ethos – though the latter drooped a bit with the onslaught of feminism. The visible manifestation of the male ethos/alcohol association is the paradoxically female spectacle even among quite young men of the 'pregnancy effect' midriff. Not a pretty sight.

Now alcohol has become imbedded in female culture. Among young women, drink, like smoking, has become part of the 'liberated, sophisticated' ethos. Research shows that girls of school age now drink almost as frequently as boys. With the rise in drinking among women has come the all too familiar cost in harm to individuals and families, though this characteristically involves less violence than the male alcohol problem.

The alcohol tolerance of women is lower than that of men probably due to the greater amount of body fat in women which means a smaller 'fluid compartment' for the alcohol to occupy. The female liver may also have a lower capacity to metabolise alcohol than that of the male. Because of these differences, women have a lower ceiling for harm-free drinking than men. There is also a special danger in pregnancy because alcohol, like many other drugs, can cross the placental barrier. Foetal brain damage may occur if the mother is a heavy drinker.

What sort of personality traits predispose people to become 'problem drinkers'? A large US study cited by the RCP showed that there were few indicators among the young as to who would succumb to drink problems in later life. In so far as there was a relationship between personality disturbances and alcohol misuse it was that alcohol contributed to the problem rather than the other way round. The greater the consumption, the greater the subsequent psychological impairment.

Alcohol-related problems tend to run in families, particularly through the male line. If various careful studies are to be believed, this seems to be due to both 'socio-cultural' influences (i.e. the environment in which someone is raised), and genetic factors (i.e. nature). The character of this interrelation has yet to be established.

Rates of hospital admissions for alcohol dependence, drunkenness offences, and liver cirrhosis deaths, are generally higher in Scotland, Northern Ireland and Northern England than they are further south. Higher still are the ill-effects of alcohol on the Continent, especially France, where consumption is even higher than Britain.

The holders of certain jobs are more prone to alcohol abuse than others. Doctors are notoriously vulnerable, with a death rate from cirrhosis of the liver three times the average. The highest risk group are publicans with a risk almost sixteen times the average. Restaurant workers, seamen, members of the armed forces and journalists are other groups at well above average risk. Within industry, company directors and salesmen suffer particularly high rates of alcohol-related harm doubtless due to the dire 'business lunch'.

What makes alcohol interesting from the viewpoint of risk engineering is that, unlike smoking, drink and the drink culture have a significant positive side. This will be evident to anyone who, desirous of a convivial tincture, repairs to a warm, friendly, oak-beamed pub, as snug as a marsupium. There, the forgiving quaff seems to ameliorate all-too regrettable frailties and cement human companionship.

Nonetheless, we have seen that for any given level of consumption there is a given level of harm. The question is: is the current level of human wreckage and suffering acceptable? The answer can only be 'no'. Or to put it in the words of the RCP's alcohol report:

If the casualty rates were to dip to the lowest level recorded in this century, they would still be worrying. If, on the other hand, emancipated adolescents were to drink more like men, and Britons, having become good Europeans, were to drink more like the French, then there are threats which are potentially appalling.

The lifestyle sub-strategy's National Programme for Risk Reduction for alcohol would consist of a clear and co-ordinated preventive thrust having four aspects: price regulation of consumption; risk-awareness through education and health warnings; 'contextual' changes; and youth-related measures. (The subject of drunk-driving will be discussed under a separate heading with accidents.)

To stabilise consumption, and preferably reduce it, the relative price of alcohol beverages needs to be raised relative to disposable incomes by perhaps 10 or 20 per cent. Special taxes on drink have been levied for over three centuries and now bring in about £6,000 million each year to the Exchequer. The money raised by an additional tax could be used to fund the Lifestyle 2000 organisation.

There is direct evidence that a price rise reduces not only 'social drinking' but also consumption among heavy drinkers. A survey showed that this was precisely what happened when excise duty was raised in the March 1981 budget. This caused the price of alcohol beverages to rise faster than the retail price index or average disposable incomes for the first time in thirty years. As a result, many people drank less. Since then, budgets have been noticeably kinder to the drinks industry – and the casualties among drinkers have risen.

Risk-awareness is the second theme of the National Programme for Risk Reduction alcohol campaign. The RCP's special committee urged the widest possible community awareness 'for it is every aspect of the community's life that is affected by excessive drinking'. Lifestyle 2000 would undertake a health campaign to alert people to the dangers involved. Particular emphasis would be on what constitutes a 'sensible' alcohol intake level, since there is surprising ignorance on this point. (Some guidelines are given in Appendix II.) The aim is to 'raise the game' of individuals by giving information to allow a correct assessment of the benefits and risks of drinking at a particular level.

Excessive hooch-swilling and attempts to bludgeon the mind into oblivion with alcohol should be portrayed in publicity for what they are – bad style and risky.

The prospects of effecting major attitudinal changes should not be overestimated, however. Education aimed at school children has proved unsuccessful in influencing subsequent drinking behaviour. Adult behaviour is even more difficult to sway, though the trend towards healthier ways of living suggests that efforts to reduce drinking may be increasingly fruitful. This is the justification for increased funding for health publicity. Part of the awareness campaign would be borne by the Health Quotient screening programme of Lifestyle 2000. This would particularly target incipiently at-risk individuals – identified by self-reported behaviour, occupation, family history, etc. – for non-judgemental support and guidance. Recent experience cited by the RCP shows that this approach employed in general hospital and medical screening centres is discernibly beneficial. It allows the would-be heavy drinker to weigh up the pros and cons of his or her lifestyle in a way which leads to positive change before it is too late.

Another aspect of the educational effort would be health warnings. These already appear on cigarette packets, of course, and the time is ripe for them to appear on bottle and can labels. Here is some suggested wording:

Warning: Alcohol is a drug which can cause physical dependence. Excessive drinking is associated with liver disease, brain damage and strokes. Driving skills are impaired by alcohol. A special tax on this product is directly helping to fund disease and accident prevention programmes.

This may be regarded as excessive and definitely kill-joy in flavour. However, public awareness that almost anybody can move into the high-risk group is so low as to warrant strong wording.

Drinking in Britain is not civilised enough. The aim of the third part of the National Programme for Risk Reduction strategy for alcohol is to make it more so by altering the 'context'. The 10-year experience in Scotland of liberalised licensing laws has largely proved a success, which, however, tends to be exaggerated by interested parties. Consumption increased only slightly in spite of many Scottish pubs now being open from 11am to 11pm and others staying open until 1am. Ill-effects in terms of disorder and social damage did not materialise. There is a general feeling that the liberalisation has contributed to a more civilised, relaxed pattern of consumption; less cramming down of 'chasers' and 'heavies' before the bell, for example.

Some of us would not have believed that one day we would be writing about the need for more civilised drinking on the Scottish pattern. But there it is, we are. Attitudes can be changed as a result of legislation. Licensing laws in other parts of Britain should be brought fully into line with those in Scotland. Northern Irish pubs can already stay open all day. Combined with price rises and health publicity, the rise in consumption which would normally accompany increased availability should be avoidable. All-day Sunday opening should be permitted, as should opening after 11pm for those pubs not too close to residential premises.

Measures related to drunk driving, discussed later, should further help to 'civilise' drinking habits, as should the increased prevalence of 'family pubs' and wine bars.

The fourth approach would be to curb youthful drinking, which amounts to under-age drug-taking. For most people the peak drinking years are their late teens and early twenties. Much damage is done by this age group and the damage is on the increase. Convictions for drunkenness among teenagers have doubled in the last twenty years. And the problem is not confined to the older members of this age group. A thousand children under 15 are admitted to hospital each year with acute alcohol poisoning.

Educational publicity aimed at the young has proved of dubious value, so this is not recommended. The law on under-age drinking should be strengthened by increased fines for those who sell to the young. A community audit could be carried out by Lifestyle 2000 to establish that there are sufficient alcohol-free entertainment centres for the young in each area such as youth clubs, coffee bars and so on.

Sponsorship of sport will be banned. The association between youth-orientated sporting activities and alcohol is distasteful and should be ended. Also ended should be cinema advertising of alcoholic drinks since audiences comprise a disproportionate number of young people. The efficacy of general advertising bans has yet to be established. A notable instance of high consumption where *no* advertising is permitted is the Soviet Union where the average lifespan of their alcohol-sozzled men, incidentally, is just 60 years, and where half of hospital patients have an alcohol-related illness.

The National Programme of Risk Reduction's four-point plan for drinking comprising a price rise, risk-awareness publicity, contextual changes and youth-related measures would undoubtedly reduce the colossal amount of damage done to society and individuals by over-indulgence in alcohol.

Crime

To speak of a 'crime wave that is engulfing society' is to do serious injustice to over half the community. Women commit less than a quarter as many offences as men and usually the crimes are of the less serious type. Their rate of offending has remained virtually static for a decade. It is a rise in crimes committed by men which, together with reporting and recording changes, is responsible for the increase of about a half in notifiable offences in the last 10 years. If society is being engulfed, it is by male criminality.

The central challenge, therefore, in any attempt to reduce the average individual risk of victimisation is to *improve male behaviour*. Over half of all crime is committed by males under 21, which means over 65–70 per cent of all male crime. We can thus be more explicit still in stating what should be our main aim: to improve male behaviour, particularly *young* male behaviour.

In the 1980s, the governmental response to the rise in crime has been to increase expenditure on police and prisons. This has had no discernible effect on the crime rate – though it is possible to argue that crime would have been worse still without higher spending on the forces of law and order and punishment. In the event, the annual crime rate had increased by 1.3 million offences in England and Wales by 1986 compared with 1979, bringing the total number of crimes to 3.85 million a year. Crime went up faster in the eighties under the Conservatives, the party of law and order, than it had in the seventies under Labour. This was by no means atypical. The Middlesex Polytechnic Centre for Criminology has calculated that in the years since the Second World War crime went up an annual average of 7.2 per cent under Conservative governments compared with 3.6 per cent under Labour. The average yearly increase was 7.5 per cent in the eighties.

If crime increases at different rates under governments of different political hues, then this seems to indicate that governments can influence the crime rate. Why did the post-war trend towards increased criminality accelerate in the eighties? Some social commentators see the explanation in an 'every man for himself' ethos coupled with an increased social stratification ill-accepted by the relatively deprived whether in the inner cities or elsewhere. In this view, crime becomes an epiphenomenon of the enterprise culture as practised by disadvantaged people such as the unemployed. Another view is that crime has risen with the increasing number of young people. A third is that ghastly housing resulting from sixties and seventies 'ugly period' planning is in large part to blame. A fourth view is that we are on the moral slide.

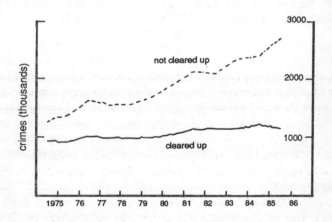

Figure 9. The relationship between crimes cleared up and crimes unsolved 1975–86
Source: *Law and Order, Five Years On*, Middlesex Polytechnic Centre for Criminology, 1987

Whatever the cause, crime is rising faster than ever and more of us are turning to crime. The number of crimes solved, however, has risen only modestly (Figure 9). Unsolved crimes now number nearly two million a year. This, in spite of a police force augmented by 7,000 new recruits between 1979 and 1986, and earning twice as much as they did in the late seventies. Spending on the police rose by a half in real terms in the seven years to 1986 to £3.2 billion annually. It was costing the British taxpayer several thousand pounds for each crime solved. Just nine offences were being cleared up on average per police officer per year.

On present trends there will be over 8 million crimes annually by the year 2000, and that is just *recorded* crimes. There will be one crime for every seven of us. And a lower proportion will be solved, perhaps as few as 20 per cent.

Our target within the National Programme for Risk Reduction programme for notifiable crimes per year is suggested to be 2.5 million. This would represent an attempt to reverse the post-war decline in law-observance and Britain's ascent of the international crime league. The target is not quite so optimistic as it sounds since demographics are increasingly on our side.

In the past decade, thanks to a baby boom that peaked in the mid-1960s, the number of youngsters in the 15-19 age group increased by 16 per cent. But between the mid-1980s and mid-1990s the number in this high-crime age-group will drop by a quarter. It is to be hoped that this will have a heart-warming effect on the crime statistics in the future.

Further reductions in the crime rate can be achieved by applying the risk engineering precepts of designing out, targeting and reconnection. Designing out in the field of crime means reducing opportunities for offending by taking preventive measures. Three suggestions commend themselves: an expansion of the Neighbourhood Watch concept; the development of thief-proof cars; and the burglar-proofing of homes.

According to the Home Office the aims of Neighbourhood Watch Schemes are these: to reduce opportunities for crime, thereby deterring would-be thieves, vandals and other criminals; to establish a community spirit so that everyone can contribute towards the protection of their property by mutual co-operation and communication; and to inform the local scheme co-ordinator or the police of any suspicious goings-on. Scheme participants, who are all volunteers, are not acting as supernumerary policemen so much as good neighbours. Where the schemes operate – and there are thousands in London alone – they have been judged a success in reducing crime, though there is some debate about this. The problem seems to be that crime tends to be pushed into areas with no schemes of their own such that the overall amount of crime does not diminish. The obvious need is to secure nationwide coverage for the Neighbourhood Watch system. This will require an increase in the allocation of police time, a modest rise in funding from central government and more local volunteers. (On this last point, the Post-Industrial Programme described in Part III could provide a mechanism for encouraging people to participate in crime prevention schemes.) There is the opportunity to develop a preventive organisation for crime around the Neighbourhood Watch idea which would be similar to the Lifestyle 2000 organisation advocated earlier for health. The crime prevention activities of the police, though laudable, are far from sufficient on their own to dent the growth in crime.

The Neighbourhood Watch idea was first put into practice in 1983. The schemes have arguably not had a dramatic effect on crime – but then neither have the police! Several factors are in their favour and might be expected to build over time. The schemes give a structure for the expression of the general public's unease about crime. They also significantly enhance the sense of community. Police-public co-operation is the crucial factor in solving crimes; police sleuthing clears up relatively few offences. As researchers from Middlesex Polytechnic's Centre for Criminology have put it: 'There cannot be good police-community relations when there is no community'.

Besides crime prevention, there could be a role for Neighbourhood Watch schemes in local road safety initiatives (see next section).

A clear opportunity to decrease lawlessness relates to motor vehicles. Thefts *from* cars and *of* cars account for 45 per cent of all thefts – and theft in general makes up more than half of all notifiable offences. Car-related thefts thus make up about a quarter of all crime. In 1983, according to *Social Trends*, one in five owners of cars, vans and motorbikes had their vehicle stolen or vandalised, or property stolen from it. Thefts from vehicles, in particular, are increasing markedly. In the decade to 1985, the incidence of this crime nearly doubled to half a million offences a year.

It is not beyond the wit of man to design an unstealable car. The Home Office is said to have had a design for an invulnerable vehicle for some time. What has prevented manufacturers from marketing a crime-proof car in the past? Insurance. If cars and their contents were uninsurable, popular outcry would have led to cars being made as thief-proof as possible years ago. Instead some cars can be entered with nothing more sophisticated than a wire coat hanger. This situation should not be allowed to persist. Standards should be introduced immediately to improve car design to make vehicles which are unstealable, preferably unenterable, and which offer low opportunities for vandalism. Any new car not conforming to these rules should be banned from British roads.

Thief-proof cars are highly desirable to cut crime – but they would also save life and limb. American statistics show that stolen cars are 200 times more likely to be involved in an accident than 'owner-occupied' vehicles.

Another opportunity to 'design out' law-breaking relates to houses and flats. At present there are no building regulations covering the intruder-resistance of new homes. These could be introduced to great advantage and might cover such things as window locks, use of toughened glass and lighting of approaches. Domestic burglary makes up almost 13 per cent of all crime and the average householder can be expected to suffer it at least once a lifetime. Reducing the opportunities for burglary can only help to reduce its incidence.

Efforts to design out burglary are growing. Besides Crime Prevention Officers, an increasing number of police forces now have Architect Liaison Officers to advise on the design of crime-proof dwellings. The disproportionately high risk of burglary on some council housing estates – which have been described as crime ghettos – have led local authorities to improve security for tenants. Surveys of 106,000 flats in London showed that blocks of flats without design defects reported no crime while those with 13 or more defects averaged one crime per year for every five dwellings. Crime rates have been halved by low-cost design changes.

At its worst bad housing design can foster 'concrete alienation' rather than a sense of community and give crooks ample opportunity for access and concealment, so that policing becomes impossible. The cul-de-sac with low-rise housing is probably the least criminogenic of lay-outs.

The risk engineering imperative of targeting should be applied to two groups in particular: young males (i.e. those under 25) and 'criminals at the top'.

Surveying the behaviour of young men, the conclusion is inescapable that they are on average more anti-social than young women. They are more likely to display bad character in any given set of social circumstances whether involving privilege or deprivation. Apart from sex crimes and violence, mugging and burglary, young men cause more drink- and drug-related mayhem, commit more vandalism and scrawl more graffiti (two skills, incidentally, in which Britain leads Europe). They are responsible for more classroom disruption, street rowdyism and football hooliganism, and kill and maim more people on the roads. If young men behaved more like young women, Britain would be a considerably nicer place in which to live. How to improve young male behaviour? One approach is to keep them busy.

Proportionately more unemployed than employed young men are involved in crime. Does lack of work therefore lead to crime? A report by the Cambridge Study in Delinquent Development followed 411 working-class young men in the early 1970s in their first three years after leaving school. It concluded that youths who were already disadvantaged by, for example, homelessness or a broken family, were more likely to be thieves or burglars – but not rapists or vandals – if they were unemployed. Lack of work did not make young people from stable backgrounds more likely to fall foul of the law. This is evidence that joblessness *does* create crime, an unsurprising conclusion supported by a Home Office study of the 1981 civil disturbances in Birmingham's Handsworth district.

The corollary to this is that the high unemployment of the eighties has had a social penalty in increased crime, particularly increased crime commited by young men.

If the young are usefully occupied they do not commit as many crimes – 'the devil makes work for idle hands'. One way of occupying the young is by teaching them skills, but as a nation we put less than a third of our 16-18 year olds through full-time education and training. The figure is 45 per cent in Germany, 58 per cent in France, 47 per cent in Italy, 69 per cent in Japan and 79 per cent in the United States. About half of Britain's male school leavers have no more than a D or E grade 'O' level or a grade 2-5 CSE. What these boys lack in academic aptitude they make up in criminality. By age 20, a quarter have a criminal record.

Our young people are our major resource for the future. Not to train them properly during their formative years is a potentially disastrous strategy from all points of view, not least the economic one. Formal education or training should be available for all those 16-18 year olds who do not want, or cannot find, a job. If they work instead, then there should be an element of compulsory training in the content of any job they take.

Many youngsters 'grow out' of crime as a result of maturity, jobs, marriage, and so on. By reducing the number of 'unoccupied' years before the transition to peaceful citizenship, the crime rate would unquestionably fall. This is a justification, though not the main one, for educating and training our young people and for creating worthwhile jobs for them. Government efforts to expand youth training schemes are encouraging. We should now attempt to develop a fully co-ordinated training strategy for the 18-25 age group.

While keeping the 18-25 age group usefully occupied is laudable, the fact should not be ignored that the peak age of offending for both girls and boys is below the school leaving age – 14 for girls and 15 for boys. Juvenile crime is a seemingly intractable problem. To tackle it, social commentators argue, education will have to be improved to bring out the personal worth of all pupils, social deprivation will have to be ameliorated, and the worst effects of family break-up, which is very much on the increase, will have to be countered in some way by greater social support from outside the family. A less acquisitive, self-orientated moral climate might be beneficial. Above all, though, the desire of individual boys and girls to behave well will have to be strengthened. It is with this in mind that a novel suggestion can be made relating to the transition from childhood to adulthood.

At present, you can legally have sex and marry with parental consent at 16, drive a car at 17, vote, consume alcohol in a pub, enter into hire purchase and other financial agreements at 18, and sit on a jury and get the traditional 'key to the door' at 21. The coming-of-age experience is thus distributed over half a decade. What I recommend is that we concentrate more of the changes at 18 in order to make more of the entry into adulthood. This leaves the way open for us to postpone conferment of adult status on those who do not behave in an adult way – which for our present purpose means in a law-abiding fashion.

How would the system, which can be called the 'majority rule', work? The crimes and misbehaviour of young people would be punished in the usual ways but in addition a points score would be entered into the record book rather in the way that drivers earn points towards a ban when they offend on the road. For example, possession of cannabis or persistent severe indiscipline in school might be worth one point, vandalism two points, burglary three, mugging four and so on. Any individual who got five or more points, say, would fail to comply with the majority rule. As such he or she would automatically suffer a three-year postponement of his or her age of majority to 21. This could 'bite' as a punishment, and thus operate as a deterrent, if it hit the social life, mobility and wallet of a young man or woman. This it would do in the case of social life because the right to drink alcohol in pubs, presently triggered at 18, would be deferred to 21. Mobility is more difficult because the current legal age for driving a car or a motorcycle over 49cc is 17. The simple expedient is to raise this to 18. (This would reduce road accidents as we shall see in the next section.) As to the wallet, the young person will not be able to hold credit cards or enter into hire purchase agreements of any kind. (If we wanted to strengthen the financial incentive to good behaviour, the state could deposit a sum of money, e.g. £100, with an investing institution on behalf of each child at birth for collection at 18 only by those who do not misbehave. Regular financial statements to the individual would be a useful reminder of the growing size of the nest-egg, i.e. what is at stake. Forfeit money could go in the victim compensation 'pot'.)

It is not recommended that the miscreant 18-year-olds be prevented from marrying without parental consent as marriage tends to be a reforming institution.

The element of compulsory training for the 16-18 age group described above would help to establish 18 firmly as the age of majority. Another useful move in this direction would be to act on the suggestion made previously (see 'Smoking') that the sale of cigarettes to under-18s be made illegal. Penalties for those selling alcohol to under-age drinkers should also be strengthened (see 'Alcohol').

The majority rule system might seem negative. To balance this, a positive component could be incorporated which would enable those who have misbehaved to 'reduce their deficit'. The kind of activity that is relevant here would be community service or sporting endeavour. The key idea would be involvement in some socially useful project.

Training to comply with the majority rule could start as early as 11 or 12 and be continued to the end of a child's school career. Though conducted at school, the early sessions should involve parents to strengthen family commitment to keeping children on the straight and narrow. Health propaganda aimed at the young on alcohol, smoking and drugs has back-fired in the past by perversely glamourising the undesirable. This might be avoided in the majority rule context by focusing on the rights and duties of citizenship and on the advantages of adulthood achieved early. At the age of 18 a youngster would receive a document confirming his or her adult status and describing the implications of this coming of age. This might go a small way to bringing it home to young people that they are now adults. At present, it is perfectly possible for some 'youths' on the dole to go on feeling not quite adult practically into their thirties. Those who suffer arrested development suffer arrest.

The possible gains from a successful crime prevention campaign aimed at the young, particularly boys, cannot be overestimated. Young offenders become old lags. As regards physical aggression in particular, boys must have it dinned into them that violence, as Brian Aldiss has put it, must be kept in the mind where it belongs. Another problem area is chauvinistic male attitudes to women, which is the thin end of the sexual assault wedge. How you change the appalling attitudes of some young men to women I do not know. A further problem is alcohol. Drunkenness offences among 18-21 year olds are two-and-a-half times greater than the average for all ages. Efforts to reduce alcohol consumption, outlined in the previous section, should help to modify this aspect of juvenile behaviour. Drunk-driving, also common among the under-21s, can be reduced by appropriate measures discussed later.

Fashions in juvenile punishment seem to fall into a 'soft–hard' cycle. We appear to be in a 'soft' phase. The recent emphasis on punishment and rehabilitation within the community for young offenders has been welcomed by most people, as has the increased use of police cautions and social counselling services. The contrasting approach involves youth custody. Home Office figures show that 80 per cent of males under 17 who receive a custodial sentence re-offend within two years. The Tory 'short sharp shock' policy for juvenile delinquents in the early 1980s has come in for particular criticism. There have been accounts of gross brutality and suicides. The harsh physical regime, which was supposed to be corrective, seemed to appeal to some of the tougher inmates. This had the disturbing consequence that these institutions were turning out some individuals who were not only unreformed but also superfit.

This might serve as a slight cautionary tale for those who urge that delinquents be exposed to compulsory national service in the armed forces. There is a blue-blooded precedent for this approach though. Male members of the royal family have been obliged to do a stint in one or other of the services ever since Queen Victoria took exception to the corpulent and licentious Prince of Wales, her son.

Apart from young men, a second group worth targeting consists of what can be called 'criminals at the top'. Included here are the fraudsters, sharks and insider dealers in the City, the tax evaders, and the corrupt in public life. The purpose in attempting to nail these people is not only to see justice done, but to improve the moral tone of society. At present, crime at the top provides some sort of slippery moral justification in some people's view for their own criminal activities. I have myself heard one petty criminal justify his actions in terms of City fraud. 'They're getting away with it. Why shouldn't I have my share?' What can be called 'top-down crime busting' would have far higher moral multiplier effects than cracking down on social security fraud, for example.

Having considered designing out opportunities for crime and targeting of key offenders, we can turn our attention to the theme of reconnection. Many criminals do not show any clear appreciation of the harm they do. This is a condition which has been described as 'anaesthetised sensibility' and it is characterised by a lack of remorse. One aim here will be to increase the awareness among criminals of the damage they cause. Another is to give the public an accurate awareness of criminal issues. Discussed here will be trends in the criminal-justice system, sentencing patterns and media reporting of crime.

The criminal justice system's concern for victims has increased. Several developments in the eighties illustrate this popular trend. Judges and magistrates are increasingly using victim compensation orders as a penalty in their own right and, indeed, the ability of the courts to expropriate villains' assets has increased. There are more safeguards to protect the anonymity of rape victims and questioning of victims in court is said to have become less brutal. The Criminal Injuries Compensation Board has increased the number of cash awards it gives to those injured through mugging, rape or other personal violence. A network of more than 300 victim support schemes has spread across the country. In 1986 these helped and advised more than a quarter of a million victims. The schemes have proven efficacy and represent one area in which we appear to lead the world. The schemes are staffed mainly by volunteer counsellors though the government gives money for full-time co-ordinators.

We could be approaching a time when every victim of violence receives compensation, together with appropriate advice and emotional support. This would be a welcome trend away from a situation where victims are first traumatised by criminals, then coldly used in the criminal-justice process, then virtually ignored.

The absence of separate reception rooms for victims (and witnesses) in court buildings is particularly unfathomable. Comfortable, self-contained facilities should be provided free of the risk of unexpected encounters between victim and accused or victim and accused's family or friends.

It is appropriate for compensation to victims to go well beyond physical injury and include consideration of psychological trauma, loss of or damage to property, and even plain inconvenience. There needs to be the strongest possible linkage between what victims receive and what criminals are forced to pay. This is 'reconnective' in my use of the word as it brings home to wrong-doers the physical and mental damage they do to their victims. Fines, although representing a financial penalty, have no moral force. Compensation orders and the like, have.

A useful way, incidentally, of collecting compensation from criminals who have jobs – and hundreds of thousands do – would be via the income tax system which is being computerised. Criminals could pay a 'Sin Tax' over a number of years. This would be set at a modest level so as not to act as a deterrent to job-holding. The message would be clear: you commit crimes, you compensate victims.

As regards seizure of ill-gotten gains, we should perhaps not go quite as far as they did in medieval England. To quote Christopher Hibbert's *The Roots of Evil*:

> In the King's courts, fines and forfeiture of goods were still common enough, and outlawry, by which the goods of the outlaw fell to the Crown, was a frequent sentence.

If we are not outlawing people, we are certainly incarcerating them. We are Europe's leaders in this respect with over 90 per 100,000 of our citizens in jail. Those behind bars in 1980 numbered 42,000. By 1987 there were well over 50,000 people in a prison system on which the Home Office spends 750 million a year. It costs twice as much to imprison a man as to employ him on the average wage. On release, half are reconvicted within two years.

To stop the prison system splitting at the seams, a full review of custodial sentencing seems desirable. The main justification for a review of both custodial and non-custodial sentencing, however, is inconsistency between courts. I know of two courts in separate but nearby towns where markedly different sentences are handed down for the same offence. The consequences are that criminals are keener to have their cases heard in the one place than the other. In Appendix III, I reproduce two actual criminal case histories involving drunk-driving. One case resulted in a woman being maimed for life; the other in property damage alone. The driver causing the latter got a fine and a two-year driving suspension. The driver who maimed a woman – and overall infringed the law to a far greater extent – received from the same court a similar fine and a mere one-year suspension. Miscarriages of justice such as this discredit the judiciary in the eyes of the public.

Take another example of judicial inconsistency: the number of individuals remanded in custody rather than released on bail before a trial. Lord Hailsham, when Lord Chancellor, pointed out that in 640 petty sessions your chances of being remanded vary from one in twenty in some courts to greater than one in four in others.

If you appear before a magistrate in Blackpool you are five times more likely to be jailed than in Staines, according to Home Office figures. Unacceptable inconsistencies like these are not confined to the lower courts and our unique system of amateur magistrates which goes back to medieval times. There is a distinct impression that property crimes are sometimes inexplicably punished more severely in some higher courts than crimes involving personal violence. The picture is of some bewigged old buffer passing down judgment on the basis of whim or outdated attitudes. But as Lord McClusky said in the 1986 Reith Lectures, media reporting of trials may not convey all the information to the laymen necessary for a fair criticism of a particular judgment. In other words a judgment may appear unfair only to those not in the courtroom. This is a reasonable point, but nonetheless public confidence in the judiciary could undoubtedly be improved as regards sentencing practice.

One way forward would be to strengthen the role of the Judicial Studies Board in establishing guidelines for sentencing. Another might be to use high technology. A computer database of current sentencing practice which could be accessed from every courtroom would help to improve consistency. All that would be involved would be establishing an information system for courts such as exists for travel agents throughout the country as regards air tickets. Judicial flexibility would be maintained but wild inconsistencies would be avoided. A pilot study seems eminently worthwhile. Each criminal brought to trial should know that he is going to get his just deserts, not more and not less, regardless of where and by whom he is tried.

A further problem with sentencing relates to the term actually served. Judges are forbidden from taking parole into account. This can mean that though a rapist, for example, may be sentenced for ten years, he may be released after just three. A researcher at Cambridge University has calculated, in fact, that in 1985 the average sentence handed out for rape was just under 43 months, and the average served was 20 months. This is not long for what is a repugnant crime involving sexual violation which can leave a psychological scar for a lifetime. What is being practised here as regards sentencing amounts almost to deception of the public who must think rapists and other criminals are spending longer in jail than they in fact are. The term 'life sentence' in particular should only be used for sentences of life imprisonment where release is not anticipated. In general, it would be desirable if judges commonly gave a recommended sentence (e.g. 'ten years') together with a minimum sentence (e.g. 'not less than eight'). This would be clearer for the public while leaving some legitimate discretion in the hands of parole-granters.

Accurate public awareness of criminal risk is an important aspect of our reconnection theme. In the analysis section it was noted that some groups, notably old people, suffer a degree of anxiety which is out of proportion to the risks they face. This can affect their lives and speaks of the need for improved dissemination of information on crime to the lay public.

Some existing publicity aimed at children is of interest because it reveals the limits of what can acceptably be conveyed. Children are warned against 'strangers'. Since in this context men are a far greater danger than women, this sleight of hand might reasonably be regarded as a piece of objectionable sexism which crops up in other crime publicity (and reporting) relating to drunk drivers and thieves, among others. More importantly, though, the publicity omits to mention that up to three-quarters of sexual assaults on children are committed by trusted males – fathers, relatives and friends. Most people would regard it as highly undesirable to inculcate fear of these men in our children. So we warn them of the next most dangerous category, strangers.

A rather similar 'transfer of fear' effect is noticeable among women as regards rape. The danger from one's nearest and dearest is unrecognised or underestimated. In as much as anybody fears murder, the same applies to this crime, with strangers bearing the burden of suspicion. Homicide comes with home and hearth; it occurs in families.

The media must bear a fair share of responsibility for the public's distorted perception of crime. Roy Walmesley in a Home Office research report on personal violence has written:

> the well-known popular press technique of following up a particularly unpleasant crime by searching for and giving dramatic coverage to another which has some similar features, inevitably creates the impression, at least in the minds of those most fearful of crime, including the elderly and those living alone, that such events instead of being extremely rare in most localities are in fact extremely common. This is irresponsible press reporting and needs to be recognised as such.

Putting crime and victimisation information into the Lifestyle 2000 risk database, previously described, would at least give journalists less excuse for slanting and sensationalising the news. But while better media coverage of crime and better crime publicity in general would be desirable, the most effective way of reducing fear would be to reduce the actual level of crime. Anxiety about the danger of becoming a victim has been shown by surveys to restrict people's lives. After dark, fear empties streets and city centres alike.

In summary, measures have been suggested here to reduce the crime rate by designing out opportunities for offending (Neighbourhood Watch schemes, thief-proof cars, burglar-proof homes) and by targeting key offenders (young men and criminals at the top of society). Miscreants can be reconnected to the consequences of their criminality by requiring them to compensate victims. Sentencing reform is recommended to ensure a one-to-one fit between the crime and the punishment. Public understanding in the area of crime can be assisted by a clarification of what sentence will be served by each criminal and by improved media coverage of criminal issues.

If measures to reduce common crimes such as burglary and car-theft are successful, then this would have the welcome effect of reducing the burden on police resources of time and personnel. Increased effort could be given to the crimes that disturb people most: sexual and violent crimes against women and children, mugging and drug offences. Though human skills will remain of key importance in the fight against crime, new technology is emerging to help the police in the form of more advanced computer systems, mug-shots on fast-retrieval optical discs, laser fingerprinting for use by scene-of-crime officers, automatic analysis of fingerprints against computer-held records and so on. 'Genetic fingerprinting' is the most remarkable development of all and permits virtually unchallengeable identification of individuals on the basis of their genetic material, DNA. Any criminal who leaves a sample of tissue, blood, semen or even a hair root can be identified. Genetic fingerprinting has been hailed as the most important scientific advance in forensic technology. The technique was developed in a British laboratory.

Accidents

Thousands die needlessly each year in accidents in the home, at work and on the roads and millions, literally, are injured. Our target within the National Programme for Risk Reduction should be to halve this toll by the year 2000.

Fatal home accidents have declined by a third in the last couple of decades but the number has levelled off in recent years at 5,500–6,000 indicating the need for a fresh initiative in this area. At particular risk are the old and the young. Among the old, falls are the leading cause of death with osteoporotic, brittle-boned women in the over-75 age group the main victims. According to *Accidents to the Elderly*, a report published by the Consumer Safety Unit of the Department of Trade and Industry:

> There does seem some value in making the walking surfaces safer about the home. Firm level outside paths, floors with non-slip finishes, particularly carpeting, and free of objects over which people can trip, particularly avoiding the use of loose rugs or mats, are to be recommended.

The scope for reducing risks to the elderly is not great but improvements should be sought not least because while the total number of over-65s will increase relatively little to the year 2000, the proportion of these in the vulnerable over-75 category will increase from 40 per cent in 1983 to nearly half by the end of the century. Increased safety publicity and encouragement of better home and product design can be recommended.

While one in twenty of the general population have an accident in the home each year requiring medical treatment, the figure is one in five for children. The main danger is to those under five years old, boys being more at risk than girls. A fair amount is known about accidents to children by virtue of the Department of Trade and Industry's Home Accident Surveillance System, an innovative survey of hospital attendances which has prompted a Europe-wide scheme, and the excellent work of the Child Accident Prevention Trust (CAPT), RoSPA and others. The accident risk to children in terms of standardised mortality is lowest for socio-economic class 1 and highest for class 5. Non-fatal accidents also increase down the social classes. These inequalities in child health are quite clear and were noted in the Black Report. For example, scalds and burns cause over 100 child deaths a year and over 40,000 injuries requiring treatment. Studies have shown links with poor housing, overcrowding and family stress. Falls, which result in 300,000 or more injuries a year, are also more common in children from poorer homes.

A factsheet from CAPT puts the situation thus:

It is a general lack of appreciation by parents of the relationship between the developing ability of the child, in terms of its mobility and behavioural development, and the hazards offered by different everyday articles and situations which result in accidents to the very young.

Also parents do not realise that a child's perceptive and motor skills are not fully developed for a number of years.

Parents, particularly in lower social classes, need to be better apprised of the dangers facing their children. There is also a case for modest grant aid for safety equipment (e.g. for fireguards and cooker guards to prevent burns and scalds).

Many homes do not seem well designed for children – or, for that matter, the old. A quarter of a million children are said by CAPT to go to hospital each year following an accident involving architectual features in the home. A proportion of these mishaps are due to bad design involving, for example, siting of cookers, stair layout and so on. Efforts to persuade architects and builders to produce 'child-softened' and 'grannie-softened' homes should be continued not least indirectly by raising the level of customer (i.e. home-buyer) awareness.

The preventive medicine organisation Lifestyle 2000, previously described, could appropriately be charged with reducing accidents in the home and elsewhere.

Accidents in the workplace are on the increase again after almost a century of improvements. In 1985, there were over 400 fatal accidents and 20,000 serious ones. There were also half a million minor accidents. In the first half of the eighties, the number of serious and fatal accidents in manufacturing rose by over a fifth and in construction by over 40 per cent. Why these rises? Economic times have been harsh, employers may be taking less trouble over the safety of their staff. Or perhaps workers in newly slimmed-down workforces are becoming more careless under increased pressure. Whatever the reason, deaths and injuries at work are rising.

The body responsible for safety at work, the Health and Safety Executive, has suffered government cut-backs in the eighties. In 1979 there were 742 factory inspectors. By 1987 the number had dwindled to 621 in spite of an increase in workload resulting from no less than eleven new sets of safety regulations coming into force. Not surprisingly, the HSE was hard-pressed to cope. Had government penny-pinching put lives at risk? Conjectural. One thing was certain though, it had not reduced the risk.

The obvious recommendation which can be made is to increase funding for the HSE – and thus renew the push for greater safety at work. The HSE itself, being essentially a preventive medicine organisation, could usefully be absorbed into Lifestyle 2000.

So far the accident scorecard reads like this: upwards of three million injuries in the home each year and more than half a million at work. Now add to this a further half a million injuries on Britain's roads, together with 5,000 deaths. Consider also the burden of fear, anxiety and family misery caused by traffic accidents, the medical and other resources needed to mop up the damage, and the 'opportunity cost' in terms of police time – and there is an overwhelming case for reducing the number of accidents on our roads. In view of this, it is all the more surprising to learn from experts like Stephen Plowden and Mayer Hillman that our road accident effort is poorly co-ordinated, ill-thought out and slow to adopt new safety measures.

Our roads are not safe enough, but they are safer than those of many other nations, at least for car drivers and their passengers. Our record is poorer as regards pedestrians and cyclists and in international terms has been so for a number of years. For pedestrian deaths, for example, as expressed per 100,000 people, Britain was ranked twelfth among the advanced nations in 1984 behind the United States, Japan, Germany, Italy, Holland and others. Our fatality rate at 3.5 per 100,000 was more than twice that of Norway at the top of the safety table.

Young pedestrians seem particularly at risk. The proportion of children in the 10–14 age group killed or injured on foot showed a steady rise after 1979 and in 1985 reached its highest level since the early seventies. As for cyclists, total casualties went up 29 per cent between 1975 and 1985 at a time when cycle traffic increased by 21 per cent. Of those killed or seriously injured in 1985, half were under the age of 20.

The young are disproportionately represented in fatality statistics indicating that road accidents frequently kill people with lots of life in front of them. Taking all types of traffic accidents together, some 2,300 young people under the age of 24 died in 1984. This represents 150,000 years of lost life expectancy. The peak danger years are 15–24, when to pedestrian and cyclist deaths are added those of inexperienced and reckless car drivers and motorcyclists.

Dr Tom Weston in his book *Don't Panic* has observed that we have greatly reduced infant mortality and fatal childhood diseases only to have an increasing number of youngsters cut down on the roads.

If traffic accidents continue at their present rate ... it means that one out of every fifty children leaving school will be dead or permanently disabled before he is ten years older. Indeed Britain's record is probably the worst in Western Europe.

The life expectancy of those in the 15–24 age group has gone down for the first time since the nineteenth century according to educationalist Brin Morgan. This is mainly due to road accidents affecting young men far more than young women.

The very word 'accident' evokes an image of uncontrollability, yet most accidents have clearly identifiable causes and could in principle at least have been avoided. This is why a strategy of accident prevention is potentially so rewarding. Our aim is to reduce deaths and injuries on Britain's roads by a half. This is in line with the views of Plowden and Hillman who wrote in 1984:

it would be entirely realistic for the Government to set a target of reducing the annual number of deaths and serious casualties in road accidents by 40 per cent within eight years.

By considering traffic accidents within a National Programme for Risk Reduction we can impart to our road safety effort the strategic co-ordination, clout and prestige which are presently lacking. Adopting the risk engineering framework, we can start by making suggestions to encourage the 'designing out' of road accidents.

Local authorities should be 'back-charged' for the medical costs of the accidents which occur in their areas. This suggestion comes from Plowden and Hillman. The intention is enormously to increase the pressure on those who control local highways to reduce road hazards resulting from poor road layout. At present the medical cost of road accidents is borne by the

NHS which is obviously not in a position to improve road safety. To keep bureaucracy for the back-charging system to a minimum, a standard 'menu' of costs could be drawn up for every type of accident severity which would be updated annually.

The opportunities for saving life and limb by good road design are immense, and even quite small changes can be valuable. Here are some examples: bigger pedestrian refuges in the centre of roads; better facilities for cyclists; speed-reducing humps on pelican and zebra crossings; the use of skid-resistant surface dressings at junctions which themselves can be converted from a straight-across to a staggered design; edge-lining of roads for night visibility; vehicle-slowing 'pinch-points' at residential road entrances; and the provision of median strips to ensure traffic channelisation. It is claimed by Friends of the Earth that for each £1 spent in recent years in London on small-scale traffic schemes there has been £4 saved in community costs such as fewer accidents. This thought is echoed by Plowden and Hillman:

> It is not unknown for particular schemes to pay for themselves several times over within a year, and a whole programme of accident investigation and prevention work is likely to achieve rates of return far higher than can be obtained from building major roads, or from most other investment whether in the transport sector or elsewhere. However, this activity has attracted far less investment than these economic arguments for it would indicate.

This recalls the business maxim that the fastest way to make money is to stop losing it. Small-scale road engineering schemes can contribute to both our wealth and well-being.

Besides road accidents, local authorities should also be back-charged for casualties resulting from falls and collisions *on pavements*. Britain's pedestrians have to negotiate an assault course of uneven surfaces, shop signs, scaffolding, lamp-posts, badly parked cars, pot-holes, uncleared rubbish, litter and dog dirt. According to a report published in 1987 by the National Consumer Council, three million adults suffer falls each year as pedestrians and half a million of these need treatment. This brings to a million the total of those requiring medical treatment each year after using our paths and roads. On the pavements, the most at-risk groups are old people and young children. Charging local authorities the full cost of treating injuries should lead to improvements, not least perhaps by encouraging enforcement of existing laws controlling obstructions and the fouling of footpaths.

At present there are no lobby organisations at local level for safer paths and roads. Neighbourhood Watch schemes could fulfil this function by identifying hazards – and hazardous behaviour – and pressing for change.

This would bolster the justification for these schemes by adding a life- and limb-saving dimension.

Another designing-out suggestion relates to accident statistics. At present, no statistics about the safety record of individual makes of car are available to the general public. The government and motor insurance companies should assemble this information for dissemination. The effect of this would be to concentrate the minds of manufacturers on safety ahead of speed, streamlining and fuel economy, and to trigger a benign 'arms race' in safety standards. A two-year notice of intention to publish safety statistics by make of car would give manufacturers time to consider the quality of their products. They might wish to install an extra set of brake lights to reduce the danger of rear-end shunts, a bleeping device as an audible complement to reversing lights as a warning to pedestrians, or whatever.

A Swedish survey of accidents by the state-run insurance group, Folksam, showed that the Renault 4 had an extremely poor safety record whereas the pre-1981 model of the Volkswagen Polo, a car of equivalent weight, was a good safety bet. On the subject of car size and safety, John Adams has written:

It has been shown that big cars are more likely to be involved in accidents than small cars, but that, if they are involved in accidents, occupants of small cars are more likely to be killed.

The publication of detailed car safety statistics might lead to increased customer preference for large cars. If this occurred, so be it. Improved data might also lead to a generation of cars coloured International Orange and with the bodywork shock absorbing capacity of a ball of fluff – unlikely, but possible. In any event, it would be an example of market forces operating on the basis of educated customer awareness.

A greater use of public transport means fewer accidents, more private vehicle use leads to an increase. In the first full year of the GLC's cheap, integrated transport policies in 1983 there were 3,500 fewer road casualties in London than in the previous twelve months, according to Friends of the Earth.

Under-development of public transport applies particularly to the railways. British Rail has carried more passengers in the eighties, but the growth in rail traffic has been greater still in France and West Germany where state subsidies are far higher and productivity lower. In assessing the value of rail against road investment, the Department of Transport refuses to take into account potential savings in accident costs. It was estimated in 1985 that on the roads the cost of each fatal accident in terms of lost output, medical services, policing and so on, was over £200,000.

From designing-out, let us turn to targeting. Three groups of relevance here are young car drivers, drunk drivers and motorcyclists. The age at which young people can drive a car or ride a greater than 49cc motorcycle, presently 17, should be raised to 18. Responsible handling of a potentially lethal vehicle is an adult activity which should be confined to adults. Raising the age limit would be consistent with the 'majority rule' idea described in the crime section where the intention was to re-emphasise 18 as the age at which adulthood is achieved.

Motorcycles are a particular safety problem. Among young men, motorcycle accidents are the premier cause of death. Stephen Plowden writing in *The Times* in November 1986 quoted a Department of Transport consultation paper as follows:

> The government's aim can be summed up as being to preserve and enhance all the good things in motorcycling – the convenience, the fun, the excitement – and to cut out the bad – the appalling risks to life and limb, the thousands of deaths and serious injuries occurring every year in accidents involving motorcycles.

Plowden added his own comments to this:

> What is missing is any sense of the government's responsibilities to third parties. Even when the only casualties in a motorcycle accident are the riders themselves, many other people are affected and the NHS picks up the bill. Thirty-two pedestrians a week are killed or injured by motorcycles; a young man on a motorcycle is eight times more likely to kill or injure a pedestrian than a young man in a car.

Training for motorcyclists – the Department of Transport's preferred option – seems not to be the answer. Plowden and Hillman cite a study carried out in Salford which showed, contrary to expectation, that trained motorcyclists had significantly *higher* accident rates than an untrained control group. Studies abroad have also failed to reveal that training has any beneficial effect. The explanation is probably that a safety benefit (riding skills) is being consumed as a performance benefit (greater speed, more exhilarating handling) with a consequent increase in risk.

Publicity is another seemingly ineffective way of reducing the toll among those on motorcycles. In Essex, for example, where the problem is tragically severe, the County Road Safety Office has been quoted in the press as saying that:

> our publicity-posters, leaflets, television, fillers, radio, whatever we tried – was not having a great deal of effect on reducing accident figures among young motorcyclists.

Delayed eligibility to ride larger motorcycles should help to reduce accidents, as will moves to curb drunk-driving, discussed shortly. What is also required, however, is a decrease in the use of over-powerful machines as there is a positive relationship between engine size and accident rates. This has been known for a long time. Stephen Plowden has cited data from an official study performed in 1958 which showed that even in the safest age group (40–49), the danger increased linearly with engine size. Riders of bikes over 350cc were nearly nine times more likely to have a fatal or serious accident per mile travelled than those riding bikes under 60cc. Stephen Plowden makes this recommendation:

> Limit the speed, power and weight of machines that even qualified riders may use to what is required for comfortable touring. The maximum speed capability should be no more than the national speed limit; the engine size probably no more than 250cc.

The Japanese have banned big motorbikes from their roads, though they continue to export them to Britain for us to kill ourselves on. An outright ban on Japanese lines, though sensible, might be regarded as over-authoritarian in this country. An alternative approach would be to require users of large motorcycles to pay for the extra damage they do by paying a special vehicle tax. If successful in reducing the popularity of bigger machines, incidentally, this would have a positive impact on the trade balance by reducing imports: wealth *and* well-being again.

Drunk drivers are another category of road user worth targeting to reduce accidents. Over a quarter of drivers involved in fatal accidents are drunk; 45 per cent of all fatal accidents to those in the 16–24 age group are alcohol-related. Convictions for drunk-driving are running at 100,000 a year, 95 per cent of offenders being male. For 'drunk driver' in publicity campaigns, read 'drunk man', and these drunk men, in general, commit more careless driving and accident offences than other drivers.

The two obvious approaches to reducing hazardous drinking are to increase the chances of detection and to stiffen penalties. Currently, drunk drivers stand a chance of being caught which may be as low as one in 250, though some would say it is higher. Either way, it is too low to act as a strong deterrent. Random breath tests, long mooted, should be brought in. Public opinion would probably regard this development as acceptable. In Australia and New Zealand, random testing at high frequency together with high-profile publicity campaigns are reckoned to have reduced alcohol-related highway deaths by 30 per cent. If the same thing happened here, it would mean 360 lives saved each year.

For drivers, the permitted level of alcohol in the blood is not more than 80mg per 100ml. If this were reduced to, say, 20mg per 100ml for those in their first year of driving after receiving a full license, then the deterrent effect on young drivers would be enhanced. A 20mg limit exists in some parts of Australia for novice drivers and young people.

When drunk-driving involves an innocent victim, a key element in punishment should be automatic compensation by the offender of the surviving victim or the victim's next of kin. This is in keeping with the reasoning in the section on crime, 'victims first'. Driving bans and fines are the commonest punishments of drunk drivers. (See Appendix III for two case histories involving drunk-driving.) Better than a fine, which has financial but no moral impact, would be a compensation order possibly involving the 'Sin Tax' method of collection previously described.

Technology makes possible a novel curb on drunk-driving recidivism. In-car breathalysers now available can prevent a car starting if the driver is drunk. The technology appears to have come of age, so much so that American judges in a number of states are already ordering offenders to drive only cars fitted with such devices. Britain should go the same way. Repeat offending is one feature of the drunk-driving problem. Offenders should pay to have a breathalyser installed in their car, and they should have to keep it there for a specified period.

Notwithstanding technological innovations like the personal breathalyser, the most important factor in road safety will remain the behaviour of individual road users. As John Adams has written:

> Accident statistics suggest that the potential life saving benefits of suppressing risk-taking desires are very large. If, for example, young men could somehow be equipped with the same behaviour patterns and attitudes towards risk as young women their accidental death rate would decrease by about two thirds.

In the analysis, it was described how risk-reducing driving styles can make 'dangerous' wet or icy roads safer than 'safe' dry roads. If drivers could be induced to display 'winter mentality' driving behaviour all year round then lives would be saved on a significant scale. How is this to be achieved? This is the great challenge facing risk engineers.

Part III
A New Renaissance

7

The Way Ahead

We live in interesting times, with the nations of the earth locked together as never before, economically and politically. The volume of international trade in goods and services has more than doubled in the last two decades. Standards of living have risen rapidly in Western Europe and America, and also notably in Japan and the newly industrialised countries of the Pacific Basin. Latin America is developing too but groans under a mountain of debt. Africa is impoverished and is the only region poorer now than it was fifteen years ago. There is a spirit of openness (*glasnost*) in the Soviet empire and China is re-emerging onto the international stage at a time when her economy is growing fast. India is feeding itself and expanding industrially, while the Middle East remains as volatile as ever.

In the middle of the world map, at the top, a small country struggles. It is an apparently played-out post-imperial power in history's backwash. It is Britain.

If the growth trends of the last 20 years are projected over the next 20, Britain will continue to be the poorest of the major industrial nations, and the gap between us and the rest will become a chasm. More than that, on trend we will be poorer than the people of Singapore and Taiwan. With waning economic power, our influence on the world and our place in it will diminish too.

The future of the British economy, as the oil years slip behind us, rests on a resurgence in the nation's manufacturing capacity together with a successful 'post-industrial' assault on the growing world market for services. This was the thrust of the 'Two Sectors/One Future' economic sub-strategy outlined in Part I.

A complementary lifestyle sub-strategy was described in Part II entailing a National Programme for Risk Reduction to eliminate – in a risk engineering mode – negative effects on the nation's well-being. Emphasis was given to improving health and reducing crime and accidents. Plainly, our relatively poor international performance has not been confined to industry and the economy. Wealth and well-being were seen to be cross-linked, particularly as regards health, where affluence is definitely life-enhancing.

The objectives of the Wealth and Well-being strategy and the policy recommendations arising from the economic and lifestyle sub-strategies are shown in Table 7. It remains for us to agree on the 'One Future' of the economic sub-strategy and identify changes which will lead to positive contributions to well-being – issues which bear critically on the second of our national objectives, quality of life.

Clearly from the economic sub-strategy I am advocating an emphasis on private enterprise as the engine of wealth creation. Let-it-rip capitalism, however, and economic expansionism are not enough on their own. I propose, therefore, that we work towards the Convivial Society. This concept, at least in my use of it, is meant to imply 'fun and profits with care.' Let us take these three aspects in reverse order before tackling the question of reform and glimpsing the future.

Table 7. Wealth and Well-being Strategy: A snapshot of objectives and sub-strategic policy recommendations

---

Objectives (for year 2000):
1. Increase prosperity by doubling national income (GDP of £700 billion at 1987 prices).
2. Improve quality of life by, among other things, improving health by 10 per cent, reducing crime by one-third and halving fatal and other accidents.
3. Restore national morale.

Economic Sub-strategy: Two Sectors/One Future

Industrial sector
- M-rated taxation to favour manufacturing
- Abolish mortgage interest relief (redirect resources to industrial investment, training and R&D)
- Raft of tactical measures (see page 36)
- New co-ordinating body for export of goods: Visible Success

Post-industrial sector
- Measures to improve Britain as tourist venue (see page 41)
- Establish London Idearium
- New co-ordinating body for export of financial, information-related and leisure/arts services, and for tourism: Invisible Enterprise
- London as 'European Capital of the Future'

Lifestyle sub-strategy: National Programme for Risk Reduction

Health
- New preventive medicine organisation: Lifestyle 2000

1. To take over NHS's preventive medicine activities
2. To mount screening programmes (using Health Quotient concept to raise individual awareness and quantitate the nation's health)
3. To make policy recommendations
4. To publicise healthy lifestyles and improve media treatment of 'risk' (Risk Factor Scale)

Smoking
- Increase tax to double prices
- Ban on advertising and sponsorship
- Raise legal age of purchase to 18
- Discourage smoking in public places and at work

Alcohol
- Increase tax to effect a moderate price rise
- Health publicity and warnings
- Civilise 'context' of drinking (e.g. fully liberalise licensing laws)
- Curb under-age drinking (e.g. strengthen penalities for sellers)
- Ban sponsorship

Crime
- Nationwide Neighbourhood Watch (for crime prevention and road safety)
- Thief-proof cars
- Burglar-proof homes
- 'Majority rule' (deferred adulthood from 18 to 21 as punishment)
- 'Top-down' crime busting
- 'Victims first' (compensation and support)
- Sentencing reform for consistency

Accidents
- Reduce home accidents (design changes/publicity)
- Improve safety at work (better resourcing of HSE)
- Back-charge local authorities for road and pavement injury accidents
- Publish car safety statistics by make and model
- Change to 18 the age at which a car or motorcycle (over 49cc) can be used
- Restrict newly qualified drivers/motorcycle riders to 50mph and 20mg per cent alcohol
- Random breath tests
- Greater resort to compensation for drunk-driving victims
- Drunk drivers to have personal breathalysers

Care

The convivial society concept, to my mind, sums up a society where people are of first importance, and theories on how to manage them and on how to manage the economy come a long way second. We do not live in an age of faith; ours is an age of personal values and human relationships. At a time when society has become more stratified than for many decades, the attitudes are tested of the two-thirds of us who are doing very nicely towards the one-third living near the poverty line.

In the convivial society, one sump of misery which should be drained is unemployment. Being without work is bad for mental and physical health and can lead to crime. The danger of family break-up is increased, as is the risk of suicide. Professor Colin Pritchard, Professor of Social Studies at Southampton University has said: 'There is no doubt that there is a strong connection between the suicide rate and unemployment.' In the past 10 years the male suicide rate in England has gone up by a quarter and in Scotland by a third. In Wales, according to Professor Pritchard, suicide is now more common than road deaths. The most marked rise has been among men in their thirties and forties.

The vast majority of the unemployed are not work-shy. This fact emerged as a result of a government programme called Restart introduced in 1986 and aimed at the long-term unemployed. The Low Pay Unit, in evidence to a House of Commons select committee on employment in December 1986, concluded on the basis of over half a million interviews that there was 'a near total contradiction of the "scrounger" myth commonly applied to the unemployed'. A similar conclusion was reached by the National Economic Development Council in a report published in March 1987 which showed, incidentally, that while earnings have increased, benefits have diminished. Doubtless some of the unemployed are work-shy and others are occupied in the 'black' economy while claiming benefits, but this should not blind us to the fact that most of the jobless are made miserable by their plight.

Britain's experience of unemployment in the eighties has been worse than that of other major industrial nations. At the beginning of the decade our rate was not much different from the OECD average (using that organisation's definitions) but by 1987 it was 50 per cent higher. The rise in joblessness since 1979 of about two million was due to the damage suffered by manufacturing industry during the early Thatcher years and to a rise in the working population of about 1 per cent a year. Robin Morris, a professor of economics, has put our problems in international perspective:

Trillions and trillions of pounds of production are being lost for ever on account of totally unnecessary unemployment, with unnecessary restraints on public expenditure, unnecessary taxes and unnecessarily slow economic growth. The tragedy is worldwide, but worse in Britain than in most other developed countries.

Mass unemployment is one of the great issues of our time, second only in importance to industrial wealth creation. The official unemployment statistics – which count only those who receive benefits – almost certainly understate the problem though by how much is a matter of definition and debate. Peter Townsend, professor of social administration at Bristol University, writing in early 1987 pointed out that surveys carried out in London suggest that 'the scale of unemployment nationally lies between five and six million rather than between three and four million.' Government statistics ignore what the professor calls the hidden unemployed such as 'discouraged' workers who have stopped looking for work or who haven't looked in the last month or so, married women, reluctant students who would have preferred work to more education, disabled people (two-thirds of whom live at or below the poverty line), and the legions of prematurely retired people who would much rather have a job. Since 1979 the number of people on the government's special training schemes has more than doubled. This and the numerous statistical changes which have been made mean that the official count is almost a million lower than it would otherwise have been.

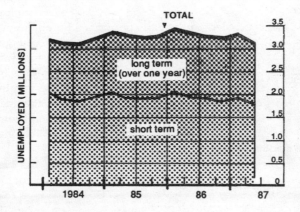

Figure 10. Unemployment by duration
Source: *The Economist*

Unemployment may come down more quickly than many suppose, as it did in the 1930s when the rate fell from 17 per cent in 1932 to 5 per cent by the outbreak of war after relaxation of fiscal and monetary policy. There will probably remain, though, the problem of the long-term unemployed who have been on the dole for more than a year. There were 1.3 million of these people in 1987 (Figure 10). One-fifth were reckoned to have literacy and numeracy problems according to the Manpower Services Commission, so many were thus not only unemployed but possibly unemployable.

The Henley Centre forecasts that unemployment will be at about the five million level throughout the 1990s. There is not enough work now and there is unlikely to be enough in the forseeable future, even given a buoyant economy and a job-creating government embarking on a programme of public works, as popular as this latter might be in some circles. One way forward would be to change our approach to 'jobs.' Some of us at least could usefully wean ourselves off quasi-Calvinistic attitudes to work. Harford Thomas in the *Guardian* has written of the Protestant work ethic, the notion that work is the prime purpose of life and the duty of man. In ancient Greece and Rome, leisure was the measure of the good life, while in medieval times, 'work and play and community jollification ran side by side'.

> It was with the Reformation and with the rise of capitalism in Europe that an ideology of work – 'the gospel of work' – came to be the overruling principle of life. But this was over a relatively short period of a few centuries, and it lacks biblical support. In the late twentieth century the work ethic is fading, though the economic system with which it was associated survives.

Most of us are still locked into work yet a surprisingly small proportion of national life is devoted to it. If you count pensioners and children, just 10 per cent of all our time is spent at work compared, for example, to sleep where the figure is 37 per cent.

One problem with the dole is that it is a demeaning aspect of welfare statism: benefits for the useless. A two-tier system of payment to the jobless would improve the tone. The lower level, dole proper, would be fairly limited in amount and would not require anything of its recipients. The higher level, designated 'post-industrial pay' would require a couple of days work a week. The keynote here would be a contribution by the 'post-industrialist' in question to the convivial society. This could involve looking after the old, clearing canals, picking up litter, acting as a neighbourhood watchman – anything so long as it is *for the good of others*. The work would need to be done well. Slip-shod performance would lead to demotion to the dole. A particularly distinguished contribution might be rewarded with a Fellowship of the Post-industrial Society!

The optional nature of participation in the Post-industrial Programme, PIP for short, distinguishes this idea from American-style 'workfare' notions based on the principle 'no work, no money', which its critics see as coercive.

At present unemployment is a demoralising trap. It needs to be a trampoline – and free of stigma. The PIP would help to reorientate joblessness. People might wish to drop out of full-time work to retrain, to take a sabbatical, as a form of early retirement, to think, to write, whatever. As long as they made a good contribution to society as well for a proportion of the week they could do what they liked with the rest of their time. By being an option for those in work, the PIP would be different from the existing Community Programme, a more narrowly conceived scheme.

The PIP scheme should be particularly attractive to Britain's rising tide of single mothers, two thirds of whom rely on benefits. Members of this group tend to have low skills and experience and limited availability, all of which makes them unattractive to employers.

Unemployment has struck most savagely in the north of England where one-fifth of jobs have been lost since 1977. Regional imbalances in terms of work and living standards are a striking feature of modern Britain – but they have been with us a long time. Paul Johnson puts this point in context:

> It is no accident, of course, that the great reservoirs of English poverty are to be found outside the south-east heartlands. No student of history can do other than acknowledge a profound respect for the constant and remorseless force of geography. Wealth and power in England, in Britain indeed, has always gravitated towards the south-east.

A survey published in 1987 forecast that in the decade 1985-95 there will probably be 900,000 new jobs. Almost half (a net 417,000) will be in the south-east and there is anticipated to be a swift turnaround in the position of London. Most of the jobs will be in services. The surge in jobs in the south is likely to reinforce the regional inequalities which have become more marked in the 1980s, unless action is taken.

The recent resurgence of parts of Scotland is a reminder that regional imbalances are not inevitable. One thinks of Edinburgh as a financial centre, Silicon Glen and a 'miles better' Glasgow. This shows it can be done outside the south-east. Local initiative, together with a judicious mix of public and private funding, seems the best formula. Ladling out cash is not the answer. Correlli Barnett:

> In the twenty years after 1962 alone aid to 'the Regions' was to mount up to a total of £20 billion (at 1982 prices), none of it adding to British productive capacity, but at best merely switching some of the growth from where it would have happened in any case to somewhere else. Moreover, even after forty years of using the life-support machine of regional aid, Whitehall still did not know what good effect, if any, had been achieved ... The rate of unemployment in the Victorian industrial areas remained in 1985 half as much again as that of the South-east – as it had been even during the postwar boom and 'full employment'.

In all likelihood, regional aid has had a net harmful effect on the economy taken as a whole. Winning is not about reinforcing failure.

What work there is will have to be shared around more equitably in the society of the future. The international four-day week is very much in line with this idea, having holy days for Muslims (Friday), Jews (Saturday) and Christians (Sunday). The trend towards shorter working weeks and longer holidays will continue but the long-forecasted leisure society where only a few people work – and then only a few hours a week – seems as distant as ever. Alas, the time is not yet at hand for the establishment of a boulevardier society of bon viveurs, socialites and intellectuals.

A major challenge for the 1990s is to transform the welfare state system from a mechanism encouraging dependence, passivity and social isolation to one encouraging self-reliance and individual achievement. The convivial society concept meets this need by emphasising *self-esteem* and *social esteem*. The welfare state is about handouts; the convivial society, hand-ups.

To adapt a phrase of E.M. Forster's: 'Only reconnect'. A worthy and convivial aim would be to reconnect people at the personal level to their ability to control their own destinies; at the social level to the communities in which they live; and at the political level to the decision-making process. This last will be dealt with briefly under a later heading ('Reform'), so let us consider community-level reconnection first.

The perceived deficiencies of the welfare state led governments in the 1980s to reduce benefits either in relative terms, by not raising them in line with wages, or in absolute terms, for example by cutting benefits for the long-term unemployed. We should have opened the throttle of opportunity before choking back benefits. A more positive approach is that advocated above involving a two-stream system, dole proper and PIP participation to serve the community. By encouraging the unemployed to make a contribution, you are, as it were, inviting them back into society.

For those in work, share-option and profit-sharing schemes, for example, are usefully reconnective. They help to diminish 'us and them' attitudes by appealing to common interest.

Reconnection at the personal level was one of the key-notes of the lifestyle sub-strategy, the intention being to reconnect people to the consequences of their actions. For example, the Health Quotient was designed to give people a clear picture of their health and thus induce beneficial lifestyle changes, while the Sin Tax was intended to establish the principle that it should be criminals rather than the general community who should compensate the victims of crime. The Risk Factor Scale which would provide a quantitative assessment of the risks associated with a particular activity is designed to increase awareness of where the major dangers lie and is also reconnective in my use of the word. It is illustrative of attempts to increase knowledge in order to permit people to make the best choices and control their own lives.

For the young, the convivial society means not so much reconnection as connection. A lack of satisfying social involvement breeds anti-social behaviour. For this reason, denial of welfare benefits to those aged 16-18 is probably well judged. Training and education is being expanded for this age group as the only publicly-funded alternative to a job (which itself should have some compulsory training element). State-subsidised idleness is an undesirable option. Interestingly, this is in line with the thinking of the original Beveridge Report which laid the foundations of the present benefit system.

Many, when surveying Britain in the eighties, will not see the makings of a convivial society so much as a new age of barbarism and social fragmentation. There is record crime, increased social and racial divisions, gross inequalities in health, and urban squalor. On this last, Edward Heath has said: 'Decay in our inner cities has now run beyond anything to be found elsewhere in the European Community.' At the domestic level, more of us are living alone than ever before and divorce has climbed to record levels to place us at the top of Europe's league. Illegitimate births have more than doubled in the last decade and now account for nearly one-fifth of total births. Abortions are running at over 150,000 a year, attempted suicides at 200,000. Neighbour noise complaints have risen nearly tenfold in the last decade to about 65,000 a year. A 'hardness' is seen as having pervaded our national life from the top, promoting greed and self-interest above fellow-feeling and compassion. Our aid-giving to poor countries has declined during the decade betokening a narrowing of our international role. Meanwhile, at home, an army of unemployed has been left in the cold.

This kind of assessment should not be overdone. There are signs of conviviality even in our divided, me-orientated culture. One thinks, for example, of the public's response to the Ethiopian famine in the mid-1980s, the increased contribution of fathers to child-rearing, the continuing interest in conserving our heritage and the environment, and the return to community-scale housing. There are 275,000 registered charities with a combined income of £10 billion. Two other encouraging signs can be mentioned: the Institute of Social Inventions was founded in 1985 'to encourage new, imaginative and feasible approaches to social problems'; and there has been a proliferation of 'mutual support groups' for a multitude of diseases and other tribulations.

The accent in Part I was on success won through endeavour, corporate and personal. But where there are winners there will be losers. A society can be judged by its treatment of failure. To adopt a medical metaphor, in raw capitalism, failure is pain. Socialism is anaesthesia – some would say, for all. The welfare state is analgesia, which arguably numbs the capacity to heal. The convivial society should offer selective palliation – something which alleviates the disease of economic failure but does not attempt a full cure. This remains a matter for self-healing in an opportunity-rich environment.

Profits

The economic sub-strategy is designed to foster free enterprise to the benefit of individuals, companies and society. As a nation we must play the capitalist game and play to win. In our favour as we move into a new economic era are our people.

The results of a survey published in 1986 by Taylor Nelson Monitor bode well for Britain's future. Apparently we have more 'new people', 36 per cent in fact, than any other industrial nation except Holland. These people reject the rat-race conformity of the old industrial era and do not give so much weight to their status as employed or unemployed, since the terms have little relevance to their individual enterprise outlook in which work is play. Their criteria for success are within themselves ('inner-directedness') but they have broad horizons. They tolerate other people's positions and they are intelligent and individual in outlook. This group is forecast to grow to 55 per cent of the population by 2010. These people will inherit the future.

Britain has a relative deficiency of the 'industrial era conformists'. Our figure is 33 per cent of the population compared to an average among industrial nations in general of 42 per cent. Japan's figure is 55 per cent. Our lacklustre performance in the industrial field may relate in some degree to this and explain the lack of commitment to manufacturing by society. We cannot withdraw from this activity, however, as we have seen.

The coming of the post-industrial era does not mean the end of consumption of goods – and does not therefore mean that Britain can afford to stop making them. It merely means that most of us will not be employed in manufacturing.

National economic success should boost average individual happiness – a crucial aspect of well-being – if the results of surveys are to be believed. 'Poor but happy' ideas notwithstanding, affluence and contentment tend to be highly correlated both within and between nations. For example, in one American study the very wealthy reported 'higher levels of happiness than any subgroup in a national random survey'. Similarly, people in richer nations tend to report themselves as being markedly happier than people in poorer nations. This was the finding of what was billed as 'the first ever global poll' which was carried out in 70 countries by the Gallup organisation in 1976. Money does not appear to make you miserable.

Fun

During the Middle Ages, nearly a third of every year was given over to religious holidays. 'Religious' they may have been, but by all accounts, stuffy they were not. That phrase quoted above of Harford Thomas's about 'community jollification' in medieval times strikes a chord. The contemporary British could do with more of this. With a feeling of achievement and personal worth, fat wallets, a restored pride in Britain, the international four-day week, and a new emphasis on revolving bow-ties and stripy socks – we can swank and swagger in the streets and have fun! All of which is very much in line with the third of our national objectives, *restoration of morale*.

'Fun' also stands for Future UNlimited. That is what we have to look forward to if we pull up our (stripy) socks.

Reform

The survey that showed we had the most new people laid to rest a myth that was sorely in need of interment, that is that the British are conservative and hidebound. The survey showed that individuals are, by and large, flexible and ready for change. It is the old establishments of politics, industry and the unions which are arthritically ill-equipped to cope with novelty. Reform is long overdue in many areas of national life. This is not to say that we should bulldoze the present to make way for the future but a few crumbling buildings are long overdue for renovation. One such is parliament.

The way we fill our Houses of Parliament is bizarre to say the least. The House of Lords is non-elected but intermittently representative of national opinion; the House of Commons is elected but typically unrepresentative. Our method of electing MPs is a particular bone of contention. The first-past-the-post electoral system has to be regarded as an aberration. In the 1987 election, the main parties polled the following proportion of the vote in mainland Britain: Conservative, 43.3 per cent, Labour, 31.5 per cent, and Alliance, 23.1 per cent. This yielded the following number of parliamentary seats: Conservative, 376 (59 per cent of the total), Labour, 229 (36 per cent), and Alliance, 22 (3.4 per cent). It took about ten times as many people to elect an Alliance MP as a Conservative MP.

Because of the distortions wrought by the present system, the Tories were elected on an overall minority vote in 1979, 1983 and 1987. In fact, every government since the war has been drawn from a political party most people voted against. This has not deterred the victorious party after each election from claiming 'a mandate from the people'. This was true even in 1951 when the Conservatives gained more seats than the runner-up, Labour, but polled fewer votes.

A great reform act has been proposed to bring in a system of proportional representation (PR) to ensure that parties win seats in proportion to their popular support. According to opinion polls this would be popular with most voters regardless of political persuasion. PR has the merit of enhancing democratic commitment because in systems of this type, which can involve multi-member constituencies, every vote counts. This increases turn-out and eliminates tactical voting. There is an end to voting *against* people, only voting *for* people. This is in line with the theme of reconnection described previously, the reconnection in this case being to a positive democratic process.

PR probably makes coalition government more likely, and some people perceive this as a disadvantage. It also could widen the range of election candidates. During the first two parliaments in the eighties there were no ethnic MPs. And at a time when we have had our first woman prime minister, the proportion of female parliamentarians was lower than in any other Western European country except Greece. The 1987 election saw something of a change: a record number of ethnic and women candidates were elected to parliament.

PR would probably help to curb local government extremism (or corruption) resulting from the monopolistic power of one party. In one London borough in 1982, Labour polled 51 per cent of the vote but got 96 per cent of the seats.

Another aspect of the British political system which attracts negative comment is the adversarial mind-set of those engaged in the political debate. Here is what Frank Cooper, a former permanent secretary at the Ministry of Defence, had to say in the *Guardian* in early 1986:

> This confrontation is second nature in politics. It is expected and sought by the media. It reaches its apogee in Parliament. It is uniquely virulent and unconstructive compared with other Western industrial democracies. It seeks to divide not to unify. It is scarcely concerned with seeking out the best solution. It is intellectually slow-moving and resistant to real change.

Writing on the 'poverty trap' by which people are virtually forced into welfare-subsidised unemployment, Norman Stone, a professor of modern history, has written in *The Sunday Times*:

> We are unique in Western Europe in retaining a system of government by which obvious long-term reforms are virtually impossible to carry through.

This is paradoxical given that we are governed by what has been memorably characterised by Lord Hailsham as an 'elective dictatorship.'

The ruling party, which may have only won a minority of the popular vote and has a majority in parliament of just one, can pass whatever legislation it likes for a five-year period, always assuming party unity remains intact. It can ignore a petition with 56 million signatures on it calling for change. It can even pass retrospective legislation penalising something that happened yesterday. This is a peculiar state of affairs for a country which gave so many basic liberties to the world. It is only surprising that there are not more calls for fundamental reform.

It can be envisaged that in the future there will be a trend towards participatory rather than representative democracy. Elections once every half-decade will probably be complemented by increased resort to referendums which could eventually usher in the days of futuristic push-button home voting. Paul Johnson has been quoted as saying:

> The actual business of political elites may not last much longer. The religious age drew to a close in the last century. The political age is drawing to a close in this one.

Meanwhile we have politics as it is now. A platter of reforms – some widely touted, several in line with our theme of reconnecting people to the policitical process – can be recommended: bring in fixed-term parliaments to end the interminable guessing game associated with election dates; centrally fund political parties to reduce the distortions wrought by vested interests; strengthen the powers of the parliamentary select committees, a superb system of watchdog bodies; reform the House of Lords by making its members stand for election; reform the idiotic Official Secrets Act; bring in a Freedom of Information Act to reduce the inimical secrecy that suffuses our national life; eliminate or improve the embarrassing honours system (the 'gong trade'); rack official statistics (e.g. relating to GDP, industrial output, unemployment, wages, national Health Quotient, and crime) to 100 when a new government assumes office to permit the public to monitor performance easily thereafter; inform members of the public in writing of how taxes are spent in the same way that councils inform ratepayers of how the rates are spent; and bring in a new Bill of Rights to protect the freedom of the individual – and, incidentally, raise his or her present status of subject to that of citizen.

British democracy though old is immature. This is evidenced by a skewed electoral system, increased centralism, excessive secrecy ('nanny knows best', even to the extent of denying us access to the Land Registry to find out who owns the house next door), erosion of civil liberties, judicial muzzling of the media (which has been likened to that operating in South Africa), adversarialism and so on. It is time our system grew up.

Improvements in the personal tax field can also be advocated. I described in Part I how workers in manufacturing industry should be given a favourable tax status ('M-ratedness'). The abolition of mortgage interest relief was also urged to help fund industrial research, investment and training. Other tax allowances could be cut and the tax system simplified. Brian Reading, writing in *The Sunday Times* in 1986 as radical US tax changes were coming in, argued for major reform:

> If all income tax allowances, other than the single and married allowances, were scrapped, and if we paid only 15p in the pound on all taxable income, the chancellor would immediately collect £2.6 billion in extra revenue. The poverty trap would be abolished. Incentives to avoid or evade taxation would almost disappear.

I would go further and abolish the married allowance as well. But either way, we need an efficient, non-penal, tax system to boost incentives and encourage a 'go-faster' culture. We are ill-advised to go on squandering £14 billion a year on undesirable, market-distorting subsidies for special-interest groups such as owner-occupiers, investors in pension schemes, farmers and the rest.

We could also usefully consider the following: abolish national insurance – which has long since become divorced from its original purpose – particularly the employers' contribution which can be regarded as a tax on jobs; bring down the retirement age for men to 60 as it is for women, a move that opinion polls suggest would be overwhelmingly popular, even among the working population who would have to pay extra to fund it, and which would eliminate a piece of sex discrimination that the European Court of Justice has held to be against Community Law; eliminate road tax and collect the money through a more equitable rise in petrol tax; end the television licence fee and fund the BBC direct. Reform in these last two areas would greatly reduce evasion. Each year £90 million is lost through non-payment of road tax alone.

Our system of education has failed us in the last 100 years or more, and is continuing to do so. International comparisons have repeatedly shown that the British are less well educated and less well trained than their counterparts in other industrial countries. A 'rule of seven' seems to apply at opposite ends of the educational spectrum. A remarkable one in seven adults has significant problems with reading, writing and using numbers according to Alan Wells, director of the Adult Literacy and Basic Skills Unit, even after 11 years of compulsory schooling. Meanwhile, just one in seven of 18-year-olds goes on to higher education, a performance which only Spain and Portugal among the advanced nations manage not to surpass. It is even the case now that more young Taiwanese and Koreans go on to higher education than young Britons.

Our educational deficiencies show up particularly starkly in the industrial field. Among managers just 21 per cent have degrees or professional qualifications of any kind. Compare this with West Germany where 63 per cent have degrees and the United States where the proportion is even higher. Among the labour force, 36 per cent of British workers have vocational qualifications of some kind compared with 67 per cent of Germans. We have invested less in education and training than our competitors. This has led to a relative educational decline which parallels – and many would argue, has contributed to – our relative economic decline. Given this, it is all the more surprising that a coherent education strategy has yet to emerge which specifies standards of attainment in all fields of education and training and which gives a time-scale for closing the gap that exists between us and most of the other developed nations.

Writing of the emerging post-industrial society, Tom Stonier sees us as needing 'a massively expanded education system to provide not only training and information on how to make a living but also on how to live'. We will all need to 'raise our game' to meet the needs of the future, but this will be particularly important for those in the bottom one-third of society lest they become locked into deprivation. It is the ever-expanding middle classes who will inherit the earth. The working-class lifestyle – early exit from education, unskilled and semi-skilled labour, trade union membership, passive consumption of entertainment and sport, smoking, nine-to-fiveism, tabloid press reading – is beginning to look very dated. Those who want to get on will have to go upmarket.

Britain's relatively weak commitment to research and development is a continuing cause for concern. Work by the Science Policy Research Unit at Sussex University has shown that our competitors' overall R&D spending has been growing at between 2 and 8 per cent a year. Ours, by contrast, has been falling an annual 0.7 per cent. Industry has tended to cut back in the eighties – as have the universities, under duress. As Professor Peter Morris of Oxford University has written: 'I don't think it is a question of us being in the scientific first division any more. I don't think we are even in the second division.'

Research is about the future, as is education. On this latter, the nation spends less than on defence. This, alas, is against the international trend. The late Dr Chris Evans pointed out in *The Mighty Micro* that combined world expenditure on education exceeded military expenditure for the first time in 1975 – 'a statistic most people find surprising.'

As a proportion of national income, our defence spending is higher than any other major Western European nation. Defence is one area of national life which could be argued to have bucked the trend of Britain's economic decline. Our military spending at nearly £19 billion a year is more than merely out of line with our world role and our diminished industrial status; pundits have pointed out that we cannot afford an army on the Rhine and other extensive NATO commitments, Fortress Falklands and a

Trident nuclear missile system.

Our profligacy in the defence sphere is startling. The 'unit of extravagance' seems to be a cool £1 billion. The abortive Nimrod airborne early warning system cancelled in 1986 was one of at least three £1 billion radar fiascos since the Second World War. As it happens, £1 billion is also how much we spent developing the Tigerfish torpedo. And each year our intelligence services cost a further £1 billion and tie down 10,000 highly trained personnel. Do we think we are a superpower?

Cheaper, but more tragic, has been the RAF's loss of low-flying aircraft. Fifty Jaguar strike aircraft, representing a quarter of the entire Jaguar force, have piled into the ground since the mid-seventies with the loss of more than two dozen lives and at a cost of nearly a third of a billion pounds. Added to this are the numerous other aircraft that have crashed in what is supposed to be peacetime.

Since the Second World War there have been 150 conflicts worldwide claiming some 20 million victims, many of them civilians. To our shame, one of these conflicts is happening close to home, in Northern Ireland. This is an abscess in perpetual suppuration. The people of the province will probably have to play a greater part in efforts to find a solution to 'the troubles'. The answer may involve something on the lines of the Swiss canton system which seems particularly suitable for divided communities. The 'solution' from the British point of view is a popular piece of national 'reshaping': ejection of Northern Ireland from the United Kingdom. According to opinion polls this would be a very popular move indeed – and it would, incidentally, save the British taxpayer some £1.6 billion a year.

Turning to the environment, our record is predictably bad. Britain's beaches and coastal waters are the most sewage-polluted in the EC. We are one of the biggest contributors to Europe's acid rain which adversely affects trees and is mainly caused by pollution from power station chimneys and car exhausts. Our countryside has been ravaged in modern times by intensive farming, forestry and urbanisation. We are notoriously lax when it comes to the dumping of toxic wastes in landfill sites and in the North Sea.

Fortunately, the prospects are not entirely bleak. We are being shamed as the 'dirty man of Europe' into reducing air pollution, one of our more disgusting 'invisible exports'. The process of cleaning up the atmosphere should in any case be aided by the decline of the smokestack industries. We are also bringing the littoral zone up to European Community standards for the benefit of our own and foreign tourists at beach resorts. Continuing food surpluses coupled with genetically improved crops and livestock should lead to reduced pressure on agricultural land. A check to inappropriate development could be offered by a Department of Environmental Protection, the creation of which has been suggested to bring a more unified approach to environmental matters.

Is it too much to hope that the last hedgerow has not been grubbed up, the last meadow given over to monocultivation or asphalt? And while we are about it, is it too much to hope that we can be given greater access to our own countryside, much of it presently cordoned off? A 'right to roam responsibly', such as they have in Sweden, has been put forward by Marion Shoard in her book *The Land is Our Land* as an alternative to our own unnecessarily exclusionist law on trespass. We have nothing to lose but our chain-link fences.

Britain does not require a revolution to change it, but there is enormous scope for the exercise of reformist zeal. This is the stirring challenge of the 1990s.

The Future

Our economic future is very much in the hands of Britain's businessmen: a lean, competitive manufacturing industry and a co-ordinated post-industrial sector hungry for success in home and overseas markets. The strategy calls for commitment, vision and attention to the 'princely' virtues of Pioneering, Reinforcement of success, Individual excellence, National roots, Clear goals and Europeanism. With all this, increased prosperity can be ours.

Britain's post-war record has not been impressive. And it did not seem to matter who was in charge. Labour and the Conservatives split between them the period running up to the end of the seventies, but neither could halt the trend of relative economic decline which was to continue into the eighties.

The central economic fact of the eight Thatcher years between the elections of May 1979 and June 1987 was that manufacturing output was higher at the start of the period than at the end. A trade surplus of about £7 billion a year had been turned into a deficit of over £8 billion. We were importing more than we were exporting; manufacturing investment was at a low level. Britain seemed to be less concerned with productive capitalism than rentier capitalism, making money out of money. Growth of the economy as a whole was below 1.5 per cent a year on average despite the blessing of offshore oil, a rather similar rate of growth to that achieved between 1973 and 1979. According to EC/OECD figures on incomes per head, we probably fell from thirteenth to fifteenth place among the capitalist industrial nations in the decade to 1985. Our fortunes have improved since, but we still have quite a lot of catching up to do.

Nor, as we have seen, has the problem of national underperformance in the post-war era been confined to the economy. We have arguably endured relative slippage as regards personal health, likelihood of criminal victimisation, some types of accidental injury, average educational attainment, the environment, social cohesion and libertarian standards. In sum, multiple relative decline.

Improvement is perfectly feasible. The Wealth and Well-being strategy comprising economic and lifestyle sub-strategies and a platter of reforms is intended to put us firmly on the upward track. It is a national strategy for the nineties.

The medium-term global economic picture looks relatively promising, even granted stock market aberrations, large trade imbalances and more than a trillion dollars of Third World debt. Beyond the short-term lurches of the business cycle, another long-term boom seems imminent based in part on a range of radical developments in technology. Food, energy and other resources are unlikely to be in limiting supply. The opportunities for wealth creation seem immense.

We live at a fascinating juncture in human history. World population passed the five billion mark sometime in 1987, yet individualism is as strong a force as ever. Of all the people in history who have lived beyond the age of 65, two-thirds are alive today. By the year 2000, half of the world's people will live in towns, up from less than three in ten in 1950. The ecologists tell us that if we do not manage the planet more responsibly we will cause the biggest mass extinction of animal and plant species for 65 million years. They warn that development should submit to the test of environmental sustainability. Meanwhile, science and technology sprint. Physicists have developed an intriguing 'from-nothing' hypothesis to explain the origin of the universe, and a 'grand unified theory' is on the cards to bring into a single theoretical framework the diverse forces of nature. Personal supercomputing is within reach and voice-activated (and handwriting-sensitive) computers will come to replace the tedious keyboard-instructed devices of today. Simultaneous language translation by machine is in sight. The experts tell us that computers using light transmission is a possibility. The interconnected 'global society' is already upon us. Man-made satellites girdle the globe; rockets pierce the heavens.

Alternative energy sources continue to be developed. Revolutionary materials such as ceramic superconductors are becoming available. Scientists are mapping the human genetic blueprint, all 50,000 genes of it, a project likely to become the largest in the history of biology ('Your genes unzipped to reveal all – man takes hold of his heredity!'). The molecular basis of cancer is increasingly understood at the genetic level in terms of 'oncogenes', an insight offering the prospect of major therapeutic advances in the future. A new generation of pharmaceuticals is emerging including novel vaccines (e.g. for hepatitis and leprosy) and anti-viral and brain drugs. We are inching towards a theory of mind.

Against this intriguing background, the nations of the earth jostle for prosperity. There is a remarkable dominance in the non-communist world of the 600 million inhabitants of what the Japanese economist Kenichi Ohmae has called the Triad – Europe, America and Japan. These three accounted for 75 per cent of the gross national product of the free world in 1960. In 1970 it was 73 per cent and even by the mid-1980s was still 72 per cent. Europe represents 25 per cent of global GNP and in Kenichi Ohmae's words 'is one of the world's three most critical and sophisticated markets.' The EC's 320 million people will have to work hard to maintain their position in the world. The 30th anniversary of the Treaty of Rome was celebrated in 1987. Britain, a late entry to the Community, has become increasingly tied to its European partners. This is inevitable but not to say that we should surrender our very individual identity. Merging with others or copying them is not the way ahead; we must invent our own destiny.

As the EC approaches its prime, a new vision is required of the future. Many feel that Europe will sooner or later have to go it alone from the United States, politically and militarily, and assume the role of independent friend rather than dependent ally – or collection of client states, as some would say. Efforts to produce a barrier-free internal European market will continue. Wise Europeans will pin their faith on free trade, worldwide.

We remain an open, vulnerable economy dealing with a turbulent world. Our economic affairs are undergoing a sea-change at the end of an era dominated by North Sea oil. Our standing in the world is not high. Lord Carrington, quoted in the mid-eighties:

We are a small offshore island in severe financial difficulties. We don't matter anymore. It's only a matter of time before they stop inviting us to economic summit meetings.

A continuation of post-war trends and a failure to exploit new opportunities implies such a hopeless future that we cannot afford to let it happen. We should be ambitious for our country; we *can* rise again. Our role will never again be that of empire-builder, of course, or even mini-superpower, but can be that of pioneer. The core of our self-esteem in the future will be economic pre-eminence and – as it should be now – radical innovation of the kind abundantly documented in Appendix I. Beyond the visionless materialism and cultural pessimism of the eighties lies a bright prospect: Britain, birthplace of the future!

Achievement beckons. The nation that gave you the first major European political revolution, the agricultural revolution, the industrial revolution, spawned the Land of the Free (albeit reluctantly), assembled and divested itself of the world's largest empire, and made countless contributions to science and civilisation, now gives you - the convivial society in a prosperous post-industrial world.

When we rise again, the last few decades of extended awfulness will be seen like an updated version of the Dark Ages where the cry that ran through the land was 'cuts' and the psychological colour was grey shading to noir. On the strength of an economic resurgence, I predict a cultural change, a new age of renaissance; a new age, that is, of popular song, literature, performing arts, conversation, invention and science.

Let me add a touch of romance to the conclusion of this book. On my right our virtuous prince, clear-sighted and eager for the success of his pioneering, M-rated kingdom revelling in industrial success. On my left the charming princess of conviviality, a recent graduate in risk engineering, generous, tolerant and humane. And ahead of them and us, wealth, well-being and a happy ending. Ladies and gentlemen, a toast: 'The Future!'

Appendix I
Best of British

A Selected List of National Achievements, Notable Characteristics and Eminent Characters

'This Scept'red Isle' (the island race with a unique national character)
Domesday Book
Magna Carta
Europe's first anti-Royalist revolution (Glorious Revolution, 1688)
Agricultural revolution
Industrial revolution
Largest empire in history
Sanitation revolution (sewers, clean water, etc.)
Therapeutic revolution (antibiotics, etc.)
Democracy, bloodlessly established
Mother of Parliaments (House of Commons, 1300)
Constitutional monarchy
Liberty, established early (Bill of Rights, Habeus Corpus Act, etc.)
Reformation (break with Rome, 1529-33)
English Bible (Authorised Version)
Discovery of quarter of the elements (more than any other single nation)
Hansard (first issue, 1608)
Pound sterling (unrivalled monetary stability between sixteenth and twentieth centuries)
World's number one language (also largest vocabulary)
World's greatest literature:
  Poetry (Chaucer, Elizabethans, Metaphysicals, Romantics, etc.)
  Rise of the novel (Richardson, Defoe)
  Nineteenth-century novels (Austen, Brontës, Dickens, Eliot, Hardy, etc.)
  Twentieth-century writing (Lawrence, Orwell, etc.)
William Shakespeare (world's greatest playwright; greatest Englishman of all time)
Pepys' *Diary*
Boswell's *Life of Johnson*
Railways
Metropolitan line (world's first underground railway)
London Underground map (emulated worldwide)
Canals (more miles in Birmingham than Venice)

163

Welfare state/National Health Service

Greenwich Mean Time

More Nobel Prizes per head for science than any other nation

Five great European wars won:

Armada

France (Louis XIV)

Napoleon

Kaiser

Hitler (we were the only allied nation to fight from first to last)

Adam Smith, David Ricardo, Thomas Malthus, David Hume

Francis Bacon

Gibbon

Newton

Dalton, Harvey, Watt, Faraday, Kelvin, Lister

Darwin

Babbage (father of the computer)

Modern analytical philosophy (Russell, Moore, etc.)

Keynes (most influential economist in the twentieth century)

Churchill (candidate for man of the century)

Four twentieth century entertainers:

Maugham

Coward

Wodehouse

Chaplin

Gave the world, *inter alia*:

Organised sport

Library service

Air force

Police

Postage stamps

Ashmolean, Oxford (world's oldest museum)

British Museum (world's oldest national public museum and one of the largest)

British Library, Boston Spa (world's largest inter-library loan service)

BBC (world's biggest producer of television programmes; World Service radio)

Television firsts (many, including first televised weather forecast, 29 July, 1949)

Decipherments:

Persian cuneiform

Mycenean Linear B

Structure of DNA

Heathrow (world's busiest international airport)

British Airways (largest international airline in non-communist world)

Inventions:
- Television
- Computer
- Jet engine
- Cement (Portland)
- Disc brakes
- Electromagnet
- Glider
- Linoleum
- Locomotive
- Power loom
- Radio valve
- Loudspeaker
- Flushing toilet
- Transformer
- Machine gun
- Safety match
- Photography (on paper)
- Rubber tyres (and latex foam)
- Steam engine
- Steel production
- Tank
- Toothbrush
- Vacuum cleaner
- Printed circuit board
- Ship's turbine
- Hovercraft
- Lead and float glass
- Optical fibres
- Carbon fibre
- Celluloid, rayon, polyethylene, polyester, etc.
- Josephson junctions
- Artificial pyrethroids (and other chemical aids for agriculture)
- Radio-microphone (the 'bug')
- Liquid crystal display
- Flexible manufacturing systems
- Viewdata, teletext, videotex
- Monoclonal antibodies
- Holography
- CAT and MRI medical scanners
- Transputer (computer on a chip)
- Transphasor ('photonic' transistor)
- Wingsail
- 'Genetic fingerprinting' (forensic DNA analysis)

'Elastic' polyester mirror (greatest optical development since the telescope)

and many more

Medical advances:

Smallpox vaccination (Jenner)

Cholera (identification as water-borne disease - John Snow)

Penicillin (Fleming)

In vitro fertilisation (first 'test-tube' baby)

Beta-blockers (heart drugs)

Anti-ulcer drugs

and many others

First commercial scanning electron microscope

First commercial pocket calculator

First commercial nuclear reactor (Calder Hall)

English longbow

Scottish bagpipes

British Navy

Royal Botanical Gardens, Kew (world's largest collection of plant specimens)

Fictional characters:

Hamlet

Romeo and Juliet

Robinson Crusoe

Frankenstein

Sherlock Holmes (most filmed fictional character)

Alice in Wonderland, etc.

Most profitable film series of all time (James Bond)

Serious music:

Elgar (and others)

Many fine performers

London as international centre

The Proms (longest and greatest of world's music festivals)

Popular music:

Beatles (most successful group of all time; seen in first satellite television link-up)

Rolling Stones, etc.

Cinema (many Oscars)

Sandwich

British breakfast

Scotch

Warm beer

The pub

Christmas cards and crackers

City of London (500 years a financial centre)

Bank of England (founded 1694)
Open University
Two of the largest companies in the world:
  BP (Britain's biggest company)
  Royal Dutch Shell
Other famous industrial and commercial names:
  Rolls-Royce (world's best-known engineering name)
  ICI
  Lloyd's of London (heart of world's leading insurance market)
  Pilkingtons (world's largest flat glassmaker)
  Wedgwood
  Jaguar
  Harrods
  Reuters
Refuge for exiles:
  Christopher Columbus
  Marx
  Freud
Discovery and settlement of many countries including:
  Australia
  New Zealand
Explorers:
  Drake
  Raleigh
  Captain Cook
  Livingstone, etc.
Hong Kong (capitalist success story)
Spitfire
First jet airliner (Comet)
First supersonic passenger airliner (Concorde)
Aviation advances ('black box' flight recorder, swing-wing, vertical
  take-off)
Longest orbital road (M25 around London)
Over 450 castles, country houses, cathedrals, etc.
Windsor Castle (world's largest castle still lived in)
Hauntings (greatest number in the world, supposedly)
Furniture:
  Chippendale
  Hepplewhite
  Sheraton
Tom Paine (*Rights of Man*), Burke, Locke, Bentham, etc.
Spawned America, Land of the Free
Sporting venues:
  Wimbledon
  Wembley

Lords
Twickenham
St Andrews
Sporting events:
  Test matches
  Boat race
  Grand National
  FA Cup Final
  London Marathon
Ancient seats of learning:
  Oxford
  Cambridge
  St Andrews
Medieval scholars
  Bede
  Alcuin, etc.
Crystal Palace (first modernist building; site of the Great Exhibition,1851, first world's fair)
Largest pier in the world (Southend)
World's oldest built road (Neolithic Sweet Track, Shapwick Heath; 6000 years old)
Many archaeological sites (630,000)
Auction houses:
  Sotheby's (world's largest)
  Christies
Theatre:
  450 years of great drama
  Royal Shakespeare Company (world's largest theatre company)
  National Theatre
  West End
  The Mousetrap (world's longest running play)
  Gilbert and Sullivan
  Famous players (Kean, Garrick, Irving, Geilgud, Richardson, Olivier,etc.)
  Andrew Lloyd Webber (most successful composer of musicals ever)
Famous schools:
  Eton
  Harrow
Most mapped and geologically surveyed land on earth
English countryside (our green and pleasant land)
Moorland ('blanket bogs', some of world's finest examples)
English gardens
English rose (flower and efflorescent maiden)
Weather records (best in world, e.g. temperature since 1659)

The Channel (world's busiest sea lane)

North Sea oil (energy from a hostile sea; world's largest concentration of
offshore platforms)

Valentine (world's oldest surviving example dated February 1477)

Literate by 1600

Innovative organisations:
  Boy Scout Movement
  Salvation Army
  Samaritans (world's largest national suicide-prevention service)
  Amnesty International
  Band Aid, Live Aid
  World Wildlife Fund
  Chiswick Family Refuge (world's first refuge from domestic violence)
  Institute for Social Inventions, etc.

Olympics (3rd most successful nation; twice hosted by London)

Festivals:
  Edinburgh International Festival
  International Musical Eisteddfod, Llangollen

Memorable monarchs:
  Boadicea
  Richard the Lionheart
  Henry VIII
  Elizabeth I
  Victoria

London (first city to have 1 million population)

Thames ('liquid history')

Edinburgh ('the Athens of the north')

Fastest war, Britain *vs* Zanzibar, 1896. Duration, 38 minutes – we won.

Charles Wells ('The man who broke the bank at Monte Carlo'; twelve
times on this Victorian gentleman's first visit)

World's largest robbery (£26 million worth of gold bars from Brink's Mat
warehouse, 1983)

World's biggest bookmaker (Ladbrokes)

Longest unbroken peace between major nations (England and Portugal)

Pope (Adrian IV, Nicholas Breakspear. Died 1159)

Great children's stories:
  Peter Pan
  Wind in the Willows
  Winnie the Pooh
  and many others

English-born Americans:
  Bob Hope
  Cary Grant
  Raymond Chandler
  and many more

Racehorses (all thoroughbreds in the world derive from 3 Arabian stallions imported into England in 1700s)

Stonehenge (1500 years older than Rome's Colosseum; one of over 900 stone circles)

Hadrian's Wall

Great ships:
  SS Great Britain (first iron ship)
  The Queens (*Mary, Elizabeth, QE2*)

Military epics:
  Trafalgar
  Dunkirk, etc.

Military personages:
  Marlborough (battle of Blenheim, etc.)
  Nelson ('England expects...')
  Wellington (the Iron Duke; 'Up Guards and at 'em')

Legends:
  St George and the Dragon
  King Arthur
  Robin Hood

Great 'place-names':
  Clive of India
  Gordon of Khartoum
  Lawrence of Arabia

Scholars:
  Joseph Needham
  Arnold Toynbee
  and multitudes more

Royal Society (world's oldest and most prestigious scientific society)

Nature (premier science journal)

World's first satellite dish (Goonhilly Down, Cornwall, 1962)

Great reformers:
  William Wilberforce (slavery)
  Elizabeth Fry (prisons)
  Lord Shaftesbury (working conditions)
  Florence Nightingale (nursing)
  The Pankhursts (votes for women)

Victorian Statesmen:
  Peel
  Palmerston
  Gladstone

World's finest private art collection (the Queen's)

Nobel Prizes for literature, peace and economics

Famous artists:
  Gainsborough

Constable
Turner
Pre-Raphaelites
Imperial behaviour:
  Gunboat diplomacy
  Stiff upper lip
  Fair play
Most successful poem: Kipling's *If* (27 languages, much anthologized)
Home for expatriates:
  G. B. Shaw
  Oscar Wilde
  Henry James
  T. S. Eliot
Cambridge University Press (world's oldest publisher, 1584)
Discovery of world's oldest shipwreck (Etruscan vessel, 600BC, Mediterranean)
First split atom

Appendix II
A Personal Programme for
Risk Reduction

I presume you want to avoid suffering a crippling illness and premature death, and that you don't want your nearest and dearest to suffer these calamities either. You probably also don't want your car stolen, your house burgled or a domestic fire. And presumably you want to remain fit as a fiddle and free of accidental injury through a long, happy life, to die peacefully in your sleep at a ripe (and still-lucid) old age surrounded by your kinsfolk, yea, even unto thy great-grandchildren. Yes? So do I.

If you are not too fussed about your own welfare, consider what you mean to others; you are your wife's husband, your child's father and your dog's best friend.

By applying the principles of the Personal Programme for Risk Reduction you can improve your chances of enjoying the good life.

- Beware of worrying too much

    Risks in most cases are lower now than ever before, and your chances of becoming a centenarian have never been greater. Don't let media reporting convince you that we live in uniquely awful times; we don't.

- Cultivate a positive mental attitude
- Reduce stress

    Mind affects body.
    Identify sources of stress in you life. Modify your behaviour to alleviate it where possible. Try not to let 'life changes' cluster (e.g. do not give up smoking, try to diet, take up a new hobby, increase your mortgage and take in a sick relative during the same week!). If you have too much on your plate, scrape a bit off.

- Do not smoke

    A high priority. Giving up

smoking improves your health
and that of others, boosts your
popularity, reduces fire risk and
swells your wallet. If you can't cut
it out, cut down. The risks of heart
disease and lung cancer increase
with the number of cigarettes
smoked.

- Maintain optimum body weight

If you are overweight, reduce your
food consumption! Of adults, over
35 per cent are overweight.

- Improve your diet

Eat *more* lean meat and poultry,
bread (especially wholemeal),
potatoes, fresh vegetables and
fruit, low-fat dairy products,
beans, fish. Eat *less* fatty meat
and fatty meat products (and grill
rather than fry), sugar (average
consumption should be halved),
cakes, biscuits and sweets, salt,
high-fat dairy products, eggs (not
more than 4 per week). Try a
vegetarian main meal at least
once a week.

- Drink only moderately
- Exercise more

Build more exercise into your routine (e.g. walk don't drive, take
the stairs rather than the lift,
mow the lawn by hand). Raise a
sweat three times a week for 30
minutes a time (e.g. jog, swim,
play squash). Vigorous exercise
can be surprisingly relaxing – but
take it easy at first!

- Family history

Identify what your grandparents,
parents and close blood relatives
are suffering from, or have died
of, and concentrate on appropriate
risk factors (e.g. smoking, diet,
exercise, stress).

- Over 35s

Have your blood pressure (and, if
possible, blood cholesterol)
checked once every five years
during a visit to your GP.

- Ladies

Cervical smear once every 3 years for early detection (and highly effective treatment) of cervical cancer. Self-examine breasts regularly for early 'lump' (tumour) detection. When out, keep keys and handbag apart; avoid dubious areas, especially at night; carry little cash; use taxis (alternatives can be a false economy).

- On the road

Drive defensively, curb aggression and tentativeness. Don't let driving expose your personality defects. Anticipate events. Use your seat belt. Don't drink and drive. Avoid using a motorcycle. Read Highway Code (latest edition).

- Car theft

Nearly 1.5 million cars are stolen or broken into each year so make your car an unattractive target by marking car number on windows, stowing valuables out of sight and using security device (e.g. lock between footbrake and steering wheel or lock between handbrake and gear lever).

- Burglary

Statistically you have a one in 25 chance of being burgled every year. Make your house an unattractive target (e.g. light approaches, fit window locks, use security deadlocks on outside doors). Ask police for (free) inspection and advice. Mark your possessions with postcode plus house number to increase likelihood of return if stolen. Photograph valuables. Tell your neighbours if you go away.

- Fire

Buy a fire blanket and smoke detectors. The value of extinguishers is more doubtful

- Personal violence

since they require presence of mind to be used correctly, are not suitable for all fires and need maintenance. (Extinguishers should conform to BS5423, or BS6165 for aerosols.) Have your electrical wiring checked for safety. Don't smoke. Ask fire brigade for (free) inspection and advice.

Perpetrators of murder, rape and assault are often known to their victims – and the crime frequently occurs indoors. Audit your acquaintances and activities. Consider changes, but don't exaggerate risks!

- Flying

Don't hang around in public areas, go through security checks as soon as possible to where there are fewest thieves and terrorists. Use your seat belt in flight in case of turbulence.

- Keep warm

Do not underestimate the British climate! Maintain a high ambient temperature (over 20°C for the very young). Wrap up well.

- Retain a healthy scepticism for advice givers

The present one not excluded!

- Generally

Dilute your risks and those of your loved ones by taking sensible precautions. Ignorance is not bliss.

Mind and Body

When you are miserable or suffering stress you are more prone to colds, 'flu and other diseases than when you are feeling 'on top of the world'. This popular belief is supported by scientific studies focusing on the immune system, that part of the body's physiology dedicated to resisting infection using defensive cells (including the white blood cells) and special chemical weapons ('antibodies'). One study carried out in Ohio showed that women who were divorced or separated had psychological problems, felt isolated - and had depressed immune systems. This last effect was most pronounced where the attachment to the former partner was greatest or where the trauma of divorce was highest. In general, the divorced have more health problems than married people, and they take more days off work. Divorce increases the risk of death from pneumonia, tuberculosis and other disorders.

If divorce is bad for you, so too is a bad marriage. Among a group of 38 married women investigated in the Ohio study, those whose marriages were poor were more often depressed. They also had lower levels of white blood cells and they rated badly in laboratory assessments of immune response.

Researchers have known for years that the loss of support from friends or relatives increases an individual's susceptibility to illness. Recently bereaved individuals are more likely to die than married people of a similar age. This recalls a common observation that among old couples one may quickly follow the other into the grave.

'Social support' is good for you. The immune system of medical students surveyed before and during examinations was found to be disrupted in those who reported stress, but even more so in those who were stressed *and* lonely. Margaret Fiske, cited in *Social Inventions* (No. 7), found that the single best predictor of moral and mental health after the age of 60 was having an intimate 'confidante'.

State of mind affects recovery as well as proneness to ill-health. One research study explored the attitudes of women who had had a breast removed as part of cancer treatment. Those women who had a positive attitude were twice as likely to survive for 10 years as those who were depressed. These days, selection of patients for heart transplants is partly on the basis of mental attitude. If you have a strong will to live you are more likely to survive and thrive.

Experiments carried out at the Common Cold Research Unit in Salisbury showed that over-serious people were more susceptible to colds than cheerful people.

Moderate exercise can improve your immune response but the severe physical and emotional strain suffered by top athletes can have a deleterious effect. Soviet scientists have reported that competitors in major athletics events in some cases have zero antibody counts.

Pet-owning is supposed to be life-enhancing. Those who keep animals are said to recover more quickly from operations than those without. This may be because they are 'taken out of themselves'. Watching a cat sleep is certainly one of life's more relaxing pastimes.

Looks can determine destiny. In medieval times there were laws that decreed that when two people were under suspicion for the same crime, the uglier or more deformed of the two was to be considered the more likely to be the guilty party. According to studies cited by psychologist Chris

Brewin in *New Scientist*, the good-looking are judged to be nicer people, their work is more appreciated, they are more likely to be offered a job when they go to interviews, and, if they commit a felony, they will probably get a lighter sentence. Pretty children are less likely to be blamed when they misbehave. It is bad luck for the ill-favoured. The less attractive you are the more likely you are to become a psychiatric patient and your physical health may be affected too. Less attractive young women (but not apparently young men) have higher blood pressure than their more attractive peers, even after the effect of any excess weight is allowed for.

Attractive women receive more visits in hospital than less attractive women, and also seem to have shorter lengths of stay. These were the findings of one study of psychiatric patients carried out by researchers at the University of Connecticut. Both male and female patients rated by others as being more attractive spent longer in the community before being re-admitted than did their less attractive counterparts. This may relate to a higher degree of social support given to good-looking people.

Keeping smart can bolster self-esteem which will help you to stay healthy. It will also enlist the social support of others.

Work carried out by researchers at Loyola University, Chicago, has shown that people with a high need for loving intimacy tend to have a greater sense of well-being and are more secure than others. They are better adjusted, particularly in their enjoyment of jobs and marriages – which chimes with Freud's notion that the essence of psychological maturity is the ability to love and to work. The research also unearthed an intriguing titbit: people whose fantasies tend towards selfless love report fewer infectious diseases.

Eating

A piece of advice: don't abandon meat-eating, it suits our physiology and digestive processes. As Marvin Harris has described in his book *Good to Eat: Riddles of Food and Culture*, our near relatives the chimps and baboons, which like us are omnivores, both enjoy a meat supper. Gorillas don't, but then these large vegetarians have longer guts than us which are better suited to high fibre diets.

Animal foods are a much better source of the protein necessary for growth and tissue repair than plants. Even those vegetable products which contain all ten of the so-called essential amino acids rarely do so in quantities and ratios which suit our needs. You would have to stuff yourself with about three loaves of wholemeal bread a day if you made this your sole source of protein. And bear in mind that recommended protein levels, lowered in the 1960s, have been revised sharply upwards more recently. Don't skimp on protein.

Besides protein, animal foods contain minerals and vitamins. They are the sole source of vitamin B12, a deficiency of which leads to pernicious anaemia, neurological disorders and psychotic behaviour. They are also rich enough in vitamin C to satisfy daily requirements.

Cutting out meat is unwise, but increasing the proportion of lean (low fat) meat is probably advisable. There is supposed to be a link between a diet high in saturated fats and an increased risk of heart disease. This is not quite as well established as some would have you believe but a reduction in intake of foods high in animal fats is sensible. Some meat products are worse than others: pork pies are said to contain two-thirds of an individual's daily fat requirement.

Fats are vital to life. Some fatty acids cannot be synthesised by the body and must be obtained from the diet. The most important of these is linoleic acid, a polyunsaturated fatty acid found in vegetable oils and soft margarines marked 'high in polyunsaturates', and also in oily fish and some nuts. Breast milk contains four times the amount of essential fatty acids as cow's milk, indicating the need for these nutrients by young babies. Adults also need them. Reduce saturated fats by all means to decrease your risk of heart disease, but go carefully with the polyunsaturated fats. One recent study carried out by researchers from the University of Edinburgh showed that the higher the level of linoleic acid in your body fat, the lower your risk of suffering a heart disease.

Nutritional science is at a stage where a reasonable attitude towards the recommendations of its practitioners is scepticism. A report by the National Advisory Committee on Nutritional Education (NACNE) published a few years ago suggested that we should all cut down substantially on our fat and sugar consumption while increasing our intake of dietary fibre. The vice-chairman of NACNE, Professor Philip James, was quoted as describing the report's recommendations as being based on 'informed guesswork'.

A final thought on eating: you use more calories in the action of consuming a stick of celery than are contained in the stick itself. What kind of food is that?

Drinking

A pamphet published by the Health Education Council (now the Health Education Authority) described 'sensible' limits for drinking. For men, two or three pints (or their equivalent), two or three times a week was within the safe limit. For women, half the volume was recommended at a similar frequency. The concept of a 'unit' of alcohol is helpful here. A Scotch, gin or glass of wine is the equivalent of one unit of alcohol, while a pint of beer or lager is the equivalent of two. This means that the HEC's safe limits equate to not more than 18 units per week for men and not more than 9 units per week for women. Both limits seem a bit on the cautious side.

Some guidelines for drinkers were included in the Royal College of Psychiatrists report, *Alcohol, Our Favourite Drug*:

1. Don't drink every day of the week – try to introduce two or three alcohol-free days. This gives the body a chance to recover.
2. Don't use alcohol as a means of helping you cope with emotional problems.
3. Don't drink alone.
4. Don't use alcohol as a nightcap to help you sleep. You will quickly become tolerant of this regular dose and then find that you have to increase it to obtain a satisfactory result.
5. Don't drink alcohol while taking other drugs, either prescribed or 'over the counter'.
6. Don't drink on an empty stomach. Try to have something to eat while you are drinking. This delays absorption of alcohol.
7. If you are participating in a drinking session try to introduce a non-alcoholic drink into your drinking sequence. It is often a good idea to quench thirst first with a non-alcoholic drink.
8. Always put your glass down between sips and try to pace your drinking so that you become one of the slower drinkers in company.
9. Sip, don't gulp your drinks.
10. If you drink spirits, always dilute them.

The RCP's advice to hosts and hostesses is as follows:

1. Make sure that non-alcoholic drinks (including water) are readily and visibly available.
2. Try to ensure that food is also available when guests are drinking.
3. Never pressurize guests into drinking alcohol. Their refusal should always be accepted.
4. Do not top up glasses.
5. If someone seems to have drunk too much, don't offer them any more.
6. If there is any concern about a guest driving after drinking arrange a taxi or a lift home.
7. If you want to give someone a special alcoholic treat then emphasize quality rather than quantity.

Fit for Life

Exercise makes you feel and look good, relieves stress, and reduces your risk of having a heart attack. It is not a very good way to lose weight, however. You need to cycle continuously at high speed for seven hours to work off a mere pound of fat. A man cycling for a couple of hours is likely to consume 600 kilocalories (which dieters simply call calories), which is only 400 more than if he had stayed home in his armchair and watched the Tour de France on the television. Even miners working at the coalface use up only an extra 860 kilocalories a day according to one study. On this kind of analysis, exercise can only make a small contribution to weight loss. It can help you to stay in shape though. Men may care to bear in mind that according to numerous polls, the physical attribute women find most attractive is a neat pair of buttocks.

Table 8. S-factor analysis of different activities

	Stamina	Suppleness	Strength
Badminton	**	***	**
Canoeing	***	**	***
Climbing stairs	***	*	**
Cricket	*	**	*
Cycling (hard)	****	**	***
Dancing (ballroom)	*	***	*
Dancing (disco)	***	****	*
Digging (garden)	***	**	****
Football	***	***	***
Golf	*	**	*
Gymnastics	**	****	***
Hill walking	***	*	**
Housework (moderate)	*	**	*
Jogging	****	**	**
Judo	**	****	**
Mowing lawn by hand	**	*	***
Rowing	****	**	****
Sailing	*	**	**
Squash	***	***	**
Swimming (hard)	****	****	****
Tennis	**	***	**
Walking (briskly)	**	*	*
Weightlifting	*	*	****
Yoga	*	****	*

Source: Health Education Council (Health Education Authority)
Notes: *No real effect **Beneficial effect ***Very good effect ****Excellent effect

Fitness can be analysed in terms of the three 'S-factors' – suppleness, strength and stamina (Table 8). Swimming is a particularly balanced activity, since it enhances all three. Cycling hard also rates highly and even digging the garden is useful. These activities tend to be associated with a low level of injuries – something which cannot be said of 'contact' sports such as rugby and football. Even jogging and squash are associated with a significant level of injuries and accidents. This is the 'downside' of sporting activities which fitness freaks usually omit to mention.

A better way of losing weight than exercise is to eat less. It requires determination. If fitness is an attitude of body, fatness is an attitude of mind.

If your will-to-exercise is weak, try a good laugh. It is said to tone up your cardiovascular system.

Out and About

When travelling on foot or on public transport you can increase your safety by observing a few simple rules. The following advice is based on information provided by the police and by such organisations as Help the Aged. It is particularly intended to improve the safety of women.

1. Avoid walking in dimly-lit areas at night. Walk with confidence and be assertive.
2. Keep your purse or wallet out of view.
3. If you carry a handbag don't let it swing loose from your shoulder.
4. If you have expensive jewellery avoid wearing it in the street.
5. Carry only small amounts of cash.
6. Don't carry your identification, cheque book and cheque card in the same place.
7. Don't put the door keys in your bag, keep them in your pocket.
8. If you are in danger, try fast talking. If you are attacked, scream and shout as much as possible – resisting or fighting back is reckoned less advisable.
9. Try to avoid going out alone. Walk or travel with friends if you can.
10. On a train, avoid compartments that are empty or have only one other person. On a bus or train sit near to other passengers. If you are pestered then ask the other passengers for assistance.

The impression created by the media notwithstanding, old ladies are not disproportionately victimised by muggers and other criminals. The old, in fact, are less likely to become victims than those in other age groups.

Bad News

Reading reports of crime, violence and accidents in the press, or seeing images of these things on the television, is harrowing and induces anxiety out of proportion to the danger to the reader or viewer. To reduce the effects of this onslaught of heart-breaking human interest stories you can try taking your information at a higher level. By this I mean giving up the daily newspapers, for example, and subscribing to a periodical news magazine. The radio can also be recommended as a less enervating alternative to the television. The effect of changes like these is to improve morale without impoverishing your understanding of contemporary events. These approaches can be particularly recommended for the old.

In general, bear in mind what might be called the Disproportionality Effect: bad events (e.g. grim news, other people's complaints about our behaviour, our children's misdemeanours) tend to have a much greater impact on us than good events (e.g. cheering news, other people's compliments about our behaviour, our children's successes).

Lightning

Is it worth carrying a personal lightning conductor to reduce your risk of incineration from above? You guessed it: no. Lightning strikes the earth about a hundred times every second and Britain gets its fair share of heavenly bolts. It is a matter of being the wrong person in the wrong place at the wrong time. Each year, about half a dozen Britons, alas, fulfil these criteria. This puts your risk of perishing in this way at rather less than one in ten million per year. Lightning follows the path of least resistance so it is more likely than not to strike in the same place twice. Apparently, your hair stands on end just before you are struck. Ask people to warn you if they see your hair acting suspiciously.

Some years are worse for lightning than others. The actor Michael Caine, of 'not many people know that' fame, has written:

According to an English chronicler, more knights were killed by a single lightning storm in 1360 than were killed at the Battles of Crecy and Poitiers.

Moral: Leave your armour at home if you decide to go out in a storm.

Thrilling Pastimes

Having reduced your exposure to risk to a low level, you may, being human, want to compensate by indulging in thrill-seeking behaviour. If this involves flying, sailing, or a similar activity, then the words of Ann Welch, author of *Accidents Happen*, may be of interest:

It is quite difficult to invent a new accident; almost every possible confusion has already occurred – a submarine has collided with a cyclist, an aeroplane towing a glider has taken off without a pilot in either aircraft, and a yachtsman has had his bowsprit run over by a train.

Flying a light aircraft, scuba diving and gliding are associated with about 30–40 fatalities per 100,000 participants per year. Sailing is safer at less than four, though the rate for motor boats is somewhat higher. As Ann Welch puts it:

... if people find their friends and fellows being knocked off at an unacceptable rate to them they either go home – and the activity declines – or take action to stop the rot.

She concludes:

There is little doubt that the biggest cause of accidents is through people getting themselves into situations for which their experience is inadequate.

Moral: Be prepared.

Risk and Sex

Danger stimulates desire. One study showed that nine out of 33 men meeting an attractive young female on a dangerous bridge rang her subsequently for a date. On a safe bridge, only two out of 33 men did so.

A Breath of Fresh Air

Deaths among elderly people peak during the 'bleak mid-winter'. Between 80,000 and 100,000 more old people die in the winter months than in summer. Hypothermia is not the main cause of these extra deaths. Most are due to heart attacks and strokes brought on by cold weather which causes adverse changes in the circulatory system, according to William Keatinge, professor of clinical physiology at the London Hospital Medical College. The initial results of a survey carried out by Professor Keatinge and reported in *New Scientist*, indicate that the higher death rate in winter is at least as marked among those living in centrally heated old people's homes and 'sheltered' housing as among those living elsewhere. It seems that old people are failing to wrap up sufficiently when they go out. If they are going to catch a bus, for example, and it doesn't turn up, they may have to stand around in the freezing cold for 40 or 50 minutes. Part of the problem is the British belief that fresh air is good for you, says the professor. This can lead to unhealthy behaviour patterns such as throwing open the bedroom windows before retiring at night.

At the opposite end of life, cold is also a danger. Every year infant mortality goes down in summer and up in winter. The greatest seasonal swing relates to children under one year old and is due to respiratory illness. In Scandinavian countries there is either no seasonal difference or a less marked one in spite of longer and more severe winters.

Margaret and Arthur Wynn in *Prevention of Handicap and the Health of Women* point out that not only is the infant mortality rate higher here than elsewhere but that there is a rising incidence down the social classes.

The much worse British result in all social classes, but particularly in poor families, is partly a consequence of the deleterious effect of cold or 'fresh air' on the progress of respiratory illness.

The national and social class differences seem partly due to the different temperatures at which homes are maintained. The Wynns again:

Some parents even in Social Classes I and II either do not protect their infants, particularly their boys, adequately from the cold or do not seek medical help quickly enough if their babies are ill...

Studies in several countries have shown that babies who have serious respiratory illness before the age of two are at greater risk of respiratory disability as adults. A final quote from the Wynn's:

In Sweden it was said that no baby should live when indoors at a temperature below 20°C (68°C) and this was regarded as too low for new, or very small, or sick babies. Such a temperature is not attained in many British homes.

Britain has one of the highest incidences of respiratory disease in the world, if not the highest. One reason is that we do not respond correctly to living in a relatively cool climate in terms of standards of housing, footwear or wrapping up against the chill. If the climate were colder – and hence more dangerous – we would be forced to indulge in more risk-reducing behaviour. As it is, our 'safer' cool climate is more dangerous to us in terms of illness and premature death than the dangerous Scandinavian climate is to the careful Swedes and Norwegians.

Longevity

In the late 1980s, the oldest man in Britain was John Evans, a 110-year old ex-miner living in South Wales. He was a life-long teetotaller and had never smoked. The oldest woman, Anna Williams, was 114. She reckoned that the secret of her long life – which had made her not only the oldest person in Britain but also the world – was eating plenty of green vegetables.

Longevity is luck to a large extent, though certain factors play their part. The most important are a disciplined lifestyle and genetics. Children whose parents have reached a good age are more likely to do so themselves.

These are the words of Malcolm Hodkinson, professor of geriatric medicine at University College and Middlesex Medical School in London, quoted in *The Sunday Times*. Women tend to live longer than men. Of a thousand boys born today, 500 can expect to make it to three score years and ten. Among girls the figure is a more encouraging 750.

Mention of luck, genetics and gender should not induce an attitude of fatalism. If you want to live out your three score years and ten, lead a longevity-inducing lifestyle by applying the principles of the Personal Programme for Risk Reduction. And as regards genetics, few things are inevitable. Identify what your parents and grandparents suffer from, or have died of, and do something to dilute the appopriate risk factors. Stopping smoking, losing weight and improving your diet, increasing your exercise and reducing stress will all help you avoid many of the leading diseases which cause premature death. You may or may not also wish to try something favoured each day by supra-centenarian John Evans: 'a mugful of boiled water with a little honey in it to take the taste of the boiling out'.

Knowledge

Beware of self-delusion in matters of health. Remember D.H. Lawrence's last words: 'I am getting better'. On the other hand, though, don't overdo self-knowledge. For example, what young person would want to know the following? You lose height progressively after about thirty years old. What is less well recognised, but obvious enough if you look around, is that your nose continues to get larger. This means that your nose to body ratio increases with age. If there was any justice in the world, this enlarged proboscis would perform better than its smaller, former self, but in fact the sense of smell declines with age. It is the first of the senses to deteriorate. This is what the future holds: anosmic semi-dwarfhood.

Crisis Posture

When you have weighed up your risks and worried yourself sick, try out the soothing, but otherwise useless, Crisis Posture. Sit comfortably. Close your eyes. Stick your fingers in your ears. Hum gently and hope for the best.

Appendix III
Inconsistencies in the Punishment of Wrong-doing

Two cases of drunk-driving are described below to illustrate the inconsistencies which can occur when miscreants are punished for wrong-doing. Both cases involved accidents which occurred in the same month within a few miles of each other in Buckinghamshire. Coincidentally, the same woman featured as innocent party in both incidents which were caused by men. The two offenders were tried in the same magistrates court.

1.) A man in his late twenties was driving home late one evening after a drinking session when he ran into a parked van with no one in it. He was uninjured, but his car and the van were both write-offs. The speed of the car was such as to cause the van to mount the pavement and crash into the van-owner's house, resulting in structural damage. The couple living in the house called the police. It was learned that the driver had been celebrating his own birthday. He claimed to have quarrelled that night with his girlfriend who would otherwise have driven him home.

The man's insurers paid the cost of replacing the van and repairing the house. In the court case that followed the accident, the man was ordered by the magistrate to pay a fine of £200 for drunk-driving and he was banned from the road for two years.

2.) The woman who lived in the house encountered another drunk driver a fortnight later. She was driving her car at about 40mph along a lane in the late afternoon when she was hit by an oncoming vehicle. The woman was knocked unconscious during the collision and sustained multiple injuries. She had to be cut out of her car by the fire brigade. The other driver, a man aged 31, bruised his ankle. Both cars were write-offs.

The man was extremely drunk at the time of the accident. He was travelling at 80mph and had strayed onto the wrong side of the road. The police investigation further showed that the man had never passed a driving test and was not therefore eligible to drive a car. He was uninsured and his vehicle lacked an MOT certificate.

The woman was hospitalised with facial lacerations, a jaw broken in five places, a fractured left foot and left wrist, and a right elbow dislocated and broken in 15 places. There was extensive bruising to her body. Surgery was necessary, as was a protracted stay in hospital. Many months later, the woman was left with severe scarring and a permanently damaged elbow which had lost two-thirds of its function and could not be straightened. Arthritis would attack the joint within five years according to medical opinion.

The woman sought compensation for her injuries and for the loss of her car from an insurance charity. There was no hope of recovering damages from the offending driver who was unemployed and of no fixed abode.

The man was fined £120 for driving with excess alcohol and a further £85 in total for having no insurance, driving unaccompanied and driving without 'L' plates. A charge of careless driving was dropped by the police for unclear reasons. The driver was banned from driving for one year.

References

Adams, J. (1986) *Risk and Freedom, the Record of Road Safety Regulation* (Llandysul, Transport Publications Project).

Barnett, C. (1986) *The Audit of War* (London, Macmillan).

Black, D., Sir (1981) *Inequalities in Health* (University of Birmingham, Christie Gordon Lecture).

Caine, M. (1985) *Not Many People Know That!* (London, Coronet).

Cambridge Study in Delinquent Development (1986). Cited in *The Economist*, 22 November.

Criminal Statistics, England and Wales, 1985 (1986) (London, HMSO).

Evans, C. (1980), *The Mighty Micro*, London, Coronet.

Gregson, Lord, (1987) 'Manufacture or Die', *Chartered Mechanical Engineer*, January.

Harris, M. (1986) *Good to Eat: Riddles of Food and Culture* (London, Allen and Unwin).

Heath, E. (1986) *The State of Britain to Come* (London, Employment Institute).

Henderson, D. (1986) *Innocence and Design, the Influence of Economic Ideas on Policy*, the 1985 Reith Lectures (Oxford, Basil Blackwell).

Henley Centre for Forecasting (1984) *Full Circle into the Future? Britain in the 21st Century* (London, Henley Centre for Forecasting).

Hibbert, C. (1986) *The Roots of Evil, A Social History of Crime and Punishment* (Harmondsworth, Penguin).

Illich, I. (1977) *Limits to Medicine. Medical Nemesis: the Expropriation of Health* (Harmondsworth, Pelican).

Institute for the Study of Drug Dependence (1986) *Drug Abuse Briefing* (London, Institute for the Study of Drug Dependence).

Johnson, P. (1975) *The Offshore Islanders* (Harmondsworth, Pelican).

Keeble, D. (1987) cited in the *Guardian*, 8 January.

Lea, R., Matthews, R. and Young, J. (1987) *Law and Order, Five Years On* (London, Middlesex Polytechnic Centre for Criminology).

Mike, V. (1986) cited in *New Scientist*, 29 May.

Mortality Statistics, Cause 1984 (1985) (London, HMSO).

Muir Gray, J.A. (1979) *Man Against Disease. Preventive Medicine*, (Oxford, Oxford University Press).

Ohmae, K. (1986) *Triad Power, the Coming Shape of Global Competition* (New York, Free Press).

Pearson, G. (1983) *Hooligan, a History of Respectable Fears* (London,

Macmillan).

Plowden, S. and Hillman, M. (1984) *Danger on the Road: the Needless Scourge* (London, Policy Studies Institute).

Pollard, S. (1982) *The Wasting of the British Economy* (London, Croom Helm).

Road Accidents Great Britain 1985, the Casualty Report (1986) (London, HMSO).

Royal College of Psychiatrists (1986) *Alcohol: Our Favourite Drug* (London, Tavistock).

Savage, W. (1986) cited in *New Scientist*, 11 September.

Shoard, M (1987) *This Land is Our Land* (London, Paladin).

Skidelsky, R. (1985–6) 'The British Disease', *Time and Tide*, Winter.

Social Inventions, Journal of the Institute for Social Inventions, London.

Social Trends (1986) 16 (London, Central Statistical Office).

Stonier, T. (1983) *The Wealth of Information, a Profile of the Post-Industrial Economy* (London, Thames Methuen).

Taylor Nelson Monitor (1986) ('New People' report), unpublished survey for National Economic Development Office cited in the *Guardian*, 7 February.

Thomas, H. (1982) *The Guardian*, 4 December.

Trades Union Congress (1986) *Britain's Housing Scandal* (London, Trades Union Congress).

Walmsley, R. (1986) *Personal Violence*, Home Office Research Study 89 (London, HMSO).

Ward, B. (1979) *Progress for a Small Planet* (London, Temple Smith).

Weiner, M. (1985) *English Culture and the Decline of the Industrial Spirit, 1850-1980* (Harmondsworth, Penguin).

Welch, A. (1978) *Accidents Happen. Anticipation, Avoidance, Survival* (London, John Murray).

Weston, T. (1981) *Don't Panic* (London, W.H. Allen).

Whitehead, M. (1987) *The Health Divide: Inequalities in Health in the 1980s* (London, Health Education Authority).

Wilkinson, J. (1986) *Tobacco* (Harmondsworth, Penguin).

Wingate, P. (1982) *The Penguin Medical Encyclopedia* (Harmondsworth, Penguin).

Wynn, M. and Wynn, A. (1979) *Prevention of Handicap and the Health of Women* (London, Routledge and Kegan Paul).

Urquhart, J. and Heilmann, K.(1985) *Risk Watch* (New York, Facts on File).

Index